Geir Lundestad was born in Sulitjelma, Northern Norway, in 1945. He graduated from the University of Oslo in 1970, and in 1974 he was appointed a senior lecturer at the University of Tromsø. Since 1979 he has been professor at the same University. He is now professor of modern history.

Professor Lundestad belongs to a new generation of Scandinavian historians of a broad international orientation. He has spent much time in the USA, e.g. as Charles Warren Fellow at Harvard University in 1978–79. His books include *The American Non-Policy towards Eastern Europe 1943–1947* (Norwegian University Press, 1975) and *America, Scandinavia and the Cold War 1945–1949* (Columbia University Press, 1980), both of which were very well received in the USA. When *East, West, North, South* was published in Norway in 1985 its success was instant. A Swedish edition came out in 1986.

East, West, North, South

Major Developments in International Politics 1945–1986

Geir Lundestad

Translated from the Norwegian
by Gail Adams Kvam

Norwegian University Press

Norwegian University Press (Universitetsforlaget AS), 0608 Oslo 6
Distributed world-wide excluding Scandinavia by
Oxford University Press, Walton Street, Oxford OX2 6DP

London   New York   Toronto
Delhi   Bombay   Calcutta   Madras   Karachi
Kuala Lumpur   Singapore   Hong Kong   Tokyo
Nairobi   Dar es Salaam   Cape Town
Melbourne   Auckland

and associated companies in
Beirut   Berlin   Ibadan   Mexico City   Nicosia

Cover design: Harald Gulli
Maps: Bon Ton A.S

© Universitetsforlaget AS 1986
Reprinted 1988

British Library Cataloguing in Publication Data
Lundestad, Geir
East, west, north, south: major developments in international politics 1945–1986.
1. World politics——1945—
I. Title II. Øst, vest, nord, sør: hovedlinjer i internasjonal politikk 1945–1985. *English*
303.4'82   D843

ISBN 82-00-18354-8

Printed in Norway
Hestholms Boktrykkeri A.s, 1481 Hagan

Contents

Foreword

Scholars who study great historical conflicts too often tend to replicate, in their own behavior, characteristics of the controversies they write about. Certainly this was true of early historical writing on the origins of the Cold War—a field dominated almost entirely by Americans— what with 'orthodox' and 'revisionist' scholars assigning responsibility for that conflict to *either* the United States *or* the Soviet Union with such passionate conviction and so little sensitivity to alternative explanations as to evoke memories of what the Cold War itself had been like at the time it began. The academic 'cold war' came to resemble the real thing.

But the historic confrontation between Washington and Moscow had never in fact been such a simple bilateral conflict. From the earliest indications during World War II that Soviet-American cooperation was not likely to survive victory, the behavior of other nations shaped relations between Washington and Moscow in both conciliatory and—more often—divisive ways. Historians of the Cold War in the United States (few exist and even fewer are allowed to publish in the Soviet Union) were slow to see the importance of such third-party actions: it was left to a new generation of European historians to make it clear that Cold War history cannot satisfactorily be written solely from a Soviet or an American point of view.

One of the best of these historians is the Norwegian Geir Lundestad, whose writings have done a great deal to reshape the debate over Cold War origins. Lundestad's first book, *The American Non-Policy Towards Eastern Europe, 1943–1947* (New York and Oslo: 1975) was an ambitious comparative study of postwar United States policy toward the countries of Eastern Europe that made clear the unique circumstances present within each of them, and the extent to which these produced variations in policies Washington and Moscow directed towards that part of the world. Lundestad then published *America, Scandinavia and the*

Cold War, 1945–1949 (New York and Oslo: 1980), a path-breaking study that not only illuminated the role of Sweden, Norway and Denmark in the intensification of Soviet–American rivalry, but also introduced the concept of 'expansion by invitation', an explanatory model that has had wide utility in accounting for the growth of United States global influence since 1945, and which Lundestad expands upon in the present volume.

It is precisely in this 'third-party' perspective that the value of *East, West, North, South* lies. There has long been a need for a clearly-written analytical overview of postwar international relations reflecting the findings of recent Cold War scholarship, but from an angle of vision distinct from that of either Washington or Moscow. This is such a book. It is, at one level, a thorough, balanced and insightful account of how Soviet–American antagonism developed, evolved, and still affects contemporary international relations. But the book gives equal attention to divisions between the 'developed' and 'non-developed' worlds, a conflict that at first only sporadically intersected Soviet–American relations, and whose linkages to them are not always clear even today.

East, West, North, South is also a perceptive critical review—but by no means a heavy-handed one—of several current issues in the study of international relations, not least those related to deterrence, economic development, arms control, and the projection of superpower influence in the world at large: here, too, Lundestad's writing reflects the combination of sophistication, balance and clarity that has come to characterize his work.

There could hardly be a better introduction to the study of international relations than this already widely-used volume by one of the most accomplished historians of the postwar era. It is a pleasure to be able to introduce it to an English-language audience.

John Lewis Gaddis
Ohio University

Author's Preface

Books that deal with international politics after 1945 are not exactly scarce. Why, then, one more? My response to that question is threefold.

In the first place, very few such surveys have been published in the Scandinavian languages. By far the greatest number are in English. This book attempts to present extensive international research to Scandinavian readers. At the same time, it is my hope that the English translation will fulfill a need outside Scandinavia.

In the second place, nearly all the existing works, also among the English literature on the subject, are limited to one or at most a few main aspects of international politics after 1945. There are many works on relations between East and West, fewer on relations between North and South, and even fewer on relations between the United States and Western Europe. Of course it has been necessary to make a selection of themes even in this book. However, there can be no doubt that the breadth of selection is great. Perhaps some readers will feel that it is too great.

In the third place, during my many years of teaching I have experienced that the existing works are unsatisfactory. To some extent their choice of themes is too limited. To some extent they are either so historically detailed that the main lines of development disappear, at least for many readers, or they are so theoretical that they do not provide the minimum of factual and chronological information that even such theoretical generalizations ought to be based on.

This book deals with relations between East and West in general, and between the United States and the Soviet Union in particular; with the arms race, relations within the Western and the Communist camps, and North—South relations (decolonization and economic issues).

It is obvious that so many themes cannot be dealt with in depth in 289 pages. The book is in many ways intended as an introduction to the sub-

ject. Even so, I believe that the method of presentation is highly significant for the insight the reader is able to acquire into international politics after 1945. This book places less emphasis on describing concrete
events than is normally the case in historical presentations. Such descriptions are readily available elsewhere.

On the other hand, correspondingly greater emphasis has been placed
on presenting long-term trends and on analyzing motivating forces and
cause-effect relationships. It is my hope that this method of presentation
will be of benefit not only to students, but to the so-called general reader
as well, whoever that may be. I believe it is important to create as much
understanding as possible of historical interrelatedness, of the major
development trends.

The method of presentation I have chosen probably makes the book
more subjective than many others. It is easier, and less controversial, to
describe than to explain. I have tried to compensate for this in three
ways. First, with regard to particularly controversial issues I try to give
the reader a summary of various interpretations of the historical topic.
Moreover, I state my own view relatively openly, so that the reader will
be able to identify it and react to it. In East—West issues I consider
myself one of the so-called post-revisionists; in North—South questions
I am more sceptical of structuralist than of liberalist theories. (These will
be encountered later in the book.) In general I have an ingrained scepticism to single-factor explanations. Finally, despite my personal viewpoints, I have tried to leave some of my most subjective hobby-horses in
the stable.

This book deals with international politics, in other words with relations
between nations. Although it covers many themes and tries to be relatively global in its perspective, it is not a comprehensive world history.
Domestic affairs are only discussed to the extent that they can shed light
on nations' foreign policies. The book is also mainly concerned with top-
level politics. This is due in part to the fact that it is at this level decisions
are most often made, in part to the fact that there is not sufficient space
to take up a discussion of decision-making processes in the various
countries. Formulations that depict nations as units, such as 'the United
States acted thus' or ' the United States believed thus', can likewise be
attributed to considerations of simplification.

The two superpowers, the United States and the Soviet Union, have
been accorded the most attention because they have been the two most

central actors during the post-war period. The United States has probably been granted more space than the Soviet Union, partly because it has been the more dominant of the two superpowers, and not least because our knowledge is so much greater about the open United States than about the closed Soviet Union.

The method of presentation I have chosen does not entail only advantages. I should like to mention some of the disadvantages. The historian keeps separate from one another events that make up an organic whole in real life. This infringement on reality is probably greater in a thematic arrangement than in a chronological one. For instance, relations between East and West, between the United States and Western Europe and the arms race are closely intertwined. Here they are analyzed in separate chapters. Certain repetitions from one chapter to another have thus become necessary. However, I have used cross-references more than repetition.

Of course not all the chapters are based on the same degree of research and reflection. Certain sections are relatively analytical, others more descriptive. This is virtually inevitable in a work of this type. I hope that the book will be well received nonetheless, and that it will satisfy a true need. If that proves to be so, advice and comments from my readers may make future editions even more satisfactory. In any case, history is never written once and for all. It must be written over and over again.

This book could not have materialized without the assistance of colleagues at home and abroad. Whereas my former books have largely been individual efforts, I felt that a survey of this type had to be based on an extensive degree of cooperation with others. I myself could have been a so-called expert on only a small portion of the material that is included.

Fredrik Fagertun has been of great help by systematically going through much of the literature that forms the basis for chapters 3 and 6. Helge Pharo and Knut Einar Eriksen have read through a preliminary version of the entire presentation and offered many useful comments. The following Norwegian colleagues have also given me good advice: John Kristen Skogan (chapter 6), John Sanness and Jan-Ivar Bjørnflaten (chapter 8), Jarle Simensen and Randi Rønning Balsvik (chapters 9 and 10), Birger Fredriksen and Valter Angell (chapter 10). Jakob Sverdrup has also commented on parts of the presentation.

For the most part, the book was written during my research leave in the 1983-84 academic year. I spent the autumn term in 1983 at the Center for International affairs at Harvard University. My stay there was most beneficial to me, as previous stays have been. I should like to thank the Center, through its acting director Joseph S. Nye, for the opportunity to visit them, and I should likewise like to thank the Center's National Security Group, led by Eliot A. Cohen and Aaron Friedberg, for allowing me to present certain of the germinal ideas in my presentation. John Lewis Gaddis has also encouraged me through the interest he has always shown in my work.

I am greatly indebted to the many libraries at home and abroad that have assisted me more than other users may have appreciated. The University Library in Tromsø and the Nobel Institute's library have rendered the greatest contributions. The office personnel at the School of Languages and Literature, University of Tromsø, have typed more 'final versions' of this book than either they or I would have thought possible. And finally, Aase, Erik and Helge did their part so that I could be away from a busy home.

Preface to the English-language edition

The Norwegian edition of this book came out in 1985. It has met with considerable success and is being used as a basic textbook at all four of Norway's universities. The book is also in use at several Swedish universities, and a Swedish edition came out in 1986.

In this English edition I have taken the opportunity to bring events up to 1986. I have also made a number of minor changes and improvements in relation to the Norwegian edition. Chapter 10 in particular has been considerably revised.

I hope the book will fill a need even in the wider international market.

I should like to thank John Gaddis for writing the foreword and Gail Adams Kvam for her translation of the book and for her patience with my revisions of the original Norwegian text.

Geir Lundestad

1. The world in 1945–1950 and in 1980–1986:
A comparison and major trends

1945–1950

The world that took shape after World War II was quite different from the world between the two world wars. One of the striking new features was the role of the United States. Even during 'isolationism', US influence had been great in certain geographic areas, such as Latin America and the Pacific. Economically, in terms of production, trade and investments, the United States had long been a superpower. Economic relations with other countries increased after WW II, but not more than the overall growth of the national product.

What was new was first and foremost the military and political role the United States would play, not only in certain parts of the world, but in virtually all parts of the globe. In 1938 the US defense budget equalled almost exactly one billion dollars. The United States was not a part of any military alliances and had no troops stationed outside US-controlled areas. During the first years after the war the defense budget stabilized at around 12–13 billion dollars. The Rio Treaty and NATO were established, with the United States as the dominant member in each of them. US forces participated in the occupation of Germany, Japan, Italy and Austria. Bases were established in many different parts of the world.

The next major development in the role of the United States evolved from 1950 onwards, primarily due to the outbreak of the Korean war. The defense budget was tripled. Numerous treaties were established with countries around the world, especially in Asia. The United States took the initiative for the establishment of the South-East Asia Treaty Organization (SEATO) and was more loosely associated with the Baghdad Pact. In 1955 the United States had approx. 450 bases in 36 countries. Complementing these military commitments was the cultural influence, which was not easily quantifiable, but which was nevertheless highly significant.

The spread of US influence was due to the fact that it was the strongest country in the world. While all the other major powers had suffered heavy material losses during the war, the US economy had prospered. The national product increased (in 1958 prices) from 209.4 billion dollars in 1939 to 355.2 billion dollars in 1945, representing almost half of the total world production of goods and services. With 6 percent of the world's population, the United States had 46 percent of the world's electricity supply, 48 percent of the radios, and 54 percent of the telephones, and US companies controlled 59 percent of the world's known oil reserves.

Until 1949 the United States had a monopoly on nuclear weapons, and after 1949 the country continued to have a considerable technological lead over the Soviet Union in both the military and non-military spheres. The United States had the world's strongest air force and the world's leading navy. The United States and the Soviet Union each had about 12 million men under arms at the end of WW II.

Although US interests were not equally great in all parts of the world, and although remnants of isolationism persisted after 1945, the United States became a global power during this period. The United States had influence in more and larger parts of the world than the Soviet Union did. This influence often went deeper in the societies affected, economically and culturally as well as politically. The US expansion was thus more comprehensive than that of the Soviet Union. Several decades would pass before the Soviet Union was able to play a global role.

The power base of the Soviet Union was not comparable to that of the United States. The USSR had suffered enormous losses during the war. Its population was reduced by approx. 20 million. Whereas steel production in the United States had increased by 50 percent during the war, Soviet steel production had been cut in half. Similar conditions existed in agriculture. In some areas they were two different worlds. The Soviet Union produced 65 000 cars a year, the United States seven million.

The Soviet Union was a superpower primarily in one field, and that was in terms of military strength, especially the number of men under arms. After demobilization the Soviet Union had more troops than the United States, although Soviet demobilization was more extensive than was assumed at the time. Whereas the United States could choose from a broad arsenal of instruments, economic and political as well as military, the Soviet Union had to depend primarily on military strength. In most countries the United States enjoyed more popular support than the Soviet Union did.

Nevertheless, it was a new development that the Soviet Union had become number two among world powers. Soviet expansion was geographically less comprehensive than US expansion. On the other hand, it was more firmly established in the areas which were most important for the Soviet Union. The country increased its territory considerably: the Baltic countries, Eastern Karelia and Petsamo, the eastern parts of prewar Poland and the northern part of East Prussia, Carpathian Ukraine, Bessarabia and northern Bukovina, southern Sakhalin and the Kurile Islands.

The Soviet role in countries beyond its neighboring areas was minimal. But with its size and geographical location, this still meant that several central areas of the world almost automatically became significant for the leaders in Moscow. Moscow insisted on virtually complete control over large parts of Eastern Europe. Europe was most important for the Kremlin, as it was for the White House, but the position of the Soviet Union was strengthened in Asia as well, where it was dominant in North Korea and would gain significant influence in North Vietnam.

In 1948-49 the Communists, under the leadership of Mao Tse-tung, were victorious in China, the most populous country in the world. However, this was a victory won with little support from Moscow. As the Chinese leader himself expressed it in 1958, without too much exaggeration: 'The Chinese revolution was victorious against the wishes of Stalin.' Nonetheless, China and the Soviet Union entered into a 30-year alliance in 1950. The leadership of Stalin and the Soviet Union within the Communist movement was indisputable, although the first cracks appeared with the break between Stalin and the Yugoslavian leader Tito in 1948.

After 1945, world politics was characterized by the conflict between the two new superpowers. Of course, unfriendly relations between the United States and the Soviet Union were nothing new. The intercourse between these two countries had not been good after 1917. Diplomatic relations were not established until 1933. Previously, however, the temperature of such relations between the United States and the Soviet Union had had little significance for the overall international climate. Both the United States and the Soviet Union were outsiders in international politics. Both countries isolated themselves, and the Soviet Union was also isolated by the other major powers.

After WW II, the United States and the Soviet Union faced each other directly in different parts of the world. They were the two main actors in the international arena; the geographic distance separating them was gone, but the political distance would soon be greater than it had ever been. During the first years after the war, the cold war between these two countries and their allies, between East and West, was concentrated on Europe, where both sides had their most important interests. The front lines froze quickly here. Outside Europe major changes could still take place without the superpowers being involved to any great extent. The civil war in China was the most obvious example of this. The Soviet Union gave little support to the Communists; the United States gave more support to its side, but compared with later events the restraint of the superpowers is striking.

The war had weakened the old major powers. Large parts of Germany and Japan lay in ruins. Germany was divided into zones controlled by the United States, the Soviet Union, the United Kingdom and France, respectively. The intention was that these four should cooperate in governing the country until the Germans at some time in the future were capable of doing so themselves. However, the split between East and West resulted in a division into a large Western part and a smaller Eastern part. This division solved the traditional German problem in European politics, a problem which had been an important factor in the outbreak of both WW I and WW II. Germany would never again be strong enough to dominate Europe. For a long time, it was assumed that Germany should be kept demilitarized. With the rapid escalation in superpower rivalry, East and West began to compete for German support. Thus even this aspect of occupation policy was subject to change.

In Japan, the United States had things its own way, despite the formal apparatus that was established to give the other allies a certain degree of influence. The war in the East had been ended with the two atomic bombs over Hiroshima and Nagasaki. A new era had begun. Here, too, occupation policy was based on the premise that the occupied country should never again be given the opportunity to start a war. The United States was so firmly decided in this matter that a provision prohibiting military forces was included in the constitution. The war, and not least the two atomic bombs, had also caused fundamental changes in the attitudes of the Japanese.

In 1945, the United Kingdom was considered the third major power. Britain's contribution to the war had been considerable; no other country had so persistently fought against Hitler Germany. Prime Minister Winston Churchill played an important role in wartime diplomacy. However, he was replaced by Clement Attlee, the leader of the Labour party, in 1945. For many people, this change symbolized a new direction, with less emphasis on world politics and more emphasis on domestic affairs.

The most important reason for the decline in the position of the United Kingdom was the cost of the war. War destruction totalled approx. three billion pounds. Assets worth more than one billion pounds had been sold overseas to contribute to financing the war. Revenue from investments abroad was halved. In 1945, the United Kingdom spent more than two billion pounds abroad, while revenues were only 350 million. In order to attain a balance, London had to ask other governments for help. In practice that meant Washington.

The United Kingdom was not the only country in Western Europe to pursue such policies. Almost without exception, they all asked the United States for support, both economic and political. During 1948-49 the European countries also exerted pressure on the United States to play a more active role in the military sphere.

Western Europe feared that the United States would return to isolationism. A new isolationism would be extremely harmful, most Europeans felt, much more so now than after WW I. Destruction had been great in many areas. The need for economic assistance was correspondingly great. It became increasingly evident that Europe needed a counterpart to the local Soviet dominance. Only the United States could provide such a counterweight.

France had suffered a humiliating defeat in 1940. Despite the efforts of General Charles de Gaulle, the country could never regain the position it had formerly enjoyed. If France was still a major power, it was so by the mercy of the others. If Paris were to play a central role in international politics once more, it would have to do so as a spokesman for a concordant Western Europe. But despite the foundation the war had laid for such cooperation, there were many barriers. France itself was divided in its attitudes; the role of Germany was problematic; Britain was only mildly interested when it came to the point.

In one area the old European major powers could still bask in the glory of the past. They had their colonies. The war was bound to mean changes for the better for the colonial subjects. But with the exception of India, where Britain had promised independence when the war was over, the colonial powers did not have the slightest intention of freeing their colonies. Reforms were one thing, independence something quite different. In 1942 Churchill had pronounced the memorable words that he had not become the King's Prime Minister in order to bring the British Empire to a close. Many British people were willing to go further

than Churchill in terms of reforms. On the other hand, the other colonial powers were even more determined to regain control over their colonies than the United Kingdom was. In fact, France and Portugal claimed
that the ties were to last forever. Colonies and mother country should
merge and become one.

1980–1986

The world looked different in the 1980s, although the changes were not
equally great in all areas. The United States and the Soviet Union were
still the world's two superpowers. The conflict between them was still a
central – most people would probably say *the* central – feature of international politics. The cold war had gradually spread to ever new areas.
In Europe, which had been so central in the 1940s, the situation had
become relatively stable. The areas of tension had been located in widely
differing parts of the globe: Korea in the early 50s, Vietnam in virtually
the entire post-war period, the Middle East from the mid-50s, Africa
south of the Sahara from the Congo crisis in 1960 to Angola and the
Horn of Africa in the 70s, Afghanistan from 1979. Serious conflicts had
arisen even in what had traditionally been the backyards of the superpowers, as demonstrated in Cuba, particularly in the early 1960s, and in
Poland in the early 1980s.

An almost continual geographic expansion of the cold war did not
necessarily mean a continual deterioration in relations between East and
West. There were periods of detente. The most important of these were
in the mid-50s, and even more so the years from 1962-63 and up to the
mid-70s. The stabilization of Europe was a primary concern. Several
important sources of conflict were resolved, or at least the level of conflict was reduced considerably. Contact between the two blocs, from
summits to trade and tourism, increased greatly.

In certain areas the two superpowers were almost as dominant as
before. This was particularly true of the military sphere. Armament had
reached a level which was beyond comprehension. Developments in
weapons technology proceeded at an ever-accelerating pace. The arms
race seemed to surge forward partly on its own momentum.

In late 1985, the United States presumably had 10 174 strategic warheads, the Soviet Union 10 223. These were supplemented with a comprehensive register of intermediate-range and tactical nuclear weapons.

22

In 1986 the two superpowers had 96 percent of the world's nuclear weapons; they were responsible for 67 percent of the weapons trade and about 50 per cent of the world's total defense budget. Total global military expenditure equalled the aggregate income of the poorer half of the world's population.

The two atomic bombs dropped over Japan had contributed significantly to the end of the Second World War. The new weapons were considered a safeguard against war and an important explanation as to why the cold war had not resulted in armed conflict between the United States and the Soviet Union directly. But at the same time these weapons gave rise to the fear that if such a war broke out, it would mean the end of human existence as we know it. In this way, too, the world became smaller.

Nevertheless, the two superpowers were on the whole *relatively* weaker than they had been 30-40 years earlier. The United States's position of leadership was not as sovereign as it had been. One reason was that the Soviet Union had become militarily equal to the United States from the early 1970s. The changes were even more dramatic in the economic sphere, particularly in relation to the United States's own allies. Of course the US economy was incomparably much larger in 1985 than in 1945. In fixed prices, the gross national product (GNP) was more than doubled. But in fact growth had been even more rapid in many other countries. In 1945 the United States had been responsible for almost half of the world's production. This high figure was partly due to war destruction elsewhere. By 1960 the US share of production had sunk to 28 percent. It continued to decline, to around 20 percent by 1985.

In 1950, France, West Germany and Italy had economies (gross domestic product) equalling 13, 15 and 8 percent respectively of the US economy. By 1980 these figures had increased to 20, 25 and 12 percent.* The European Community had created an economic and to some extent a political unity which helped to give Western Europe strength of a different order to what it had had in the years just after the war. According to some estimates, the total production of the EC was even larger than that of the United States. The United States had been a driving force behind European integration, but during the 1970s Washington's attitude would become more ambivalent. Time had shown that it was not

* There are major methodological problems involved in comparing the size of various economies. Comparing Western and Communist countries is particularly difficult. In this presentation emphasis has been placed on arriving at figures which can form a basis for comparison over a period of time.

at all certain a united Western Europe would have such a high degree of mutual interests with the United States. Only Britain fell further behind in relation to the United States. In 1950 production in the United Kingdom had equalled 15 percent of that of the United States. By 1980 this figure had sunk to 12 percent.

These economic shifts were bound to have political consequences. The Bretton Woods system that had been constructed to liberalize international trade was subject to great pressure and partially collapsed in the 1970s. Exchange rates fluctuated, and plainly protectionistic elements began to appear in the policies of many countries. The United States had neither the dominant role nor the political faculties needed to establish a new system. In the military sphere the Western European allies had to be heeded in a different way than previously. The United States could no longer determine NATO policies and strategies more or less on its own. Western cooperation would face considerable difficulties.

As a result of detente in Europe and the increased strength of Western Europe, the will for political independence grew stronger. This was evident first and foremost in France in the 1960s under de Gaulle. Nationalism in France had specifically French roots. The role of West Germany became increasingly important. As the war faded into the background, and as West Germany became clearly stronger economically than Britain and France, its capacity and will for independence grew. West Germany's new independence was most clearly demonstrated through the German *Ostpolitik* of the late 1960s and early 1970s.

Japan's economic strength was even greater than that of West Germany. In 1950 the Japanese economy (GDP) had equalled 10 per cent of the US economy. By 1980 this figure had risen to 37 percent. In 1985-86, the Japanese GDP was in the process of surpassing that of the Soviet Union. This tremendous growth would thus make the Japanese economy the second largest in the world. Politically, however, Tokyo remained hesitant and was closely bound to Washington. Japan was unwilling to play the role of a political and military major power. But in comparison with the period of US occupation in the 1940s, the Japanese were, of course, much freer now. It was only a question of time before Japan's economic status as a major power would have wide-reaching political and military consequences.

The role of the Soviet Union was diminished at least as much as that of the United States. There had been latent tensions in relations with China all along. In the 1960s this discord became open and accelerated rapidly. Significant armed encounters took place. Relations became so poor that first Moscow and then Peking sought support in Washington against the other side. The discord between the Soviet Union and China would have enormous consequences. In military terms, the USSR had to tie up great numbers of troops, approximately one-third of its total number, along the border to China.

The political consequences were even more important. Communist unity disintegrated. The split between the Soviet Union and China was echoed in most of the Communist parties of the world. It also contributed to enabling other Communist countries to act much more freely, as illustrated in Eastern Europe. Tito had long since struck out his own path. Little Albania first allied itself with China, then chose to stand entirely on its own. Romania would come to follow a relatively independent course in foreign affairs. Extensive liberalization attempts took place in Czechoslovakia and in Poland. Although 'law and order' were reinstated in these two countries, the conformity of the first decade after the war had come to a lasting end.

Whereas the Soviet Union had previously exploited its allies, it now became necessary to render sometimes considerable assistance in order to secure their support in various circumstances. The most obvious example of this was in Cuba, where Moscow paid out 9 million dollars a day at the most. Large sums were injected into Poland, too. And whereas the United States had had a standard of living which exceeded that of Western Europe, this was not the case in the Soviet Union as compared to Eastern Europe. Most countries in the area were better off than the Soviet Union.

The colonial empires collapsed; reforms were not enough. The British had started it all in India. Despite all the reservations made at the time, it became apparent that India had set an example not only for the United Kingdom and not only for Asia. The floodgates had been opened. Processes which even liberals had expected to take decades now took years. Those which should have taken years took months. In the Belgian Congo, for instance, as late as in 1958 no preparations for political independence had been made. Two years later the country was free.

The British led the way not only in Asia, but in Africa as well, where in 1957 Ghana became the first independent country south of the Sahara. Nothing could prevent 'the course of history.' If such an expression could be used with any validity, it would have to be in relation to the process of gaining independence after WW II. France tried to retain its colo-

25

nies. In Asia that resulted in defeat in Vietnam in 1954; in Africa the end of the line was reached in Algeria in 1962. The strength of the nationalist movements was, of course, an important reason for their victory. But the ability and not least the willingness of the colonial powers to retain their colonies were also diminishing. The pressure from the international community was considerable. The dictatorship of little Portugal had the strongest will and persisted the longest. Angola and Mozambique did not become independent until 1975.

Whereas the UN in 1945 consisted of 51 member countries, this number had reached 159 by 1986. Most of this increase was accounted for by the new countries of Africa and Asia. The expectations linked to independence had been high. The disappointments were all the greater when it became evident that the political changes did not result in economic improvements to any great extent. Most of the countries in the South were poor before gaining independence. They did not become richer afterwards.

If the differences were large among the groups known as East, West and North—and particularly within the North—the same was true to an even greater extent in the South. Politically most of the countries of the South, though not all of them, chose to remain neutral in regard to the conflict between East and West. On the other hand, there were several ways of being non-aligned. Economically they were not all equally poor. In the 1970s the oil-producing countries, organized in OPEC, proved that in at least one area the South was in a strong position. Some of the oil countries were among the richest in the world, although the differences among them were great here as well. A few other developing countries, particularly in Eastern Asia, achieved considerable economic growth, proving that the barriers between rich and poor were far from impassable.

As mentioned, the rivalry between East and West spread to ever new areas in the South. In part this expressed an ability and a willingness on the part of the superpowers to play an active role. But in part it was also a question of groups within the various areas who themselves wished to use these powers for their own purposes, for instance to win support against neighbors and other external enemies or to exploit the major powers in an internal power struggle—of which there were many as time went by.

But here, too, the limited influence of the superpowers became evident. Local determinants often played the most important role for the outcome of this type of conflict. This was particularly true when the superpowers neutralized each other, but not only then.

During the 1970s both the United States and the Soviet Union suffered several humiliating 'local' defeats. In South Vietnam, over 500 000 American soldiers and more bombs than were dropped during all of WW II could not prevent North Vietnam, supported by the National Liberation Front, from assuming power. Large-scale weapon support could not prevent the Shah of Iran from being ousted and an anti-American Moslem government from taking over in 1979. The system of alliances in Asia disintegrated. SEATO—established in 1954—was dissolved in 1975. The Baghdad Pact (later CENTO), which had been established in 1955, disappeared in 1979. By the time they were dissolved both of these organizations had had a dormant existence for a number of years.

The impotence of the superpowers was most clearly and most frequently demonstrated in the Middle East. Despite the fact that neither the United States nor the Soviet Union had any desire for war, armed conflicts were numerous and extensive. Alliances changed rapidly. In 1971 Egypt entered into a wide-ranging agreement with the Soviet Union. The following year 20 000 Soviet soldiers were thrown out. In 1973 Egypt and Syria waged war on the United States's closest partner in the area, Israel. After Israel had won, Egypt initiated a process of collaboration with the United States, which resulted in termination of the agreement with the USSR and the establishment of peace with Israel.

In Africa, too, conditions shifted rapidly. Even the superpowers could find more than enough of a challenge in adjusting to local conditions, not to mention working according to set, long-term plans. At the close of the 1960s the Soviet Union, despite many efforts to win friends, was almost out of the picture in Africa. Ten years later Moscow's position was quite favorable. No one could know how long this would last. Gains one day could turn into losses the next. This was illustrated in the Horn of Africa. During the course of the 1970s, Ethiopia gradually moved away from cooperation with the Western powers towards a friendship and cooperation agreement with the Soviet Union. Somalia, on the other hand, terminated its agreement with the Soviet Union and struck out a political course that was friendly towards the West.

Even in their respective neighboring areas the superpowers had problems in maintaining their established positions. The United States experienced a Cuban crisis in the early 1960s and a confrontation with Nicaragua in the 1980s. The difficulties of the Soviet Union in Eastern

Europe were no less serious than those of the United States in Latin America. In 1986, after seven years of fighting, the Red Army was still far from establishing effective control in Afghanistan. There was reason to believe that the problems would only continue to grow in the neighboring areas of both the superpowers.

In the 1940s as well, local forces and actors had been of great significance for the outcome of an issue. The civil war in China provided the clearest example of this. In the 1980s local factors were even more significant. This applied not only to East-West issues. In matters between North and South, political independence gave the various countries increased opportunities to strike out an independent course. Economically the international framework was still very important, but under the surface local variation flourished. The reasons for poverty varied from one area to another, the rate of economic growth likewise. No simple formula could capture the local complexity.

Thus the two main threads have been spun. On the one hand, we have the tremendous power and mutual rivalry of the superpowers: they had become capable of bringing human existence, as we know it, to an end in the space of a few minutes. The struggle between the two blocs had forced its way into even the most remote parts of the world. On the other hand, we have the diminished position of the superpowers, in many cases even their impotence: no one was too small to take a blow at the superpowers. The greater the size of their armaments, the less they seemed capable of controlling local events. And in a more general sense, a multitude of local conditions often made the East-West conflict seem largely irrelevant.

2. The cold war in Europe, 1945–1949

Three main theories about the Cold War

Why did antagonism develop between East and West after the Second World War? There are nearly as many answers to that question as there are scholars who have researched the subject. Nonetheless, their answers can be grouped according to three schools. These main schools are often called the traditionalists (Herbert Feis, William McNeill, Arthur M. Schlesinger Jr.), the revisionists (William Appleman Williams, Gabriel Kolko, Lloyd Gardner) and the post-revisionists (John Gaddis, Daniel Yergin, George Herring). All three schools are represented among scholars today, although they have dominated during different periods. The traditionalists held sway almost alone until the mid-60s. Then a strong revisionist wave took hold, to be succeeded by post-revisionism in the course of the 1970s.

The scholarly debate on the origins of the cold war has been dominated by Americans. Soviet writings have tended to reflect official attitudes. In Western Europe, generalized accounts long took precedence over specialized studies. Most of these accounts have been clearly traditionalist in tone (André Fontaine, Raymond Aron, Desmond Donnelly, Wilfrid Knapp), although a few have shown revisionist inclinations (Claude Julien). Various kinds of post-revisionist ideas became noticeable during the 1970s (Ernst Nolte, Wilfried Loth, Geir Lundestad).

Many factors distinguish the three schools. Three questions are particularly pertinent in defining them: Who was responsible for the cold war? Which side was most active in the years immediately following WW II? What are the primary motivating forces, particularly for US foreign policy?

Few people, if any, maintain that all the blame can be placed solely on one side. After all, this is a question of interplay among several actors. However, the traditionalists hold the Soviet Union primarily accountable for the cold war. The revisionists place the responsibility on the United States, whereas the post-revisionists either do not say much about this question, or they stress the mutual accountability of the two countries more than the other two schools do.

The question of blame is closely linked to an analysis of which side was most active in the years immediately following WW II. According to the traditionalists, US policy was characterized by passivity. Washington emphasized international cooperation within bodies such as the UN and attempted to a certain extent to negotiate between the two major antagonists, Britain and the Soviet Union. Demobilization of the armed forces was effected at a rapid pace. Not until 1947 did Washington change its course, and then as a response to Soviet expansion in Eastern Europe. The Truman Doctrine and the Marshall Plan were the turning points.

The revisionists present an entirely different picture. Even before the war had ended, the United States had tried to limit the influence of the Soviet Union and of leftist forces throughout the world. The United States had such comprehensive goals that it came into conflict even with the United Kingdom. In order to attain their goals, the Americans employed a number of different instruments, from atomic bombs to loans and other forms of economic support. The Soviet Union is considered defensive in orientation. Soviet policies in Eastern Europe were to a great extent a response to American ambitions in the area.

The post-revisionists agree with the revisionists that important elements in US policy had fallen into place before the Truman Doctrine and the Marshall Plan. They also agree that the United States implemented a number of different measures to promote their interests. But they maintain that the revisionists are too eager to perceive the use of these measures as motivated by anti-Soviet considerations. They also reject the idea that Soviet policy in Eastern Europe can be considered a result of US ambitions.

With regard to the motivating forces behind US policies, the traditionalists emphasize the US need to defend its own and Western Europe's legitimate security interests in the face of an expansive Soviet Union. These security interests coincide with the defense of democratic rights. The revisionists, however, perceive US policy as determined primarily by the needs of capitalism and a fundamental anti-Communism. The post-revisionists claim that all these motivating forces played a part. They also include a number of additional factors, such as the role played by public opinion, the Congress, and various pressure groups. The relative strength of the various factors varies from author to author, but the post-revisionists consider economic conditions less significant than the revisionists do. On the other hand, they disagree with the traditionalists' almost total dismissal of such motivating forces for US policy.

Perception of the motivating forces behind Soviet policies does not distinguish the schools to the same degree as attitudes toward the United States do. There is, however, a tendency for traditionalists to perceive Soviet policy as motivated by considerations of ideology and expansionism, whereas the revisionists place greater emphasis on the security needs of the Soviet Union. Once more the post-revisionists stress plurality and emphasize their view that one type of explanation need not exclude the other.

Some structural explanations for the Cold War

Historians can describe what happened and suggest explanations as to why something happened. Causal explanations, in particular, often contain an element of attributing guilt or responsibility. But any discussion of guilt and responsibility is also influenced by the author's appraisal of how advantageous the outcome of a situation was. Whether the outcome was good or bad is, however, a political conclusion the individual reaches on the basis of his or her political orientation. In this type of appraisal the judgement of historians is no better than anyone else's. On that basis, this presentation will describe US and Soviet policies and attempt to say something about the motivating forces behind these policies. The question of blame will not be explicitly considered, despite the place it has been granted even in historians' writings.

The outbreak of the cold war can be analyzed on several different levels. A number of features were determined by the international system as such, others were linked to ideologies, nations and individuals. The more general explanations will be considered here; the more specific ones will be considered in the section on motivating forces behind the superpowers' policies.

One theory is that conflicts are inevitable in the international system. The normal state is rivalry rather than harmony. The international community differs from the domestic situation within individual nations in that there is no effective central power having more or less a monopoly of the use of force. Of course major powers can cooperate, but when they do so it is most often to face a joint threat. When the threat no longer exists, cooperation normally dissipates. In this perspective the antagonism between East and West is a new variation on a familiar theme.

There is a lot to be said for this general theory, but it should be remembered that in the course of history there have been lasting periods of conflict in which the tension was kept at a relatively low level. The years from 1815 to 1914 may serve as an example of this. The coalition between the United States, the Soviet Union and the United Kingdom was dissolved after Germany and Japan were defeated in 1945. A similar situation pertained after the Napoleonic wars and after WW I. But the objection can be raised that the tension between East and West after WW II reached a higher level than after earlier, corresponding conflicts.

Other structural conditions may shed light on the high level of tension. The changes that resulted from WW II were enormous. The most important change was the vacuum created by the defeat of Germany and Japan. This theory is most clearly presented by Louis Halle in his book *The Cold War as History:* '. . . the decision to eliminate German power from Europe rather than make . . . peace was the basic cause of the cold war . . . It is evident that such a vacuum can hardly persist, even for a week. It had to be filled by something.' Both the United States and the Soviet Union were capable of filling the vacuums in Europe and Asia, and the two new superpowers were both drawn into them. Since there was no mutually acceptable way of filling them, conflict was the inevitable result.

Ever new vacuums would arise during the post-war period. Conditions in Central Europe and Eastern Asia were scarcely stabilized before the colonial empires began to crumble. As the new nations of Asia and Africa suffered from a lack of domestic stability and as the former colonial powers were often unable to fill the vacuums which arose, the stage was laid once more for a conflict between the two superpowers, the United States and the Soviet Union. To an increasing degree, the most important conflicts between East and West took place in Asia and Africa.

The tension between the United States and the Soviet Union was naturally also affected by the fact that the two countries had differing political and economic systems. The systems were not only different; the two countries mutually denounced each other's system. The ideological gap was bound to make cooperation difficult and a sober analysis of the adversary nearly impossible. This had been evident even before WW II. Relations between the United States and the Soviet Union were poor

32

then, too. The new element was that the two powers now confronted each other face to face in several parts of the world.

The assertion has even been made that these were different types of people confronting each other: on the one side the Russians, who have often been described as insecure, fearful of the outside world, and with a clear inferiority complex towards the West; on the other side the Americans, who supposedly represented the opposite qualities—optimistic, superior and expansive.

This factor cannot be discounted, although many historians are sceptical about explanations based on distinctive national characteristics. The picture was certainly not uncomplicated. The Americans may well have felt that they were God's chosen people, but the threat of evil was ever present, as the Communist witch hunt showed. The isolationism of the period between the wars did not indicate a strong feeling of confidence towards the rest of the world. However, the political climate was far different from that of the Soviet Union. 'Enemies' of the United States lost their reputations; 'enemies' of the Soviet state lost their lives.

The differing political and economic systems are a more concrete factor than the various personality types. The fact that the United States was capitalist and the Soviet Union communist was significant. A few comments are needed, however, to shed light on the fact that there were certain complications involved in even this apparently obvious explanation of the antagonism between the United States and the Soviet Union.

In the first place, social democracy did not necessarily represent a sort of middle course that could tone down the conflict, even though many people were convinced that this was so. Relations between Britain and the Soviet Union were no better than between the United States and the Soviet Union. Until the spring of 1946, the Labour government in London was more sharply criticized by Moscow than the Truman administration in Washington was. On several vital issues regarding Germany and Poland, antagonism was even greater between Britain and the Soviet Union than between the United States and the Soviet Union, although the two Western powers had relatively close ties. And, as we shall see, many of the new initiatives in US policy—such as the Truman Doctrine, the Marshall Plan and NATO—were measures that were eagerly applauded by the British government. In fact, they were not only endorsed, but even to a certain degree initiated or at least encouraged by the British.

In the second place, the alliance during the war had created an atmosphere which was bound to influence the climate in the post-war years. The Soviet attitude towards the United States—as expressed during the war in Stalin's declarations, in his correspondence with Roosevelt, and in the Soviet press—mellowed somewhat. Even so, this shift was quite insignificant compared to the change in the United States. A minority continued to be extremely suspicious of the Soviet Union, but the vast majority changed their minds dramatically. The American press regularly printed articles praising the Soviet Union. The conservative weekly *Life* magazine proclaimed that Lenin was 'perhaps the greatest man of modern times'. Nor was there any reason to fear the Soviet Union, because the Russians 'look like Americans, dress like Americans, and think like Americans'.

In 1943 and early in 1944, nearly all the experts on the Soviet Union who had been sceptical towards Moscow before the war felt that it should be possible to cooperate after the war. Gallup polls showed that as late as in August 1945, 54 percent of the American population believed that the Soviet Union was to be trusted and felt that the USSR would cooperate with the United States. This was only one percent less than the highest level during the entire war, which was registered in February 1945. Thirty percent said that the Soviet Union could not be trusted, while 16 percent had no opinion.

Thus a majority believed that it would be possible to continue to cooperate after the war. Even more, no doubt, hoped to avoid conflict. The transition from war to cold war is sometimes made too automatic. It was politically impossible to go directly from one to the other. Only gradually did leaders and public opinion lose this optimism and prepare themselves for a new conflict.

The past bound East and West together, but only parts of the past. For there were also other experiences, which in the short term had limited influence but which would soon become more important. From a long-term Soviet perspective these included all the invasions from the west, from the Vikings to Hitler, and in a more short-term perspective all the unfulfilled promises of the Second Front in 1942, as well as what Stalin considered suspicious contacts between the Western powers and Hitler Germany. Moscow's conclusion was that in order to ensure its own security the Soviet Union would have to rely solely on itself.

The Americans were equally interested in what they could learn from the war. An important lesson was that aggression had to be contained as early as possible. Encouraged by previous successes, Hitler's ambitions had grown continually. Feelings of guilt in the United States about their former isolationism reinforced this way of thinking.

The war had definitively ended American isolationism. Pearl Harbor had shown that the United States was vulnerable to attack. The Pacific and Atlantic oceans did not make an attack on the United States impossible. New long-distance bombers and new weapons, not least the atomic bomb, made the world even smaller. The United States had to play an active part in order to prevent new wars and to create a world in accordance with American interests.

Who acted where?

The United States would come to play a part in politics throughout the world, although the American influence was not equally pervasive in all parts of the globe. Soviet policy was less ambitious geographically, but the desire to dominate was even stronger in the areas which were most important to Moscow. The clash was between two different views. The United States and the Soviet Union, East and West, quite simply had conflicting interests in several countries and regions.

US policy

The Americans had always considered themselves something special. In their own opinion, they represented principles that were not primarily in the interest of the United States, but rather in the interest of the entire world. These principles had been proclaimed by President Wilson in his Fourteen Points during WW I. Even isolationism was a way of emphasizing the unique nature of the United States. The issues of European strife had no bearing on the country. The main dividing line in international politics was between the United States and all other major powers, not between groups of major powers. There was a constant fear that American ideals would be defiled by foreign influence. The strength of the United States was underestimated.

The war had shown that it did make a difference to the United States who controlled Europe. The country had closer ties with some powers than with others. But the belief that the United States had a special mission persisted. Wilson's Fourteen Points were reiterated in modified versions in the Atlantic Charter of August 1941 and in the Declaration on Liberated Europe from the Yalta Conference in February 1945. They also formed part of the background for the new international organizations.

With the enthusiasm that new converts often have, the United States was going to create a new foundation for peace and cooperation between nations. America was going to protect the world against the power politics of the old major powers—politics that had drawn the world into so many conflicts. The key phrases were international cooperation, self-government by the people, anti-colonialism and freer trade between nations.

In the political sphere the United Nations was to be the central body. It was to be supplemented by others, such as regular meetings between the foreign ministers of the major powers. The United States would participate in international politics in an entirely different way than previously. The country was to be a global power. No issue would be foreign to Washington any more. The so-called Bretton Woods institutions, the World Bank and the International Monetary Fund, were to be central actors in the economic sphere. Through an active lending policy and stable exchange rates they were to increase international trade, promote economic growth and in so doing perhaps contribute to ensuring world peace.

Although many leading Americans understood that the major powers would have unequal influence in various parts of the world, the overall ideology represented a sharp break with anything resembling the outdated policy of spheres of interest. As President Franklin D. Roosevelt expressed it in reference to the Yalta conference: 'It spells the end of the system of unilateral action, exclusive alliances, and spheres of influence, and the balance of power and all the other expedients which have been tried for centuries and have failed.'

Under this ideal surface, concrete policies were adapted to US interests and other practical realities. The UN system would be strongly dominated by the United States and its friends. Free trade favored the country with the strongest economy. Despite its high ideals, the United States would both have its cake and eat it too. There were not to be spheres of interest, but the United States would continue to have a high degree of control over Latin America. Colonies and mandates were to be placed under international supervision, with the exception of the areas the United States was to have command over. The Rhine and the Danube were to be internationalized, but not the Panama Canal. Free trade was to be combined with protectionism where this best suited the United States. The Soviet Union was to have little say in the occupation of Italy and Japan, but the United States tried to have more of a say in the former enemy countries of Eastern Europe.

The war had undoubtedly suppressed most of the scepticism towards the Soviet Union. But there were always 20 percent or more who maintained that the United States could not trust the Soviets. As early as in the autumn of 1944 there were obvious signs that the climate was changing. In the State Department, the experts on the Soviet Union recovered their old scepticism. The lack of Soviet support—and sympathy—for the Polish uprising against the Germans in Warsaw during the summer and autumn of 1944 was particularly important in this context. According to expert opinions, the Kremlin seemed determined to gain control of Poland, Romania, and Bulgaria. The war had not after all altered the policies of the Soviet leaders. The experts on the Soviet Union were supported by the Secretary of the Navy, James Forrestal, although the military establishment as such was not at all among the most staunch critics of the USSR. As 1945 went by, the signals of tough Soviet policies in Eastern Europe became clearer. Scepticism towards the Soviet Union was strengthened and spread to ever new parts of the administration.

President Roosevelt was one among many who hoped to achieve cooperation with the Soviet Union. He was also one of the few who understood that it would be necessary to make considerable concessions to the Soviet Union in Eastern Europe in order to continue this cooperation. However, he did little to prepare public opinion for this type of concessions. The general public wanted good relations with Moscow, but there were few indications that they were willing to sacrifice American ideals in Eastern Europe. In private, Roosevelt could accept the system of spheres of interest that Stalin and Churchill agreed on in October 1944, but it would have been political suicide to have publicly advocated this course of policy with regard to Eastern Europe.

Just before his death in April 1945, Roosevelt's view of the possibilities of continued cooperation with the Soviet Union was in the process of changing. The new President, Harry Truman, intensified this scepticism, although during the first few months of his administration he was understandably uncertain as to exactly what policy to pursue.

From the time of the meeting of foreign ministers in London in September-October 1945 there was an open split between the United

The Percentage Agreement between Churchill and Stalin

We alighted at Moscow on the afternoon of October 9, and were received very heartily and with full ceremonial by Molotov and many high Russian personages.

. . . . .

At ten o'clock that night we held our first importtant meeting in the Kremlin. There were only Stalin, Molotov, Eden, and I, with Major Birse and Pavlov as interpreters.

. . . . .

The moment was apt for business, so I said, 'Let us settle about our affairs in the Balkans. Your armies are in Roumania and Bulgaria. We have interests, missions, and agents there. Don't let us get at cross-purposes in small ways. So far as Britain and Russia are concerned, how would it do for you to have ninety per cent predominance in Roumania, for us to have ninety per cent of the say in Greece, and go fifty-fifty about Yugoslavia?' While this was being translated I wrote out on a half-sheet of paper:

Roumania
Russia . . . . 90 %
The others . . . . 10 %
Greece
Great Britain . . . . 90 %
(in accord with USA)
Russia . . . . 90 %
Yugoslavia . . . . 50-50 %
Hungary . . . . 50-50 %
Bulgaria
Russia . . . . 75 %
The others . . . . 25 %

I pushed this across to Stalin, who had by then heard the translation. There was a slight pause. Then he took his blue pencil and made a large tick on it, and passed it back to us. It was all settled in no more time than it takes to set down.

Of course we had long and anxiously considered our point, and were only dealing with immediate war-time arrangements. All larger questions were reserved on both sides for what we then hoped would be a peace table when the war was won.

After this there was a long silence. The pencilled paper lay in the centre of the table. At length I said, 'Might it not be thought rather cynical if it seemed we had disposed of these issues, so fateful to millions of people, in such an offerhand manner? Let us burn the paper.'

'No, you keep it,' said Stalin.

Winston S. Churchill, The Second World War. Volume VI: Triumph and Tragedy. London, 1954, pp 197-198.

States and Britain, on the one hand, and the Soviet Union on the other. Now public opinion and attitudes in Congress began to change in earnest. The hopes for cooperation had been high. The disappointment at not having succeeded was thus even greater. From having believed that the Soviet Union was perhaps not so unlike the United States, a large part of public opinion swung to believing that Stalin was a new Hitler. Not much time was required to move from one extreme to the other.

The United States could not achieve the comprehensive policy goals it had laid out. Although the Americans may have underestimated their own strength before WW II, there were indications that they overestimated it after the war. These indications would become stronger as the post-war period progressed.

This was probably mainly due to the ambitious nature of the goals, for the means which were available were considerable. The United States had a monopoly on nuclear weapons. There was a definite expectation in Washington that the atomic bomb, by its mere existence, would have a moderating effect on the Soviet Union. For instance, it would have a deterrent effect with regard to possible Soviet plans for an attack on Western Europe. However, there were few people in Eastern Europe who could see any positive virtue in the new weapon. (The atomic bomb will be discussed in more detail on pages 145–148.)

The United States had a wide-reaching network of bases throughout the world. The Pacific was considered an enormous US-dominated lake by many. In Europe, the United States had forces in the occupied countries and set up important bases on Greenland and the Azores and in Iceland. These were established primarily on the basis of US commitments in the occupied areas, and on the basis of their significance for the defense of the American continent, but their purpose changed with the international situation. When Secretary of State James Byrnes announced in September 1946 that US troops would participate in the occupation of Germany as long as the occupation persisted, this was not directed primarily at Germany, but at the Soviet Union. His declaration put an end to the uncertainty as to how long the United States would have troops in Europe, an uncertainty due in part to Roosevelt's statement at Yalta that the US troops would have to be recalled within two years. Roosevelt had assumed that American public opinion would not tolerate this type of commitment in Europe for a longer period of time.

Roosevelt himself had advocated that post-war economic support to the Soviet Union ought to be linked to the policies pursued. Washington attempted to influence Moscow's policies through economic measures. Firstly, Lend-Lease aid was reduced abruptly in May and again in August, 1945. This was partly to express dissatisfaction with Soviet policies, particularly in Eastern Europe. Then the preliminaries for the loan negotiations were prolonged, and when the negotiations were finally initiated at the beginning of 1946, the conditions were extremely stiff. It was not possible to reach agreement. Loan policy was also used actively in relation to the countries of Eastern Europe in the hope of attaining political influence, but to little avail once more.

The distribution of economic support gives a good picture of Washington's involvement and priorities. During the period from July 1945 to July 1947, the countries which would later participate in the Marshall Plan received various American loans and credits amounting to 7.4 billion dollars. The corresponding figure for Eastern Europe was 546 million, including 106 million to Finland. Britain received 4.4 billion, the Soviet Union 242 million in so-called Lend-Lease pipeline deliveries. Stopping them would have damaged US interests almost as much as Soviet interests. France received 1.9 billion, Poland 90 million. Italy received 330 million, Czechoslovakia 73 million, the Be-Ne-Lux countries 430 million, Bulgaria and Romania nothing.

Loan policy was closely linked to Washington's evaluation of what was a politically acceptable government. The most Moscow-oriented regimes received little or nothing. In the autumn of 1946 US aid to Czechoslovakia, the bridge-builder among the Eastern countries, was abruptly cut off. Prague's foreign policy had become unacceptable to Washington. In the autumn of 1947 complaints about the bridge-builders among the Western countries, the Scandinavian countries, became ever stronger, although there was no question of cutting off economic aid to countries participating in the Marshall Plan.

The decisive factor was a country's foreign policy stance. Governments which were far from perfect in terms of democracy could increasingly count on support if they opposed the Soviet Union and Communism. This was evident in US policy towards Greece and Turkey: in 1946 Washington was willing to increase economic assistance to these two countries, the Sixth Fleet was built up in the Mediterranean, the firm stand towards the Soviet Union in Iran was a signal for Greece and Turkey as well, and the United States was prepared to give the British the weapons they might need to fight the left-wing guerillas in Greece. In the autumn of 1946, the Truman administration decided to do whatever was necessary to prevent the guerillas from winning and to get the Turkish government to resist Soviet wishes with regard to boundary changes and a stronger position in the Bosporus-Dardanelles.

When the British economic situation in February 1947 was such that they had to withdraw from the area almost entirely, the Truman administration was ready to take over. The administration did not need to be convinced, as Congress and public opinion did, that major outlays were necessary. The striking new element was that assistance was linked to a general principle that US policy would support 'free peoples who are resisting attempted subjugation by armed minorities or by outside pressures'. This was the Truman Doctrine.

Nor did the Marshall Plan represent anything dramatically new in Washington's relations with Western Europe. The economic assistance given during the years 1945–1947 was, in fact, greater per year on the average than it was during the Marshall Plan from 1948 to 1951. But the Marshall Plan was innovative in its organizational form, and it was given in a few large portions, not in many smaller installments (see pages 178–180).

The establishment of NATO in April 1949 was a more wide-reaching change. As we have seen, the ties to Europe were considerable before 1949, so even the changes in US military involvement in Western Europe can easily be exaggerated. Nonetheless, for the first time in peacetime the United States entered into a military alliance with countries outside the Western hemisphere.

In March 1947, Britain and France had signed the Dunkirk treaty, which was formally directed against Germany—a situation that was realistic enough, particularly for France. The Soviet Union was not mentioned, but lurked in the background, particularly for Britain.

As early as the turn of the year 1947–48, Britan, with the support of France, Belgium and the Netherlands, began to campaign for a more direct US contribution to the defense of Western Europe. As had been the case with the Truman Doctrine and the Marshall Plan, the Europeans' eagerness to link the United States more closely to Europe was an important precondition for the US stance.

According to the British, the defense of Europe could not be effective without US participation, preferably in the form of membership in a joint organization. At this time Washington was not prepared to make any commitment regarding participation. A vicious circle was in the making. The United States wanted to see what the Western Europeans established before deciding how strongly to support it. Western Europe would perhaps not be able to accomplish anything of substance if the US did not in advance guarantee comprehensive assistance.

A number of events during February—March 1948 contributed to a change of course by the United States, so that it decided to take part in negotiations on the establishment of an Atlantic defense system: the coup in Czechoslovakia, the Finnish—Soviet cooperation agreement, the fear of a Communist victory in elections in Italy. From Germany came the alarming report by US commander General Lucius Clay that a conflict could erupt there. What seem to have had the most immediate effect, however, were rumors that the Soviet Union might suggest a type of Finnish pact with Norway. (Nothing came of this. For that reason, these rumors were long given little emphasis in analyses of the background for NATO.)

Even after US-British-Canadian negotiations had resulted in an agreement to establish some form of Atlantic security system, a year passed before NATO was established. The Americans disagreed among themselves as to what course to pursue. Such leading members of the Truman administration as George F. Kennan and Charles Bohlen were sceptical about an Atlantic treaty and wanted a more loose-knit association between North America and Western Europe. The military were unenthusiastic because they feared that Western Europe would attain too much influence on US strategy and make excessive demands on what were after all the limited resources of the United States. The Congress had to be consulted. The Democrats were uncertain as to what the outcome of the presidential election in the autumn of 1948 would be. In addition, time would show that although all the countries of Western Europe wanted to tie the United States more closely to Europe, they disagreed on just how this should be done. (Relations between the United States and Western Europe are discussed in more depth on pages 176–180.)

There were definite limitations to both Washington's use of instruments to promote its aims and its foreign policy commitments. The atomic bomb was used primarily to end the war with Japan (see pages 145–146). There could never be any question of using it to threaten the Soviet Union directly. No one was prepared for such a rapid change from wartime cooperation to cold war. Lend-Lease was not stopped primarily to frighten the Soviet Union. It was a program of assistance for all the allies, and the President had promised Congress that he would terminate it as soon as the war was over. Loan negotiations were carried out with little confidence that anything of significance could be accomplished. Conditions were not particular to the negotiations with the Soviet Union and Eastern Europe; return services of various kinds were also required from the many countries of Western Europe that had received assistance from the United States.

The limitations of US foreign policy involvement were made evident by demobilization and through attitudes towards the defense budget. Rapid demobilization undermined the US position, but there was no way of stopping it. It had to be carried out. Anything else was considered political suicide. The army was reduced from 8 million men at the end of the war to 1.5 million in the summer of 1946. The corresponding figures for the navy were 3.5 and 0.7 million. A large part of the remaining troops were merely waiting to come home. The defense budget sank drastically. The political leaders, following Truman's lead, felt that the upper limit to what the United States could bear in defense expenditure was 12-13 billion dollars. This was a high figure compared with the pre-war period. But considering the extent of US occupation commitments, and not least compared with later defense expenditure, this was a small sum.

Although US involvement was global in principle and although it was far more comprehensive than Soviet involvement, the depth of US commitments varied considerably from place to place. As we shall soon see, Washington was willing to limit its role in Eastern Europe to the advantage of the Soviet Union. The surprising thing about US policy towards China was how little was done to prevent a Communist victory in the civil war (see pages 62–65). To some extent, the United States tried to limit its involvement even in Western Europe. Washington encouraged European integration, in part to reduce Western European dependence on US assistance (see pages 185–186). The United States also wanted to limit the number of members in NATO and opposed membership by Greece and Turkey.

Soviet policy

The Soviet Union, too, represented a global ideology. For Marxists it was almost a law of nature that the world would become Communist one day. But from a Soviet point of view in 1945 that goal would inevitably seem a long way off. The Soviet Union faced the task of widespread reconstruction, and the country far from equalled the United States in terms of strength.

This did not mean that the Soviet Union lacked ambitions. Some areas were more important than others, and the possibilities of increased influence were greater in some places than in others.

America, Africa, and even most of Asia were of little significance for the Soviet leaders. Few attempts, if any, were made to establish Communist regimes there. Africa illustrated this situation most clearly. There was only one Communist party in all of Africa, and that was in South Africa. The shaping of colonial policy was for the most part left to the mother countries' Communist parties. Stalin's interest in Latin America was also minimal. In Japan, Moscow was willing to accept the US-supported occupation regime without much protest. Support for the Communists in China was lukewarm (see pages 65–67). Revolutionary attempts were made in Southeast Asia, but there is no definitive assessment as to the Soviet stance regarding the revolts there in 1948 (see pages 68–69).

The alternative to Communist control was to support nationalist leaders. But after a brief period of a few years, these leaders were denounced as lackeys of the colonial powers. This was the case with Gandhi and Nehru in India and to a lesser extent with Sukarno in Indonesia (see pages 68–69).

At first the Soviet Union seemed inclined towards cooperation in Western Europe. The Kremlin only half-heartedly tried to change the occupation regime in Italy in order to increase its influence there. The large Italian and French Communist parties were advised to take part in broad coalition governments, partly in order to meet the enormous tasks of reconstruction. The Communists became constitutional and moderate.

In contrast, the Soviet position was strong in North Korea and in Outer Mongolia. Attempts were made to increase influence in other border areas. The Soviet Union was interested in acquiring the provinces of Kars and Ardahan in Turkey, as well as in attaining as much control as possible over the Dardanelles. Moscow tried to use Soviet troops in northern Iran to build up a loyal regime there. In China, Stalin wanted to regain the rights Russia had lost after being defeated by Japan in 1904-05.

Roosevelt thought the changes in China were a reasonable price to pay for Soviet participation in the war against Japan. Thus agreement on

Legend:

·········· Germany's borders in 1939
xxxxxx Iron curtain
■ Soviet conquests
▨ Countries in which communist regimes were established in 1945–48
■ Italian territory transferred to Yugoslavia

NORWAY

SWEDEN

GULF OF BOTHNIA

FINLAND

U.S.S.R.

EAST-GERMANY

POLAND

WEST-GERMANY

CZECHOSLOVAKIA

AUSTRIA

HUNGARY

ROMANIA

YUGOSLAVIA

BULGARIA

ALBANIA

GREECE

Territorial changes in Europe after the Second World War.

this point was reached during negotiations at Yalta. In return, Moscow recognized Chiang Kai-shek as the legitimate ruler of China. Churchill was kept out of these discussions, a fact which illustrated the weakened position of the United Kingdom. In March-April 1946, a firm Western reaction combined with tactical Iranian concessions resulted in a Soviet withdrawal from Iran. The demands with regard to Turkey were toned down. The same was true of more tentative wishes that had been expressed concerning joint bases with Norway on Spitsbergen and acquisition of the Italian colony Tripolitania (Libya).

However, all these 'concessions' had a price. Restraint in areas which were important to the West was to be reciprocated by similar restraint by the West in Eastern Europe. Stalin was relatively clear on this point. The most important objectives were established as early as December 1941, in talks with British Foreign Minister Anthony Eden. The Baltic countries were to be reincorporated in the USSR, the Polish border was to follow the Curzon line, the Soviet Union wanted bases in Romania and Finland. In return, Stalin expressed his willingness to support British demands for bases in Western Europe, e.g. in France, Belgium, the Netherlands, Norway and Denmark.

This was not the last time Stalin himself clearly expounded on Soviet policy. The gist of the percentage agreement with Churchill in October 1944 was that the Soviet Union was willing to grant the British a free hand in Greece if the Kremlin was granted the same freedom in Romania, Bulgaria and to a lesser extent Hungary. Stalin's message to Churchill on 24 April 1945 illustrated the same line of thought, this time with regard to Poland:

> Poland is to the security of the Soviet Union what Belgium and Greece are to the security of Great Britain ... I do not know whether a genuinely representative Government has been established in Greece, or whether the Belgian Government is a genuinely democratic one. The Soviet Union was not consulted when these Governments were being formed, nor did it claim the right to interfere in those matters, because it realises how important Belgium and Greece are to the security of Great Britain. I cannot understand why in discussing Poland no attempt is made to consider the interests of the Soviet Union in terms of security as well.

Stalin did not waver when it came to the border changes mentioned in the conversation with Eden. Even when the existence of the Soviet regime was at stake, these were minimum demands.

Poland was the most important Eastern European country both for the Soviet Union and for the Western powers. For the Soviet Union it was a buffer towards Germany and the West. An attack from the West would have to go through Poland. Britain had gone to war to defend Poland. That made it difficult to accept complete Soviet dominance. Both in London and in Washington, Poland was considered a test of whether and to what extent the Soviet Union would accept independent regimes in Eastern Europe.

From the summer of 1944 it seemed obvious that Moscow was determined that Soviet sympathizers, in other words the Lublin group, should be in control in Poland. Criticism of the exile government in London, recognized by the Western powers, became harsher. The London government's forces in Poland were pushed aside and partly suppressed by the advancing Red Army. Local administration in the liberated areas was left in the hands of those who were loyal to the Soviet Union. In January 1945 Lublin was formally recognized by Moscow as the government of Poland. When it became evident that Stalin's Poles would not stand much of a chance of winning free elections, the elections which were presupposed both at Yalta and at the Potsdam Conference were postponed indefinitely.

Developments in Poland were an indication of how things would develop in Romania. In March 1945 Moscow imposed a change of government to the advantage of the circles that were loyal to the USSR. The Soviet Union enjoyed more support in Bulgaria than in Poland and Romania, which were traditionally anti-Russian. For this reason the Kremlin's methods were more indirect in Bulgaria, but the tendency was unmistakable: purging of the political opposition and increased control by Soviet sympathizers.

Even in the three countries mentioned, the Soviet Union was willing to make minor concessions to the Western powers. For instance, it appears that Stalin was prepared to accept the Eastern Neisse as the border between Poland and Germany. The Poles insisted on the Western Neisse. The United States and Britain accepted the western border without Stalin really being tested on this point. The Soviet Union was also willing to accept Western-oriented politicians in the governments of all three countries, although in a minority. When Washington and London protested against the biased elections that were planned for Bulgaria in

August 1945, Moscow agreed to postpone them. Monarchy persisted in Bulgaria until the autumn of 1946 and in Romania yet another year.

Moscow's flexibility was greater in Hungary and especially in Czechoslovakia, although limits were set for the freedom of action of these countries, too. In Czechoslovakia there was widespread support for a course that meant close military and political cooperation with the Soviet Union. Economically and culturally, on the other hand, Czechoslovakia was oriented towards the West. Soviet forces were withdrawn in December 1945. Free elections were held in May 1946. In contrast to most of the countries of Eastern Europe, the Communist party enjoyed a strong position in Czechoslovakia, receiving 38 percent of the votes. The extent of Soviet intervention was limited until the summer of 1947.

In Hungary, too, there were free elections. They were held in the autumn of 1945 and represented a victory for the Smallholders' Party, whereas the Communists made a poor showing. During the first year after liberation, at least, the broad coalition government enjoyed considerable freedom of action, although it was gradually limited by the Soviet occupying power. From early in 1947 it was evident that Moscow would take complete control of Hungary.

There were Russian troops in Finland and Austria as well. But in these countries developments took an entirely different course than elsewhere in Eastern Europe. In terms of foreign policy, Finland would emphasize close cooperation with the Soviet Union. The Communists were represented in the Finnish government, although they were in a minority. In terms of domestic policy Finland functioned like a Western democracy. After the peace treaty was signed in 1947, the Russians withdrew except for a base in Porkkala, which was retained until 1955. Part of Austria was under Soviet occupation, but in contrast to Germany the country was administered as a single unit. In the elections of November 1945 the Communists received only 5 percent of the votes. The country even participated in the Marshall Plan.

Soviet dominance in Eastern Europe was mainly based on the presence of the Red Army in the area. The widespread impression in the West was that Soviet demobilization was quite limited. For various reasons Stalin found it advantageous to exaggerate Soviet strength willfully. The number of Soviet troops had probably declined to 2.8 million by 1948. This figure was still higher than the corresponding figure for the United States, but much lower than was thought at the time. Even so, it was more than enough to retain control over Eastern Europe. Developments there cast long shadows into Western Europe.

As we have seen, the Soviet Union was willing to make certain concessions to the Western powers, who in turn were prepared to limit their influence in Eastern Europe, and agreements were entered into which reinforced Moscow's position in the region. They ranged from ceasefire agreements and the percentage agreement in 1944 to the agreement on the governments of Bulgaria and Romania in December 1945 and the peace treaties in 1947. Both Washington and London were aware that Western control over Italy and Japan had to be paid for to a certain extent with return favors in Eastern Europe, although of course both sides tried to have their bread buttered on both sides.

The United States and Britain admitted that Eastern Europe was more important to the Soviet Union than to themselves. It was reasonable that the Soviets had considerable influence there. The border changes did not represent major problems. Nor was a certain orientation towards Moscow in foreign policy, such as in Czechoslovakia, particularly problematic during the very first phase of the cold war.

Despite such concessions on both sides, the distance between them was considerable. Conflict over Eastern Europe would destroy the cooperation established during the war. Neither Washington nor London was willing to relinquish fully their influence in the area. The Soviet Union, on the other hand, had limited geographic objectives in Europe, but in at least the inner ring of countries the Kremlin was firmly set on establishing quite complete control.

Free elections were the largest obstacle. The problem was that in the countries which were of most importance to the Soviet Union the Communists were weakest. There was little doubt that the Peasant parties would win free elections in both Poland and Romania. Moscow would not accept this type of result, while the Western powers could not allow the opposition to be simply pushed aside. In Poland and Romania it was impossible to combine free elections with a government friendly to the Soviet Union, at least if the Western powers were to define what were free elections and the USSR what was a government friendly to the Soviet Union. There was no basis in domestic policy for a 'Czech' or 'Finnish' pattern in anti-Russian Poland and Romania. Soviet interests were also greater in these two countries than in Czechoslovakia and Finland.

US requirements as to what could be considered 'friendly' governments rose continually. The same thing happened on the Soviet side, although with the difference that the consequences of not fulfilling these requirements could be even more dramatic. During the initial period after the war, non-Communists were represented in all the governments of Eastern Europe and were even in the majority in several of them. They gradually lost influence. The pace varied from country to country, but by the autumn of 1947 most non-Communists were pretty much in the same boat. Of the prominent peasant leaders, Petkov in Bulgaria had been hanged, Maniu in Romania sentenced to prison for life, and Mikolajczyk in Poland and Nagy in Hungary had to flee from their home countries. From the summer of 1947 Moscow began to pursue a more active policy in Czechoslovakia as well. The coup in Prague in February 1948 arose partly from local conditions but undoubtedly enjoyed Soviet support. In 1948–49, comprehensive purges were initiated within the various Communist parties, purges which ended with death even for several leading party members (see pages 209–210).

From the autumn of 1947, Moscow's attitude towards Western Europe changed as well. The French and Italian Communist parties were severely criticized for the passive policies they had pursued, although they had done so with the Kremlin's support. Now comprehensive strikes and demonstrations were launched, even though they were probably intended more to weaken the effect of the Marshall Plan than to take power in these two countries.

The Problem of Germany

The antagonism between East and West spread from Eastern Europe to Germany. The war against Hitler's Germany had drawn the two sides together. After the country was defeated, they agreed on important principles as to the course of development for Germany. It was taken for granted that Germany would remain demilitarized. Even though the three major powers had discussed dismembering the country into several small states as late as at Yalta, in the following months all three would commit themselves to keeping Germany one unit. Dismemberment would entail the danger of a new nationalistic movement being created by a rally call for unity. The three also agreed that clear limitations had to be placed on the German economy. The United States promoted the Morgenthau Plan for a short time, to the effect that all heavy industry was to be closed down. Even after this plan was abandoned towards the

Allied Zones in Germany and Austria.

end of 1944, their mutual point of departure was that Germany should not have a higher standard of living than the average in the European countries.

At Yalta the United States, Britain, and the Soviet Union had grudgingly agreed to allow France to administer one of the zones of occupation, but it was to be carved out from the US and British zones. This rather humble start did not prevent France from pursuing a distinctive course. None of the other powers so strongly emphasized the importance of keeping Germany weak. Paris was opposed to a possible German central government attaining anything more than purely symbolic func-

51

tions. The best solution would be to dismember the country, but France had entered into the discussion at such a late stage and had so little influence that this goal was unattainable. Instead the Saar province was to be annexed to France, whereas the Ruhr and the Rhineland regions were to be partitioned off from the rest of Germany and placed under international control in a manner that allowed France to play a central role.

Unlike France, the Soviet Union wanted a strong central government in Germany. This was natural from a Soviet way of thinking. A strong central government could also be an instrument for procuring larger reparations from Germany. Finally, there was the fact that the Soviet Union controlled a much smaller part of the country than the three Western powers combined. Through a strong central government Moscow could attain a certain influence even in the other zones.

The Soviet Union naturally had a particular interest in the payment of reparations. The Germans were to pay for the tremendous destruction they had caused. At Yalta Roosevelt and Stalin accepted the sum of ten billion dollars as a basis for discussion concerning reparations to the Soviet Union. Moscow would return to this question again and again. The United States—and to an even greater extent Britain—was afraid that it would be impossible for the Germans to pay such large reparations as the Soviet Union wanted, and that in the end it would be American and British taxpayers who would be called on to keep the Germans alive if they had to transfer excessively large sums to the Soviet Union. London and Washington could recall unpleasant lessons from WW I to this effect. At the Potsdam Conference in July and August this difficulty was partially, but only partially, resolved by agreeing that most of the reparations were to be taken from one's own zone of occupation.

It is difficult to find clear patterns in the policies of the major powers with regard to Germany immediately after the war. Several courses competed with one another. This was perhaps most evident on the part of the Soviet Union. Moscow advocated German unity and even a strong central government. At the same time, the Soviets pursued policies which were bound to undermine both the desire for unity and the possibilities of attaining political influence. Their hard line in terms of reparations was poorly received by the Germans. The merging of the Communist party and the Socialist party in April 1946 was a sign that the Soviet Union was beginning to organize its zone according to the Eastern European pattern.

Churchill did not want to accept the ten billion in reparations to the

Soviet Union, even as a basis of discussion. The British were sceptical, too, towards the conditions of the Potsdam agreement regarding reparations. In the discussions as to how high industrial production should be in Germany, the British pressed for the highest figures. This was mostly because the Ruhr, the major industrial area, was in the British zone, and the British were afraid their weak economy would suffer because of outlays in Germany. The object of not weakening Germany too much in relation to the Soviet Union was another contributory factor.

On 3 May 1946, General Clay stopped payment of reparations from the US zone. The background for this action was the fact that it had proved impossible to administer Germany as a political and economic unit. France was the country which was most strongly opposed to any coordination, and Clay's halt in the payment of reparations was aimed not only at the Soviet Union, but just as much at France. Gradually, however, the United States and Britain began to accept that the Saar region be linked to France. They still opposed partitioning the Ruhr and the Rhineland from the rest of Germany.

On the part of the United States there were obvious differences between the local authorities in Germany who, in order to facilitate their tasks then and there, advocated a more lenient policy, and the State Department in Washington, which was concerned about the reactions this course would evoke in other countries. For instance, these differences had manifested themselves in the negotiations regarding the level of industrial production: the US local authorities adovocated a level slightly lower than the British proposal, whereas the State Department originally pressed for a level which was lower than that suggested by both the Soviet Union and France. (The stand taken by these two countries was partially determined by the fact that they themselves wanted to reap part of the benefits of increased production.)

Nevertheless, the tendencies in allied policies towards Germany were clear. The United States in particular would follow an ever more lenient course. In July 1946 Washington proposed that those who wanted to could merge their zones with the US zone. Britain soon accepted, but both France and the Soviet Union declined. The establishment of the so-called Bi-zone illustrated two things: in the first place, that consensus as to Germany was in the process of disintegrating entirely, and in the second place, that the United States had assumed leadership in the West, here as elsewhere.

The major breakthrough for a new policy towards Germany was Secretary of State Byrnes' speech in Stuttgart on 6 September 1946. Byrnes not only made it clear that US troops would participate in the occupation as long as it lasted; furthermore, the German economy had to be made self-sufficient so that the country would not be dependent on supplies from abroad. The Germans would also have to be granted self-government to an increasing extent.

At the Potsdam Conference it had been decided that Poland was to administer the territory as far west as Oder-Neisse, but a final decision regarding the Polish-German border was to be made in connection with a German peace treaty. The Western powers had seemed to reconcile themselves to the fact that the temporary border would become the final border, but in Stuttgart Byrnes stated that it was not at all certain this would be the case. This initiative strengthened the US position in Germany, while the Soviet Union, which had tried to secure a foothold in relation to both Germany and Poland, now gave its full support to the Poles.

Germany was no longer an adversary. Increasingly, it became a prize the major powers competed for. The more intense the cold war became, the greater was the interest in granting new concessions to the Germans. Moreover, it became increasingly evident that Europe could not be rebuilt economically unless Germany was granted a larger role. The Western zones thus played an important role in the establishment of the Marshall Plan in 1947.

The cold war made it more difficult for France to continue its independent course in Germany. In April—May 1948, Paris assented in principle to merging the French zone with the US-British zone. A constitutional assembly was to be convened and a federal German government to be established for the three Western zones. French policy regarding the Ruhr and Rhineland regions was abandoned. In return, agreement was reached that the Ruhr should have an international controlling authority, although a relatively weak one.

Seen from Moscow, these developments were ominous. The Soviet Union was excluded from the Ruhr and from most of Germany. The tremendous economic potential of the Western zones was about to be released. US assistance was being poured in. In June the Western powers implemented a monetary reform which made it unmistakably evident that Germany was no longer an economic unit. The new West Germany would be integrated into Western European cooperation, but that did not improve the situation, as the country could easily become the dominant member.

The Berlin blockade was Moscow's reponse to these events. The first obstructions of traffic to West Berlin were introduced in April 1948. From July 25th the blockade was complete except for air connections. This was Moscow's most dramatic action after the war. For the first time force was used to promote changes in an area where Western troops were stationed. However, Moscow allowed itself a certain scope for maneuvering by arguing that the measures were due to repairs. Thus the blockade could be lifted when the repairs were completed. Soviet objectives were not at all clear. A maximum objective may have been to prevent the creation of West Germany and to achieve control of all of Germany by the four powers. A minimum objective may have been to isolate West Berlin in order to bring the city under Soviet influence.

The Western powers improvised by establishing an airlift, a measure which was expected to be temporary but which proved to be protracted. The airlift exceeded everyone's expectations. The Soviet Union could not stop the traffic without resorting to more direct use of force. Nor could Moscow prevent the developments leading to the creation of a West German state. The blockade of West Berlin hastened the establishment of NATO and weakened the Soviet position in Western Europe. The Western blockade of East Germany in response to the Berlin blockade had a certain effect as well.

In May 1949 Moscow agreed to end the blockade without having achieved anything except minor concessions. The day after the blockade was ended, the three Western military governors approved the new West German constitution. Ten days later the new state was formally established. In October East Germany followed suit.

Motivating forces behind US and Soviet policies

It is almost always easier to describe what happened than to explain why something happened. The difficulties are especially great in relation to the motivating forces behind Soviet policies because of the scarcity of material available. Concerning the United States, the problem is rather the opposite: an abundance of sources.

The United States
A number of different factors were of significance for the Americans. The question of national security was one of them. This could be observed even in US policy towards Eastern Europe. The region in itself was

not of particular strategic importance to the United States. However, two circumstances diminished the distinction between important and less important regions. In the first place, many leading politicians in the Roosevelt and Truman administrations asked themselves whether 'relinquishing' Eastern Europe to the Soviet Union would not merely result in the pressure being transmitted to the next layer of countries. Then the strategically important Western Europe would be threatened. This layer-by-layer theory was accepted by more and more policy-makers in Washington during 1944-45. In the second place, and this may explain why the theory so easily gained ground, the lesson of WW II was that aggression developed gradually. Hitler had not been stopped in time; this mistake should not be made a second time.

In 1945–46 the conflict concerned Eastern Europe and to some extent Germany. In 1947–48 Washington began to fear Soviet expansion into Western Europe. The main threat was not direct aggression. The chances of a direct attack were small, although they could not be disregarded entirely. Most politicians believed that an exhausted Soviet Union wanted to avoid a destructive conflict with the West. However, considering the long shadows Soviet control of Eastern Europe cast over Western Europe, the chances were greater of Moscow succeeding in less dramatic ways, as a result of political pressure, economic chaos and active local Communist parties. Czechoslovakia was an example of this type of expansion.

A number of events during the winter and spring of 1948 contributed to the impression that Western Europe was threatened (page 42). The attitude of Western Europe itself was important; as we have seen (pages 40–42), there was fairly constant pressure on the United States to play a more active role in European politics. This involved first economic assistance, then political and moral support and finally direct military guarantees.

The influence of Britain was especially important. This country had the best relations with the United States and worked most actively to draw the United States closer to Western Europe. Another important consideration was the fact that it was less necessary for the United States to play a new role in foreign policy as long as others could represent US interests. Washington and London did not see eye to eye on all matters. They disagreed as to colonial policy, international trade, the question of Palestine and a number of other issues. Nevertheless, they had an important mutual interest in containing Soviet influence. As long as Britain was able to fulfill this function, there was less need for the United States to do so.

However, the position of the United Kingdom changed dramatically in the years immediately after the war. The British had to retreat on a number of fronts. In India, the colonial system began to collapse. The British withdrew from Palestine when the political problems piled up and their economy did not allow them to be actively present. Even more important in terms of the cold war was the reduced presence of the British in Greece and Turkey and in Germany. The economic problems of the United Kingdom were the immediate cause of the proclamation of the Truman Doctrine in March 1947. When the British could no longer hold back the leftist guerillas in Greece nor support the Turkish government against Soviet pressure, the Truman administration saw that it had to take over.

In Germany, too, the weak British economy was an important reason for their close cooperation with the United States, as evidenced for instance by the merging of the two countries' zones in 1946. In more comprehensive terms, it could be argued that both the Marshall Plan and NATO were measures that were established because the Western Europeans could not solve their economic, political and military problems by themselves.

A number of different domestic conditions also influenced US policy. There was a strong ideological desire to spread the American gospel to other countries. America was God's own country, with a duty to proclaim her values to others. Everyone wanted democracy and freer trade, or at least would have wanted them if they could have expressed their wishes. The more subdued version of this message was the emphasis on US responsibility to defend democracy against an expansive Communism.

There was widespread political agreement in the United States as to the main course the country pursued after the Second World War. However, some groups were more active than others, depending on which issue was most pressing. Ethnic considerations played a part. The many Polish-Americans were especially active with regard to Eastern Europe in 1944-45. The Italian-Americans played a corresponding role with regard to Western Europe. These groups in turn enjoyed support in wider circles, such as the Catholic Church.

After the 1946 election, Congress was controlled by the Republicans, and even though they were often even more anti-communist than the Truman administration, they were sceptical to most things that cost

57

money. Anti-communism was to be inexpensive. Thus considerations of party politics influenced US policy. In order to compensate for the insufficient appeal 400 million dollars for Greece and Turkey had on a Congress bent on saving, the Truman Doctrine was presented in extra dramatic terms. Other concessions had to be made to the Republicans in general and the chairman of the Senate Foreign Relations Committee, Arthur Vandenberg, in particular. The Marshall Plan was pruned here and there; Western Europe had to promise to do more on its own both economically and militarily; the United States avoided automatic military commitments towards Europe.

After such concessions the Truman administration managed to get its most important measures passed in Congress, usually by a large majority. The opposition which existed came from both the left and the right. On the left it was centered around former Vice President (1941–45) and Secretary of Commerce (1945–46) Henry Wallace and his supporters. Wallace was dismissed in the autumn of 1946 because of his more conciliatory attitude towards the Soviet Union. However, most of the opposition came from the right, and was linked to the name of Senator Robert Taft. The right wing was even more anti-communist than the majority, even more nationalistic, but also even more cost-conscious. The Marshall Plan cost the American taxpayer far too much. NATO limited US military freedom of action. Taft and his supporters represented the mild postwar variant of American isolationism.

Economic considerations, too, influenced US policy. A recurrent question was whether the US economy would slide into a new depression when the war was over. Many people believed that this type of setback was likely, even more believed that it was possible. It could be avoided or possibly softened by foreign policy measures. Exports could be increased, and possible surplus capital used for investments abroad. Important raw materials the United States lacked could be imported from abroad. The motives of pure self-interest behind these policies were reinforced by the ideology they were a part of. The dominant circles were convinced that tariffs and regional trade blocs were detrimental not only to the United States but to all countries, and that they were also an important explanation as to why war and conflict arise between nations.

Several factors moderated these economic considerations. In the first place, most people quite soon became more optimistic with regard to the possibilities of avoiding a new depression. In the second place, the United States was one of the countries in the world which was least dependent on its foreign trade. In absolute figures, the United States had by far the largest volume of foreign trade in the world, but in relation to total production, export and import each represented less than 5 percent. This figure was much lower than for the countries of Western Europe. The United States was also more self-sufficient in terms of raw materials than almost any other country. US dependence on other countries did not increase significantly until the 1970s.

The business world was not more sceptical to the Soviet Union than other people were. Many branches, such as the aviation industry, obviously profitted from international tension and large defense budgets, but most of the business world was more interested in keeping taxes down than in increasing the defense budget.

The vast majority of exporters were interested in increasing trade with the Soviet Union: here was a market that could really amount to something. Thus these circles advocated both increased trade with and large credits to the Soviet Union. The many restrictions imposed on trade with the Soviet Union from the end of 1947 did not represent the attitude of big business in the United States.

The most important basis for US policy seems to have a tendency to be forgotten, namely the tremendous power of the United States at the end of the war. History affords few examples of overwhelming power that does not express itself in active policies. Considering US strength in 1945, it was almost inevitable that the country should try to shape the international environment in its own image to a considerable degree.

The Soviet Union

Stalin and the other Soviet leaders often stressed the fact that Soviet policy in Eastern Europe was motivated by considerations of national security. There is little reason to doubt that this was the case. During the preceding 30 years alone, Russia/the Soviet Union had been attacked by Germany twice. Besides this, there had been Western intervention in the civil war and war with Poland. The First World War had caused the fall of the Czar's regime. The Second World War had nearly resulted in a collapse of Stalin's rule.

National security considerations would necessarily carry a lot of weight with any leader in the Kremlin. But Stalin made higher demands than most leaders. This had become evident in his domestic policy through the many extensive purges. Now the position of the Soviet Union in terms of foreign policy was to be secured. The only problem was that what was security for one country tended to be insecurity for another. This was true both in relation to the neighbors who were no longer to be given the opportunity to represent a threat and in relation to the Western powers.

On rare occasions Stalin could give credit to the Western powers. After the Second Front was finally established at Normandy in June 1944, he proclaimed that 'one cannot but recognize that the history of warfare knows of no other similar undertaking in the breadth of its conception, in its giant dimensions, and in the mastery of its performance.' *Pravda* took the unheard of step of publishing the figures for the help the Soviet Union had received from the West during the war.

But these were rare exceptions. Stalin's scepticism of the Western powers was considerable. It did not diminish as the war drew to a close. In March-April 1945, Stalin accused the Western powers of having made a separate peace in Italy, which would give the Germans the opportunity to transfer troops from Italy to the Eastern front. At the end of April, the Red Army in Austria built up large defense installations. At that time the Germans were nearly defeated. It actually appears as though the Soviet leaders were now afraid that the Western powers would make a separate peace with Germany which applied throughout Europe, rather than just for Italy.

In August 1945 the leaders in the Kremlin began to openly emphasize their conviction that even though the danger of fascism was over, the Soviet Union could not reduce its vigilance on that account. The attacks on capitalism were increased. References to the mutual interests of the three major powers ceased. Stalin's so-called election speech in February 1946 was an expression of this new orientation. (The Western leaders were cautious in their public descriptions of the Soviet Union, with few exceptions. Their private opinions were another matter. Thus the Truman administration tried to create the impression of a greater distance to opposition leader Churchill's attack on the Soviet Union in March 1946 than the actual attitude of the administration would indicate.)

Soviet control in Eastern Europe was not only a military *cordon sanitaire* in relation to the West, but also an ideological barrier. The Soviet Union would no doubt be capable of closing its borders to undesired influences, but adding an extra margin here could not hurt. Consideration of the many Soviet soldiers in Eastern Europe certainly played a part as well.

In addition, the risk that Moscow's policy in Eastern Europe involved was very small. It is quite possible the Soviet leaders had the impression that the Western powers were prepared to 'relinquish' the region to them if a number of more or less cosmetic concessions were made. Little in the actions of the Western powers indicated otherwise, at least before the Yalta Conference. After Yalta it must have been evident to the Kremlin that both the United States and Britain intended to pursue an active policy, particularly with regard to Poland, but also in other countries. Former Foreign Minister Litvinov probably expressed genuine confusion when he said to an American journalist in June 1945: 'Why did you Americans wait until now to begin opposing us in the Balkans and Eastern Europe? ... You should have done this three years ago. Now it's too late and your complaints only arouse suspicion here?'

Economic considerations played a role in Soviet as well as in US policy. The Soviet Union acquired substantial benefits in Eastern Europe and in other border areas, such as in China. Through trade agreements, joint companies, reparation payments and war spoils, considerable resources were transferred to the Soviet Union.

Soviet expansion was also in accordance with communist ideology. Stalin's 'socialism in one country' had been an admission that, in direct opposition to Lenin's expectations, the Communist revolution had been limited to the Soviet Union. Now, at last, history had begun to take its proper course. But expansion in Eastern Europe was much less a historical necessity than it was an expression of the possibilities created by the advance of the Red Army. Power was an important condition for the policy pursued, even though the Soviet Union's power was considerably less and geographically more limited than that of the United States.

3. The cold war becomes global, 1945–1962

During the years 1945–1949 the cold war was concentrated mainly on Europe and the areas bordering on Europe, such as Turkey and Iran. This chapter will first show that the superpowers' involvement in other parts of the world in the years immediately following the war was relatively limited. This was particularly true for the Soviet Union. The argument then proceeds to analyze how the cold war later spread to ever new areas, first to Asia, then to the Middle East and Africa, and finally to Latin America as well. In the 1960s the cold war had become global.

The United States, the Soviet Union, and Asia, 1945–1950

The Civil War in China

Although Japan and the European powers had controlled parts of China, they had never managed to dominate it to the same degree as they did most of the remainder of Asia. China was a vast country and the most populous in the world. The Chinese could play off the various great powers against each other. During the post-war period, China would illustrate the limitations even of the superpowers' influence.

Many Americans had had a certain fondness for China for a long time. Europe was the old world; like America, Asia belonged to the new world. Businessmen, missionaries and teachers had flocked from the United States to China in their thousands to spread American ideals.

This sentiment towards China had also been evident during the war. Washington had insisted that China should be one of the major powers, thus becoming a permanent member of the UN Security Council. Although despair as to the ineffectiveness of Chiang Kai-shek's war against the Japanese could reach considerable levels, the Americans always remained determined that he should be the future leader of this major power. China suited Washington's plans for the post-war period perfectly. In relations between East and West, China, under the leadership of Chiang, would support the United States against the Soviet Union. In colonial questions, too, China would undoubtedly side with the United States, primarily in opposition to Britain. China represented an important market which could become even more important in the future. Parts of American opinion still sympathized more with fledgling Asia than with aging Europe.

Chiang's regime was authoritarian, corrupt and ineffective. Even so, there was no alternative. Leading circles in Washington considered Mao Tse-tung a communist who did have an independent streak, but who nonetheless cooperated with Moscow.

The United States gave considerable support to the Kuomintang. From 1945 to 1947 total economic assistance amounted to 1.4 billion dollars. Even so, it was not enough to keep the regime functioning. From 1947-48 Chiang was on the defensive. The Truman administration and the Congress responded with the China Act of 1948. In the rhetorical language of Washington, it declared that the US objective was to 'maintain the genuine independence and the administrative integrity of China, and to sustain and strengthen principles of individual liberty and free institutions in China through a program based on self-help and cooperation.' An additional 275 million dollars were given as economic assistance and 125 million for military supplies.

Nevertheless, there were clear limitations to this assistance. The US troops that were in China at the end of the war were withdrawn, and only indirectly and to a diminishing extent used to support the Kuomintang army. New troops were not sent in to prevent a Communist victory in the civil war. In 1948 the Truman administration only half-heartedly granted further assistance to Chiang. The administration was particularly sceptical about the military part of the program of assistance, but was also in doubt as to whether there was any purpose in sending further economic assistance.

The new assistance was in part a concession to the military and to rightist circles in Congress. Again and again Taft and his conservative Republicans had asked why one policy was to be pursued in Europe and a different one in Asia. If it was right to curb communism in Europe, it must be right to do the same in Asia. Although public opinion had long been opposed to escalating the US involvement in Asia, in 1948 there were unmistakable signals that this attitude was in the process of changing.

The opposition wanted more forceful rhetoric and an increase in Washington's economic and military assistance. They were also in favor of sending American military advisers to China, suggesting a figure of about 10 000. But even the strongest pro-Chiang circles denied that they wanted to send US combat forces to fight on the side of the Kuomintang.

The sizeable, yet limited, support by the United States may seem surprising in the light of the comprehensive US involvement in Europe and not least in comparison with the US interventions that would later follow in Asia.

A primary reason was that China was certainly important, but it was far from equal to Europe in importance. Within the Truman administration, both the State Department and the military establishment agreed that efforts to stop the Communists in China had to be subordinate to the policy of containment in Europe. Europe was primary in terms of both strategic and economic significance. During the Second World War, Germany had to be defeated before Japan. The same priority was evident now. Even those who in theory felt that Asia ought to be at least equal to Europe in importance supported the 'Europe first' policy in practice, although this course was less pronounced for them than it was for the administration.

A second reason was that US resources were limited, especially when Europe was to be granted top priority. Demobilization had reduced the US armed forces to a bare minimum. They were not even sufficient to fully realize US commitments in the occupied countries. There was no desire, least of all among those who opposed the administration's China policies, to induct extraordinary forces or to increase the defense budget in order to procure resources for a more active policy in China.

In the third place, China was a vast country, and the tasks involved could easily become equally vast. The 10 000 'advisers' there was talk of sending were intended to be just that. Few people, if any, wanted the United States to become involved in another war such a short time after WW II. In a sense, the tasks in China were more comprehensive than in Europe, where the task was primarily to deter Soviet expansion, not to support troops in combat. Moreover, no one could know how many 'advisers' could be needed to prevent a communist victory in China.

In the fourth place, there was uncertainty as to what the Soviet response would be if the United States began to send in troops. A US intervention could easily result in a corresponding Soviet reaction. Since the Soviet Union had not yet given military support to the Communists, the United States would be left with the responsibility for having let a local conflict develop into something that could threaten world peace.

Finally, Washington was dissatisfied with Chiang Kai-shek and his policies. Rightist regimes could receive, and did receive, support from the United States to an increasing extent, but in China there were few indications that this assistance had much effect. Chiang was already getting considerably more assistance from abroad than Mao was. The problems of the Kuomintang were internal. Popular support seemed to decline, but that did not increase the willingness to implement reforms that could strengthen the basis for popular support for the regime. Aid could not compensate for political disintegration. This had long been the conclusion among most of the US experts on China. To an ever increasing degree it was also shared by Truman and his leading advisers.

If US support to Chiang was limited, Soviet support to Mao Tse-tung was even more limited. The Soviet Union gave little or no military assistance, with the exception of the Japanese weapons that were left behind in Manchuria when the Red Army withdrew in 1946. It is likely that Moscow gave a certain amount of economic support, but it must have been much less than the amounts the Americans gave to their side. (If any, it was also less than the value of the spoils taken out of Manchuria during the withdrawal.)

There is little reason to doubt that the Soviet Union preferred Mao to Chiang, but this ideologically based involvement was kept at a very modest level. In the Sino-Soviet pact of 14 August 1945, Moscow recognized Chiang as China's legitimate leader. This recognition was formally sustained until 30 September 1949. There was little mention of the war in China in the Soviet press. Not until 3 October, 1949 were the Chinese Communists praised on the first page of *Pravda*.

In October 1949, former Secretary of State Marshall, who had recently left the cabinet, stressed that with regard to Soviet assistance to the Communists: 'I never could see any trace of it ... Well, as far as I could see, what they were preparing themselves for was a case before the United Nations, where they could appear clean as driven snow and we would have our hands muddied by every bit of propaganda they could manufacture.' Mao Tse-tung would later express a similar view.

An important reason for this lukewarm attitude was that like the Americans, but to a much greater extent, the Soviet Union had limited resources. Moscow wished to concentrate the resources that were available on Europe—again even more clearly than Washington—particularly in Eastern Europe and Germany. China came further down on the list of priorities.

It is true that Moscow hoped to strengthen its position in parts of China. In many ways a relatively weak China could serve Soviet interests. Only then could Moscow secure the influence in the Sino-Soviet border areas it openly hoped to obtain. The first step was to regain what Russia had lost in the war with Japan in 1904-05. This was achieved at Yalta and confirmed in the Sino-Soviet pact of August 1945. The southern part of Sakhalin was returned to the Soviet Union. Port Arthur was again to become a Soviet navy base. Dairen was internationalized under Soviet leadership, and the railroad in Manchuria came under Soviet influence. Moscow's supremacy over Outer Mongolia was recognized, and the Soviet Union acquired control over the Kurile Islands, including the southernmost islands, which had not previously belonged to Russia.

In 1944, Islamic rebels had established an independent republic in East Turkestan. The Soviet Union was obviously in close contact with them, and not until 1949 was the republic reintegrated into China. Even more surprisingly, Moscow made a separate trade agreement with Manchuria as late as in July 1949. As it was evident that all of China would soon be under the Chinese Communists' control, this had to be interpreted as a blow at them. The local Communist leader, Kao Kang, was later sharply denounced by Mao. In Sinkiang, too, Moscow emphasized the expansion of Soviet regional interests.

Moreover, it is likely that in the years immediately following WW II Stalin expected Chiang to be victorious in the conflict with Mao, which may have been conducive to moderation, in part to retain the privileges mentioned. The US stance was probably significant as well. The Soviet Union wanted to avoid a direct conflict with the United States. How Washington would react to Soviet interference in China was unknown. Moderation there could moderate the consequences of the conflict over Eastern Europe to some extent. When the Communists showed dramatic progress during the civil war, the need to provide assistance disappeared. Developments were moving in the right direction anyway. Why strain relations with the West under these circumstances?

Finally, it is likely that the conflict with Tito (see page 211) came to influence Moscow's evaluation of the Chinese Communists. At a time when Stalin had become extremely suspicious of anything that could appear to be national communist dissent, there was a lot to worry about in China. There were evident signs of independence in the ideology of the Chinese Communists. Like Tito, Mao rose to power mostly on his own. Both of them had little to thank Moscow for on that account. Mao had had even less contact with Moscow than Tito had, and he would govern a much larger country than the Yugoslavian leader did. There must be reason to believe that Stalin had less confidence in the fruits Sino-Soviet cooperation would bear than the official statements after Mao's victory gave the impression of.

Local factors led to the Communists' victory in the civil war. Support for Mao increased rapidly. The majority of the peasant population had long been on his side, and corruption, incompetence and a lack of willingness to institute reforms gradually limited Chiang's support, even among the urban bourgeoisie. Or as Mao summed up the principles of the guerilla war: 'The people are the sea—we are the fish.'

Other Countries in Asia

Both Washington and Moscow obviously placed greater emphasis on events in Europe than in Asia. This was evident not only in China, but in other parts of Asia as well.

For the Truman administration, what mattered was supporting the regimes in Western Europe, as Washington's attitude towards the European colonial powers showed. On the one hand, the US stance was clearly anti-colonial: the colonial empires had to be dissolved. On the other hand, the United States wanted to contain communism and stabilize conditions in Western Europe. This often required a cautious course with regard to decolonization.

During the first phase of the war the Roosevelt administration had spoken out in favor of hastening India's independence, but even during the war Washington increasingly left the initiative to London. Churchill did not want any American interference. Relations improved as the British made a clear commitment that India would become independent after the war. When the Labour government took over in 1945, it further accelerated the process. That diminished the differences between Washington and London even more. The United States supported Britain's plans to keep Hindus and Muslims together. When this proved impossible, both countries were in favor of partition into two nations, India and Pakistan.

The priority given to stability in Europe became even more evident in relation to France and the Netherlands. The United States had fewer mutual interests with these two countries than with Britain. Roosevelt had favored the establishment of an international trusteeship in Indo-China. He felt that France, through its exploitation of the region, had proven itself unworthy of ruling the country again. This idea died with Roosevelt. France regained control over Indo-China.

Washington's insistence during the first years after the war that military assistance to France should not be used in Indo-China was reduced. It soon became evident that support to France also assisted the French in their colonial war in Indo-China. Washinton still maintained that France ought to pursue a far more liberal colonial policy, but found it increasingly difficult to build up the country in Western Europe and at the same time pressure it to make concessions in Asia. The latter objective had to yield. This conclusion was strengthened as it became more evident that the independence movement in Vietnam was controlled by communists.

If anti-colonial considerations should have shown themselves anywhere in their purest form, that would have to have been in Indonesia. The Netherlands were not a major power in a European context. The Indonesian independence movement was clearly non-communist. Even so, US policy until 1948 was primarily aimed at attempting to negotiate between the two sides. Only when violence escalated and both the UN and Congress began to take an interest in the conflict in earnest did the Truman administration change its course. Then Washington threatened to halt all economic and military assistance to the Dutch. This was an important factor behind their decision to grant Indonesia independence. (Decolonization will be dealt with more thoroughly in Chapter 9.)

During the first few years after WW II, Moscow showed a certain degree of openness towards nationalist movements in Asia. Even in Zhdanov's so-called two-camp speech in September 1947 there were certain non-camp exceptions. Vietnam and Indonesia were perceived as 'associated' with the socialist camp. India, Egypt and Syria had sympathies with the Eastern bloc, but were obviously not a part of it. However, for the most part the world was divided into two blocs: 'the imperialist and antidemocratic camp, on the one hand, and the anti-imperialist and democratic camp, on the other'.

Verbal attacks on the new nationalist leaders soon increased in intensity. Moscow expressed the view that it made little difference whether the British administered India or whether they did so indirectly through their lackeys, Gandhi and Nehru. From 1949, Indonesia's Sukarno, who had previously been treated more warmly, was denounced in strong terms. Those who did not show complete support for the East belonged to the West. At the same time, Stalin and the other Soviet leaders became increasingly less interested in what was happening in the new nations of Asia. Expression of official attitudes in these matters was left to lower levels in the hierarchy, such as the press and scholars.

It was difficult to count on communist take-overs, as the local Communist parties other than in Vietnam were rather weak. Even so, communist revolts broke out in Burma, Malaya, Indonesia and the Philippines in 1948. A similar occurrence had taken place earlier in Hyderabad in India.

The role of the Soviet Union is not at all clear. It is uncertain whether the Soviet leaders had inspired the revolts. The conference in Calcutta in 1948, where Moscow's directives were supposedly given, was not a very suitable forum, as participation far exceeded the ranks of the Communists. It seems more likely that the overall international climate, and the resulting division into two camps, stimulated both the Soviet Union and the local movements to strike out a more radical course. The progress of the Communists in China may also have been of great significance. Moscow did little or nothing to quell revolts once they had broken out, but except for articles in the press and speeches they did not give any active support either. In the press, interest seems to have been greater for a broad front against the colonial powers, such as in Malaya, than for revolts against established independent governments, such as in Burma and to some extent in the Philippines. Sympathy for the revolt in Indonesia was something in between.

Even for Moscow, France was more important than Vietnam. At least this must have seemed to be the case for the Vietnamese Communists. Nothing was to be done that could possibly weaken the position of the French Communists. To a great extent policy was left to the French comrades themselves, who wanted to attain a compromise, particularly while they were members of the French cabinet. After war had broken out between France and Viet Minh in December 1946, Moscow declared that:

'The further development of Vietnam depends to a significant degree on its ties with democratic France, whose progressive forces have always spoken forth in support of colonial liberation.' Until 1950, the Soviet Union gave little or no material assistance to the Vietnamese Communists.

Signs of Re-evaluation in the Superpowers' Asian Policies

The Communist victory in China inevitably led to a re-evaluation of Moscow's Asian policies. It was one thing to have been lukewarm towards Mao and his forces during the civil war. When victory had been achieved, the best had to be made of the possibilities which undoubtedly presented themselves. In 1948, China had not been mentioned in the main speech during Moscow's celebration of the October revolution. In the following year, Malenkov declared that Mao's victory would lead to a new and higher stage in the peoples' struggle for independence in Asia and other parts of the world.

The Chinese on their part stressed that in the cold war no nation could take a stance between the imperialist bloc led by the United States and the anti-imperialist bloc led by the Soviet Union. Mao proclaimed that neutrality was only camouflage. In February 1950 the two countries signed a 30-year alliance and friendship pact. Among other things, they promised each other mutual assistance in the event of attack by Japan or a country allied with Japan.

The Soviet Union would give up its territorial privileges no later than in 1952. Moscow also granted a 300 million dollar loan on reasonable terms. But tensions were noticeable even at this stage. It was strange that Mao had to spend three months in Moscow at a time when he was urgently needed in his own country. Nor was 300 million dollars a very large amount. Poland had just been granted a 450 million dollar loan on even better terms. It can not have been absolutely necessary to retain Soviet privileges for a few more years, either. Nor can the cooperation which was to be established have been a godsend for the Chinese if it was to follow the pattern established in Eastern Europe.

On 18 January 1950, Peking recognized Vietminh as the government of Vietnam. Moscow soon followed suit. The Kremlin had formerly explained to their Chinese comrades that recognition was to be given only after they had won control of the country. Now, all at once, this established practice could be broken.

In 1949-50, there were clear signs of changes on the part of the United States as well, but until the outbreak of the Korean war this re-evaluation was less comprehensive than that of the Soviet Union. After the Communist victory on the Chinese mainland, the Truman administration planned to let events take their course as far as Taiwan was concerned. Washington expected the island to be conquered and did not intend to use military intervention to prevent such a result. Some policy-makers even felt that it might then be appropriate to recognize the new leaders in Peking.

That was not the course events would take. Attitudes in Congress and in large parts of public opinion made diplomatic recognition difficult. Economic assistance to Taiwan continued. From the spring of 1950, military supplies were sent as well. Leading Republicans spoke in favor of sending troops to the island; the US navy was to halt any attempt at invasion. However, on this issue the administration held firmly to its original stand.

The 'fall of China' made it necessary for the Truman administration to pursue a more active policy in Asia. Further communist expansion would represent a foreign policy defeat for the United States and a domestic setback for the Democrats. In December 1949, Truman approved National Security Council (NSC) 48/2. This document aimed at creating a basis for escalation of economic and military assistance to Asia. It established that special attention was to be paid to the situation in Vietnam.

For a long time, Washington had tried to get Paris to make concessions to non-communist nationalists. France finally agreed to grant Vietnam formal independence. In practice, this did not mean major changes as French control remained about the same as previously. Nevertheless, in February 1950 the United States recognized the new government under the weak, French-oriented Bao Dai. Washington was now prepared to increase assistance, and in May the first military assistance was given directly to France in Vietnam.

Japan was the most important country in Asia from an American perspective. Japan's significance increased even more after the Communist victory in China. US occupation policy had gradually changed because of the importance of Japanese resources for the West in the cold war. (Japanese-US relations will be discussed further on pages 202–203.)

The changes in US Asian policies were, however, relatively small before the outbreak of the Korean war. Europe was still far more important than Asia. In Asia the main emphasis was on Japan, the Philippines and other strategically important islands off the Asian mainland.

US strategic interests in Asia were clearly defined in 1949-50. Secretary of State Dean Acheson stated in January 1950 that the US defense perimeter went from the Aleutians to Japan and continued to the Ryukyu Islands and the Philippines. Several important areas were thus outside this line: Taiwan, Indo-China and South Korea. There was a considerable amount of debate about US policy in regard to Taiwan, but as far as the Asian mainland was concerned Acheson had broad support at the time. Disagreement as to the content of his speech would become much stronger at a later date. General Douglas MacArthur, supreme commander in Japan and highly activist during the Korean war, declared as late as two days after the outbreak of the war that whoever thought US troops ought to combat communism on the Asian mainland 'ought to have his head examined'.

This did not mean that the countries which were beyond the defense perimeter were not of interest to Washington. Economic and military assistance was given to them as well. The increase in assistance to Taiwan and Indochina has already been mentioned.

US commitments were even more direct in South Korea. With the collapse of Japan, Korea was divided into two zones of occupation at the thirty-eighth parallel. The Red Army moved in in the North, the US Army into the South. The Soviets molded their zone in their own image. They were supported by large groups of communists and radicals in the relatively industrialized North. The political situation was much more chaotic in the South, with as many as 200 political parties and groups. The Americans would support the reactionary Syngman Rhee, and the favoring of the right became more evident as Rhee was faced with ever increasing problems. In January 1950, Acheson stressed that although South Korea lay beyond the US defense perimeter, an attack on the country would be a matter for the UN.

When the Red Army was withdrawn from North Korea in 1948, the Pentagon felt that South Korea was a place were money could be saved on a tight defense budget. The last US troops were withdrawn in June 1949. In January 1950 the Congress voted down a proposal by the Truman administration for economic assistance to South Korea, but by promising a little extra support for Taiwan the administration persuaded the Congress to reverse this decision.

There were many reasons for Washington's restraint in South Korea.

The most important US interests were undoubtedly linked to the islands off the Asian mainland. Moreover, intervening in Korea seemed illogical when the United States had not intervened in China. In a sense, the statements of Acheson and others were rationalizations which arose from the policy that had already been pursued, particularly in regard to China.

Evaluations of the relative local strengths varied, but many Americans expected South Korea to be able to withstand North Korean attacks. It was considered unlikely that the Soviet Union or China would be directly involved in an attack on South Korea. Finally, Syngman Rhee, despite the increasing support he gradually enjoyed, was viewed with scepticism in Washington. He was far from democratic, but there was no other strong anti-communist alternative. The United States even feared that South Korea might attack North Korea, and to prevent this the Americans withheld deliveries of heavy military equipment such as planes and tanks.

US policy also rested on a specific analysis of the relationship between nationalism and communism. Nationalism was a growing force on the Asian mainland. It was important that the United States should not become antagonistic to nationalistic forces, but be able to use them against communism. In this context, and partly to soften the consequences of China's fall for US domestic politics, the Truman administration developed the theory that in the course of time there might be a breach between the Soviet Union and China. Acheson claimed that the most important interference in Asia was Soviet attempts to win control over parts of China. Thus 'we must not undertake to deflect from the Russians to ourselves the righteous anger and the wrath and the hatred of the Chinese people which must develop'. In the long term, nationalism would be victorious in China. US policy showed—despite many general statements that could indicate otherwise—that Washington still distinguished between important and less important regions, and that the United States was capable of perceiving differences within the communist bloc.

The Korean War

Many clashes had taken place between troops from the two parts of Korea. However, the North Korean attack on 25 June 1950 was of a completely different magnitude than these minor skirmishes. It seems highly likely that Moscow not only knew about, but had also given its consent to the attack. Even though the Red Army had been withdrawn, many Soviet military and civilian advisers remained, and they were to be found both centrally and locally. North Korea was dependent on the Soviet Union for weapons, and had received supplies as late as in April-May 1950. The North Korean leader Kim Il-sung did show signs of independence, but he seems to have had good relations with Moscow. Considering the position of Stalin and the Soviet Union within the communist movement, it is unlikely that an attack would have been made without having been cleared with the Kremlin.

But there is a difference between initiating and having given consent to plans. Khrushchev may well be right when he claims in his memoirs that the initiative was taken by the North Koreans. There were strong wishes in both North and South for a reunification of Korea. The North Korean leaders may have hoped that an attack would lead to a revolt in the south that would make the war short-lived.

In terms of great power politics, there was little reason to believe that the United States would intervene directly. The country had kept out of the civil war in China, and, as we have seen, there were numerous declarations that Korea was beyond the US defense perimeter. A successful drive would not only result in a unified communist Korea, but might also stop the ever stronger integration of Japan into US military strategy. Khrushchev claims, moreover, that Mao had consented to the Korean plans. That may be, but considering the tremendous domestic tasks facing China, it seems unlikely that the Chinese role can have been particularly active. Perhaps Stalin wanted to demonstrate to the Chinese that he, too, could actively support national liberation movements.

Although the risk involved in an attack was considered small, such a conflict meant a clear increase in Soviet involvement in Asia. Conditions in Europe were somewhat stabilized, and Moscow could devote more attention to what was happening in Asia.

The United States responded to the North Korean attack with air and naval forces. When this proved insufficient, ground troops as well were sent in. Thus the United States was at war on the Asian mainland after all. The American commander was Douglas MacArthur. The United Nations, with the Soviet Union absent from the Security Council, supported the US action. Forty-five states came to give aid of some sort to the American-led defense of South Korea.

What can explain this change on the part of the United States? There is often a difference between theory and practice. It was one thing to say that there would be no direct military response. It was another matter to keep to that policy in practice. Washington's declaration that South Korea was beyond the US defense perimeter was to a certain extent based on the expectation that the South Koreans themselves were able to withstand an attack from the north. This proved not to be the case.

Even before the war broke out, US involvement in Asia was growing. The domestic political situation in the United States further undermined the original stance of the Truman administration. Verbal assaults for having 'lost China' to the communists became steadily harsher. In February, Senator Joseph McCarthy had begun his attacks on communist influence within the administration. If South Korea now fell, too, that would undoubtedly sharpen the tone even further, just a few months before Congressional elections. Moreover, Truman liked to consider himself a man who could act swiftly and decisively, a characteristic he could now demonstrate. He received overwhelming support from the Congress and public opinion.

It was more or less assumed that Moscow was behind the North Korean attack. In Western capitals, the usual analysis had been that the Soviet Union would probably try to gain control of new areas, but that this would happen by indirect means. Now, however, the Kremlin had resorted to very direct methods nonetheless.

The policy of containment required a Western response. A large-scale attack across a clearly defined, even though temporary, border revived the memories of the 1930s. The lessons from those years were unambiguous. Aggression had to be stopped as early as possible. If not answered in Korea, it would only result in new advances in more central areas. Japan and Western Europe might be new goals, and confidence in the United States would be weakened in these areas if the country did not oppose communist aggression in Korea. Thus the experience of Hitler lent support to the domino theory that if one domino fell, the next one would also fall. Such thoughts were a central element in the decision to send US troops into Korea.

During the first two to three months, the Americans had their hands full just making sure they were not thrown into the sea. But after MacArthur's amphibious landing at Inchon on 15 September, their luck turned full circle. The Americans were soon crossing the thirty-eighth parallel. This violated the statement issued just after the war broke out that the US objective was to return to the situation that had existed before the war.

This change was to a certain extent a result of pressure by MacArthur and highly conservative circles in the United States, but for the most part the administration agreed with the new policy. The objective had always been to unify Korea. Now the opportunity presented itself. The communists had actually created this opportunity themselves, according to Washington. The United States would not have crossed the dividing line without provocation, but once the North Koreans had done so, it was only reasonable that they had to take the consequences of their actions. Korea was to be united as a non-communist nation.

The goal was Yalu, the river bordering on China. That showed how the nature of the US involvement had changed. US troops had first been withdrawn from the Asian mainland. Now they were back. Not only were they back; for the first time Americans were fighting directly against communist forces. This took place in Asia, not in Europe. After October Ist it took place on communist territory.

Washington had received signals that China might intervene if the United States went beyond the thirty-eighth parallel. The US position was quite confusing. Troops were not to cross the dividing line if that would result in Chinese intervention. But certainty as to whether or not they would intervene could only be achieved by crossing the line. China was considered weak in military terms and preoccupied with internal problems. A second reason why the Truman administration placed little emphasis on the signals it received was that the State Department in particular still clung to the earlier analysis that Peking would understand that it was Moscow, and not Washington, that was the true antagonist.

The Chinese response came in November in the form of massive forces. Seen from Peking, the worst possibility must have been that MacArthur would not stop at the Yalu, but advance into China. This was not inconceivable, in the light of new demands for support to Chiang Kai-shek. But even a united non-communist Korea was probably unacceptable to Mao. Such a country would cooperate not only with the United States, but probably with Japan and Taiwan as well.

The Soviet Union was not interested in an armed conflict with the United States. Moscow did not need to intervene as long as the Chinese could prevent a North Korean defeat. But it must have irritated the Chinese that they had to fight with poorer equipment than even the Koreans had. When new weapons came from the Soviet Union, it appears that Peking had to pay a relatively high price for them.

The Chinese intervention put an end to any hopes that Washington, and the State Department in particular, had had of a possible breach between the Soviet Union and China. Now their evaluations swung to the opposite extreme. With a slight exception for Tito's Yugoslavia, communism was considered a monolithic entity. A victory for a communist movement anywhere in the world thus necessarily entailed a loss for the West.

There were still a few who felt that a breach between the Soviet Union and China would come at some time in the future. Surprisingly enough, Secretary of State John Foster Dulles was among them when he assumed office in 1953. But the conclusion was still the same: China was to be kept isolated. By China becoming even more dependent on the Soviet Union, the possibilities for a breach would increase.

US policy towards China became even harsher than towards the Soviet Union. Any mention of diplomatic recognition was taboo. Trade and all contact was almost totally discontinued. As early as from the outbreak of the war, the US navy was to prevent a communist take-over in Taiwan, but Washington's assistance to Chiang now increased rapidly. It consisted not only of economic and military assistance, but of subversive operations on the Chinese mainland as well. Support for reconquering the mainland, however, was out of the question.

There were still clear limitations on US anti-communist involvement in Asia. Nuclear weapons would not be used in Korea. General MacArthur was dismissed in April 1951, partly because the Truman administration had decided that the war should not be escalated further. The Yalu River was not to be crossed. The supply lines in China would not be bombed. Military assistance from Chiang was not to be accepted in Korea, and support to Chiang was to be limited.

In the spring of 1951, the war in Korea stabilized itself at approximately the thirty-eighth parallel. Neither side went in for new major offensives. Nevertheless, it took two years and political shifts in several capitals before a ceasefire was established.

Changes in US Policy in Asia

The war would cause major changes in US and Soviet policies. The changes were greatest on the part of the United States. (Changes in relation to strategy, rearmament in Western Europe, and the size of the defense budget will be described in more detail on pages 149–151.)

For the most part, the Truman administration continued to concentrate its attention on Europe. The US military response in Korea became as comprehensive as it was only after it had become evident that Korea was not a diversionary maneuver for an attack in Europe. In the course of two to three years, the US defense budget was tripled, but only a small portion of these resources went to the war in Korea. The largest share was used for a buildup of forces in the United States for the purpose of preventing, and, if that did not succeed, fighting a war in Europe. The US troops in Europe were reinforced with four new divisions. Europe was still far more important to Washington than Asia was.

Although the main emphasis was still on Europe, US military involvement increased considerably in most parts of the world. The increase was even greater in certain areas after the Korean war than it had been after WW II. Before the Korean war, the United States was only bound by one military treaty outside the Western hemisphere, and that was NATO. After the outbreak of the war, the United States entered into treaties and made commitments in a number of different regions. The number of bases rose sharply.

As early as during WW II, it had become evident that Australia and New Zealand would orient themselves towards Washington, and away from London, in security matters. Australia in particular showed an interest in a separate security system in the Pacific. In 1951 the Truman administration was ready to consider this type of scheme. The intention was to work out an agreement between the United States, Japan, the Philippines, Australia, New Zealand, and perhaps Britain and Indonesia as well. The US army was still sceptical about commitments on the Asian mainland. That was the reason that Thailand, for instance, was not included.

It proved impossible to achieve such a comprehensive system. There was particularly strong opposition to including Japan. After the peace treaty with Japan was signed in 1951, the United States and Japan made a separate defense agreement which gave the United States the right to have bases in Japan. A second agreement was made with the Philippines. Then the United States, Australia and New Zealand entered into the ANZUS pact in September 1951. Britain was not a party to ANZUS. This emphasized the power shift to the advantage of the United States that had taken place in this part of the world as well as elsewhere.

The Eisenhower administration would place even greater emphasis than its predecessor on building up a bulwark against communism in Asia. Although the alliances and agreements here were considerably less stringent in their composition and commitments than NATO, the idea behind them was basically the same. Definite lines had to be drawn up. If the Soviet Union or one of its allies overstepped these lines, the West, led by the United States, would respond in military terms. The more countries that were included in these agreements, the stronger the West would become and the smaller the chances of communist aggression would be.

As early as in the report on the first 90 days of the administration, Secretary of State Dulles could declare that '. . . the Far East has received a higher priority. Furthermore, it has been made clear that we think our friends in the Far East, from Japan, Korea and Formosa to Indo-China and Malaya face a united enemy front, which has to be met by a common attitude and greater cooperation among the separate links of freedom'.

In August 1953, the United States entered into a defense agreement with South Korea. It was to guarantee the security of South Korea, and was necessary in order to get the country to agree to a ceasefire in the Korean war. Taiwan, too, had long been eager for closer contact with the United States. The Eisenhower administration stepped up its verbal support for Chiang Kai-shek. The US fleet was withdrawn from the Formosa Strait. This would supposedly make it easier for Chiang to carry out operations on the mainland. But Washington was still not willing to support an attempted invasion, and without US assistance an invasion was impossible. In September 1954, the Communists began to bombard the island of Quemoy, which was located just off the mainland and far from Taiwan, which controlled it. Despite initial reservations on the part of President Eisenhower, Washington agreed to enter into a security agreement with Taiwan in December. The agreement was unclear as to Quemoy and Matsu, but these islands could at least partially be said to fall within the scope of US defense commitments.

The Korean war and the setbacks France experienced in battle against the Vietminh troops resulted in a rapid escalation in US military assistance to the French in Indo-China. In 1954 Washington paid about 80 percent of the French war expenses. US advisers were also brought in.

Despite this assistance, the war went badly for France. In the spring of 1954, the French position was about to collapse, partly because of the battles around Dien Bien Phu and partly because of the domestic political situation in France. Paris would have liked a military victory, but became increasingly more interested in finding an alternative that could end the war. Washington still placed greatest emphasis on avoiding a communist victory. In order to prevent a French defeat, the question of US intervention was raised. Vice President Nixon, the navy and the air force supported this option. However, Eisenhower was sceptical, as were the leaders of the US army, who felt that the Korean war had only emphasized the difficulties of fighting a war on the Asian mainland. As Britain and the Democratic leadership in the Senate were also opposed to US intervention, Eisenhower dropped the idea.

At the subsequent conference in Geneva, both sides had to make concessions. France granted complete independence to North and South Vietnam, Laos and Cambodia. The communist regime persevered in North Vietnam, and the chances were high that the elections which were to be held in Vietnam within two years might result in communist dominance over the entire country. For the time being, however, the North Vietnamese had to be content to control a smaller area than they had expected and less than what developments in the war had given a basis for. Both the Soviet Union and China were interested in an end to the war and contributed to getting North Vietnam to accept the agreement (see pages 98–99).

After the Geneva meeting, the United States remained intent on saving what could be saved from communism. The most important step in that context was the establishment of SEATO, the South East Asia Treaty Organization. SEATO had fewer members than Washington had hoped for. India and Indonesia had no desire to belong. The British protested against including Taiwan. France would not accept South Vietnam, Laos and Cambodia. According to the Geneva agreement, they were to be neutral in any case. Nonetheless, they were partially covered by the SEATO pact. The members were the United States, the United Kingdom, France, Australia, New Zealand, the Philippines, Thailand and Pakistan. In the United States there was widespread support for this new addition to the pact system. The treaty was ratified in the Senate by a vote of 82 to 1.

In Europe, too, the pact system was expanded. In 1948–49 the United States had opposed including countries in NATO that did not border on the Atlantic Ocean. Italy was the only exception, although many members of the Truman administration were sceptical even to Italian full membership in NATO. In 1952, the links to the Atlantic Ocean were weakened even more by the inclusion of Greece and Turkey. In 1955, after the French national assembly had rejected the plans for a European army with German participation, West Germany became a member of NATO (see page 189).

There was considerable continuity from the Truman to the Eisenhower administration both in Europe and in Asia. The expansion of NATO and transference of the pact model from Europe to Asia had begun under Truman. The Korean war was the major breakthrough. It made evaluations of Soviet intentions even more negative than previously. Through an accelerated pace of rearmament, the United States also acquired an instrument to pursue an even more ambitious course, with more and more comprehensive commitments in ever new regions.

In principle, the Republicans were not quite as oriented towards Europe as the Democratic Truman administration had been. This was particularly true of the Republican right wing, which had roots back to the isolationism of the period between the wars and to the 'Asia first' policy during WW II. Eisenhower and Dulles belonged to the more international and Europe-oriented group, but showed a certain consideration for the minority in the party.

The change in administration meant that a larger share of Washington's program of assistance went to Asia, although a reduction in Europe at this stage was natural for many reasons. Asia's share under the Mutual Assistance Act increased from 12.6 percent in 1953 to 54.5 percent in 1954. During the Dien Bien Phu crisis it had also become evident that leading persons in the Eisenhower administration were more willing to intervene than the Democrats in the Senate were. But these differences can easily be exaggerated. As mentioned earlier, Senate support for SEATO was overwhelming.

After the establishment of SEATO, the largest gap in the alliance system was in the Middle East and western Asia, between Turkey in NATO and Pakistan in SEATO. Both Washington and London were eager to create a pact in this region. The first plans had been launched as early as in 1952, during the Truman administration. For the Americans, the objective was primarily to create a front against communism. Britain was still the dominant major power in the Middle East and had considerable strategic, political and economic interests in the area, even after the withdrawal from Palestine in 1948. To some extent, the United States perceived the British presence as a factor that contributed to making the countries there more radical, thus making the establishment of a front against communism more difficult. A weakening of the British role could also lead to a strengthening of the US position. These different perspectives, combined with the complex local conditions, made progress difficult, but in 1955 the Baghdad Pact was established with the United Kingdom, Turkey, Pakistan, Iran and Iraq as members.

The United States was only indirectly linked to the new system. The main reason was that the pact resulted in a polarization in the Middle East. Those that were not included, and that was the vast majority of the countries in the region, tended to be in a position of rivalry in relation to those that were members. Washington wanted to maintain relations with the countries which at least partially considered the Baghdad Pact the extended arm of British colonialism. When it came right down to it, Dulles actually felt that it would be best if even Iran waited to join. A certain amount of time ought to pass from the US-British coup in the autumn of 1953 against Prime Minister Mohammed Mossadeq until

Iran joined the Western side directly. But the Shah of Iran saw things differently, and he had his way.

The new organization was not a great success. The British felt betrayed by the Americans. Iran and Iraq were the only countries that did not already belong to a pact. In July 1958, General Abdul Karim Kassem seized power in Iraq and withdrew the country's membership. The Baghdad Pact was reorganized as CENTO, the Central Treaty Organization, although it did not become more central even with its new name.

The US bloc build-up was accompanied by denunciations of neutrality. Dulles, in particular, issued many harsh statements. In his opinion, neutrality was not only 'old-fashioned' and 'short-sighted', but also 'immoral'. It was everyone's duty to cooperate in the struggle against the forces of evil in the world. At first sight this resembled the two-camp theory that Zhdanov had proclaimed on the Soviet side as early as in 1947. However, Dulles championed the idea at a time when, as we shall see, the Soviet Union was in the process of abandoning it.

India was the most important of the non-aligned countries. The United States and India had differing views on several issues during the Korean war; they disagreed as to the peace treaty for Japan, and not least about the establishment of SEATO, which brought the United States into a close relationship with India's rival, Pakistan. Many US policy-makers felt that Nehru was naive in thinking that he could practice neutrality.

However, the US attitude was not as literal as Dulles' diatribes might seem to indicate. The United States gave considerable economic assistance to countries such as India, Indonesia, Egypt and Yugoslavia as well. As we have seen, Washington was interested in establishing some type of relations even with the more radical Arab countries in the Middle East. On the whole, the US attitude towards neutrality became more conciliatory as the 1950s progressed.

In Africa, the United States was content for quite some time to leave the responsibility to its allies, the colonial powers of the United Kingdom, France, Belgium and Portugal. The Eisenhower administration showed little interest in hastening the process of independence in Africa. For the most part it emphasized the need for moderation on both sides. After the countries had become independent, the administration stressed the advantages of continued cooperation with the former colonial powers.

The Kennedy administration would place more emphasis on having good relations with the countries of both Asia and Africa than its predecessor had done. The attacks on neutrality ceased. Interest in the new

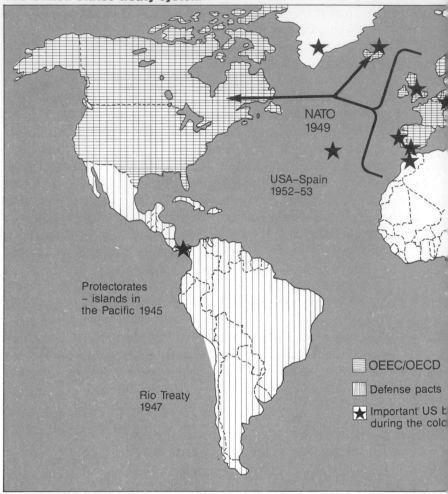

nations grew. Economic assistance increased, as did pressure on the colonial powers to complete the process of independence. Portugal's policies in Africa were of particular interest in this context. Even so, there was no question of a clear break with the past. For instance, Portugal was still an important ally because the United States was dependent on continued base rights on the Azores.

84

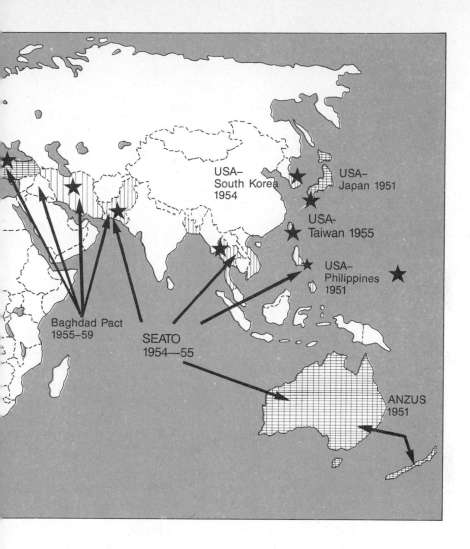

USA–
South Korea
1954

USA–
Japan 1951

USA–
Taiwan 1955

USA–
Philippines
1951

Baghdad Pact
1955–59

SEATO
1954—55

ANZUS
1951

The Soviet Union tries to play a global role

The other superpower, too, tried to press complex local conditions into an East-West pattern. Gradually, however, Moscow began to pursue a more friendly, active policy towards the many countries that had entered the international arena. This became evident first in Asia and the Middle

East, then in Africa. The Kremlin would try to get a foothold in Latin America as well. However, the overall conclusion must be that in the 1950s and 1960s, Soviet influence in the Third World could not equal US influence in any way.

A new policy in Asia and the Middle East

As early as in 1949-50, Moscow had become less exclusively oriented towards Europe in its policies. As we have seen, the communist victory in the civil war in China, the outbreak of the Korean war and the conflict in Indo-China were significant in this context. However, all of these events could be accounted for within the two-camp theory. It was a question of helping one's 'socialist brethren' in the fight against imperialism.

To some extent, the Soviet Union was drawn into new regions by events which were beyond Soviet control. But it was also a question of a conscious change in Moscow's policies. The first sign of movement away from a pure East-West division could be noticed while Stalin was still alive. In his *Economic Problems of Socialism in the USSR* of October 1952, the Soviet leader had even cautiously suggested that peaceful co-existence between East and West might be possible. Moreover, the split in the imperialist bloc could become so great that the countries which came into the greatest opposition with the United States would seek to improve relations with the Soviet Union. This theme was made even more explicit by Malenkov at the Nineteenth Party Congress that same year.

Stalin's death in March 1953 gave an impetus to this cautious re-evaluation. The new leaders were much freer to make a break with a policy that had unquestionably had negative aspects. There could be no doubt that the two-camp theory had barred the Soviet Union from contacts with and influence in the new nations. The number of new nations was growing rapidly, and the vast majority of them chose to remain neutral in East-West matters. At worst, a negative Soviet attitude could press them into the comprehensive alliance systems the United States was in the process of building up. At best, a re-evaluation could result in closer cooperation against 'imperialism and colonialism'. The Chinese, too, were interested in pursuing a more active policy towards the new nations.

Moreover, the material basis for a new course of policy was more favorable. The wartime destruction had meant that at first resources had to be channelled into the enormous tasks of reconstruction. In 1950, at the close of the fourth five-year plan, the 1940 production level had been exceeded for almost all types of goods. Production continued to increase at a rapid pace throughout the 1950s. The Soviet Union could finally begin to use economic assistance and trade as policy instruments in Asia and Africa. The country was also much stronger in military terms now that it had developed the atomic and hydrogen bombs.

Moscow ceased to describe Nehru and Sukarno as lackeys of imperialism. Terms of abuse that had previously been common in descriptions of these nationalist leaders were now reserved for reactionary leaders, such as Chiang Kai-shek and Syngman Rhee. The Kremlin began to show interest in entering into trade and cultural agreements with the leaders who had previously been so harshly denounced. In 1954, Afghanistan became the first non-communist country to receive economic assistance from the Soviet Union.

These new signals harmonized in 1955. In that year, Nehru visited the Soviet Union, and then both Khrushchev and Prime Minister Nikolaj Bulganin toured India, Burma, and Afghanistan. Substantial economic assistance was given. Moscow expressed its support for the Bandung conference, which was held by Asian and African countries (see page 258).

The Kremlin's attitude towards the Arab countries in the Middle East was the best example of how hesitant this change of course was. At first, Stalin had tried to compete with Truman in being most strongly pro-Israeli. In the UN, the Soviet Union voted in favor of partitioning Palestine, and barely lost the race with the United States to be first to recognize the Jewish state. During the subsequent Israeli-Arab war, Moscow pronounced the Arabs the aggressors, and weapons were sent from Eastern Europe to Israel. The point of departure for Soviet policy seems to have been the desire to get Britain out of the Middle East as quickly as possible.

Soviet-Israeli relations soon cooled, however. Israel followed a clearly Western-oriented course, despite its socialistic domestic policies. The Kremlin's suspiciousness towards the Soviet Jews also made good relations difficult. At the end of his life, Stalin expressed unmistakably anti-Semitic views.

Even so, Moscow hesitated to improve relations with the Arab countries. The fact that many of them pursued reactionary policies is one explanation. But when King Farouk of Egypt was overthrown in 1952 and replaced by progressive military leaders, the Kremlin was sceptical even of them. The large *Soviet Encyclopedia* from 1952-53 described the coup as organized by 'US-British imperialists' and the new leaders as 'a group of reactionary officers'. The most important consequence of the overthrow seemed to be that it foreshadowed increasing 'clashes of interest' between the United States and the United Kingdom. Soviet relations with Syria and with Iraq in particular were even poorer than with Egypt.

Nevertheless, the domestic radicalization of several of the Arab countries, the polarization in the wake of the Western attempts to build up a system of alliance, and, most important of all, the Arab-Israeli conflict opened up unique opportunities for Moscow in the Middle East.

In 1954, Moscow used its veto in the UN Security Council for the first time to support the Arab countries in opposition to Israel. However, the red-letter year in the Middle East, as in Asia, was 1955. Gamal Abdel Nasser, who proved to be the dominant member of the group of military leaders who took over after Farouk, tried to buy new weapons. The Western powers showed little interest in selling, in part because they wanted to limit the sale of weapons to an area as full of conflict as the Middle East was, but also because they were dissatisfied with Nasser's negative attitude towards the build-up of a Western pact system. Thus Nasser turned to the east. Moscow was now prepared to pursue a more active policy. A 200-million-dollar weapons deal was camouflaged as a Czech-Egyptian agreement. When a turnabout did come, it could be dramatic. The Egyptian Communists who did not support Nasser were denounced in the Soviet press as 'provocateurs who call themselves communists.'

However, the Soviet role was still modest. Although its influence was increasing, it was still far from equal to that of the West in the Middle East. Its limitations were evident during the Suez conflict in 1956 and again during the Middle East crisis of 1958.

In July 1956, Nasser nationalized the Suez Canal. This was mainly a reaction to US and British statements that they were not willing to give Egypt support for building the Aswan Dam as they had earlier held out expectations of. Among other things, the two powers reacted to Nasser's overtures towards the east as evidenced in the weapons deal and in Egypt's recognition of China.

The attempts to achieve a peaceful solution to the dispute over the Suez Canal were unsuccessful. In October, Britain and France, in cooperation with Israel, went to war against Egypt. Britain had substantial interests in the canal, both in its operation and in the canal as a link between Europe and Asia. The British Government was also highly irritated by Nasser's attempts to reduce British influence in the Middle East. Disapproval of the Egyptian leader was at least equally strong in Paris. The French Government was convinced that the rebel forces in Algeria received a substantial share of their supplies from Egypt.

The Soviet Union kept a low profile during the first phase of the conflict. Later on, Moscow threatened to use nuclear missiles against the two Western powers and to send Soviet volunteers to support Egypt. However, these threats came so late that there was little or no danger of them being implemented. The US stance seems to have had more significance for the French-British decision to call off their military action even though they had not achieved the victory they had hoped for (see page 190). The invasion of Egypt also produced strong reactions in many other countries, including Britain and France themselves.

The British–French fiasco undermined Britain's position in the Middle East. Moscow's threats represented a considerable propaganda victory in the Arab countries, and the Kremlin's influence was on the increase. In response to this situation, Eisenhower proclaimed the so-called Eisenhower Doctrine in January 1957. In a message to Congress, the President maintained that US troops would be used to protect nations in the region from countries that were 'controlled by international communism'. The Eisenhower Doctrine was to do in the Middle East what the Truman Doctrine had done in Greece and Turkey ten years earlier. The United States was to fill the vacuum the British–French defeat had created.

When Washington and London sent troops to Lebanon and Jordan respectively during the following year to support the conservative governments there against the after-effects of Kassem's seizure of power in Iraq, Moscow could only protest. The intervention of the two countries was as much an attempt to keep pro-Nasser circles from power as it was aimed against international communism. But the Soviet Union had neither the will nor the ability to neutralize such a direct intervention.

Quite contrary to what the Western powers had expected, hefty disagreements soon broke out between Kassem and Nasser. The Kremlin would have liked to have stayed on good terms with both sides, but could hardly keep out of the bitter dispute. The choice fell on Iraq. One reason seems to have been Kassem's more radical domestic policies, emphasizing major economic reforms and cooperation with the communists. Moscow could not entirely ignore domestic policies in its evaluations of the various countries of the Third World.

Nonetheless, there was never a question of a break with Nasser. The Soviet Union still gave substantial economic assistance to Egypt, for instance for the completion of the Aswan Dam. After the Iraqi Communists made an unsuccessful takeover attempt in 1960, their influence dwindled rapidly. Then Moscow turned back to Egypt, or the United Arab Republic, as the union between Egypt and Syria was named. The Union lasted from 1958 until Syria broke out in 1961. Changes took place quickly in the Middle East. No one was able to control events there.

A new policy in Africa

The Soviet attitude towards the struggle for liberation in Algeria (1954-1962) illustrated some of the problems the country had to face in relation to the Third World. On the one hand, the Soviet leaders wanted to support 'wars of national liberation'. This was ideologically correct and could lead to considerable political gains not only in Algeria, but elsewhere in Africa and Asia as well. These considerations must have been reinforced by the fact that China in 1958 effected diplomatic recognition of the National Liberation Front (FLN) as the legitimate government of Algeria. On the other hand, there was consideration of France and to a certain extent of the United States as well. Even though General de Gaulle had an anti-communist stance in many questions, he was a nationalist in relation to the United States. Moscow could not have been interested in doing anything that would bring Paris and Washington closer together. Both countries would have reacted sharply to Soviet support for the FLN. The result was that here, as so often before, least emphasis was placed on ideological considerations. The Kremlin kept a low profile in the Algerian question. The FLN was not officially recognized until Algeria received its independence in 1962.

If US interest in Africa south of the Sahara was modest for a long time, that of the Soviet Union was even smaller. This was particularly the case during the colonial era, but even after independence the Soviet Union acted hesitantly, although the country had good cards to play in the shape of its fundamental opposition to the Western colonial system.

In 1956–57, Ghana was the first colony south of the Sahara to be granted independence (page 243). However, it took two years before a Soviet ambassador came to Accra. The country's leader, Kwame Nkrumah, was considered a collaborator with the Western powers and a petty bourgeois politician. The re-evaluation which had taken place with regard to nationalist leaders in many Asian countries and in the Middle East seems to have been delayed here. In addition, Moscow had little expertise on this region. An African division was not established in the Soviet foreign ministry until 1958. The first trade contracts of any size were signed in 1959-60.

Guinea under Sekou Touré was a more promising partner for cooperation than Ghana under Nkrumah. Ghana maintained close contact with its former colonial ruler, the United Kingdom, but Guinea, as the only country in Africa, broke with France in 1958. Tribal rivalry was not as strong in Guinea as in Ghana, and Touré was the African politician Moscow knew and liked best, despite certain disagreements with him as well. The new nation was soon recognized. President Voroshilov described it as 'an important step on the path of the liberation of Africa from the colonialist yoke.'

Whereas the Soviet Union showed understanding for France's position in Algeria, which was highly significant to Paris, there was less need for caution in regard to a Guinea which had broken with France. But Touré had no plans of trading French dominance for Soviet dominance. Because of the break with France, he probably became economically more dependent on the Soviet Union than he liked. However, he did not tolerate any meddling in the domestic affairs of his country, and during the Cuban crisis in 1962 he refused to allow Soviet planes to refuel in Guinea on their way to Cuba. The progressive regimes in Africa were seldom as progressive as Moscow had hoped for. As compensation for a certain degree of disappointment in Touré, the Soviet leaders could be pleased that Nkrumah after 1960 pursued more radical policies than previously. Good relations were also established with Mali, and with Algeria after it became independent.

The Congo crisis in 1960 was the first clear signal that the cold war had spread to Africa south of the Sahara. The crisis would confirm a pattern that had already shown itself in Asia and the Middle East: although Moscow was in the process of becoming an important actor in ever new parts of the world, Soviet influence was seldom equal to that of the Western capitals, particularly Washington.

Before the Congo became independent in 1960 (page 249), it had had little contact with the Soviet Union and Eastern Europe. As so often elsewhere, Moscow mainly left the formulation of colonial policy to the communists in the mother country, in this case Belgium. After independence, the Soviet Union considered Prime Minister Patrice Lumumba a possible 'progressive' politician. But after the administration of the country had collapsed and Belgium intervened, Moscow chose at first to leave further initiatives to the UN.

However, relations between Lumumba and the UN deteriorated rapidly. That increased both the temptation and the possibilities for the Soviet leaders to play a more active role. They decided to help Lumumba, thus coming into conflict with the policy of the UN under the active leadership of Secretary General Dag Hammarskjøld. Transport planes and other supplies were sent, and several hundred advisers from Eastern bloc countries turned up in the Congo.

Once more, events would prove that Moscow had little luck. In September 1960, Colonel Sese Seko Mobutu seized control, with support from the United States and Belgium. Lumumba was imprisoned and the advisers from the Eastern bloc sent home. There was little the Russians could do to prevent this. In February 1961, Lumumba was killed. This contributed to the Kremlin increasing its support for a separatist government in Stanleyville. Assistance arrived in the form of political declarations and military assistance given through Egypt and Ghana.

The local situation was extremely complex. For a while, Moscow seems to have been afraid of being out-maneuvered by China in terms of relations to progressive forces. However, most of the countries of the Third World supported the role the UN tried to play.

In contrast to the Soviet Union, the United States would enjoy ever increasing influence. Several years of unrest went by before Mobutu carried out his second coup in 1965 and declared himself president with complete control, to the extent that complete control was possible in such a vast, divided country as the Congo, or Zaire, as the name was changed to in 1971.

The Cold War reaches Latin America

If the Soviet Union had been slow in establishing itself as a serious actor in Asia and Africa, it took even longer in Latin America. Since the Monroe Doctrine of 1823, Washington had considered the western hemisphere its backyard. Through the establishment of regional systems, such as the Rio Treaty in 1947 and the Organization of American States in 1948, the United States had formalized its role as the only major power in this part of the world. Not only was the Soviet Union barred from entrance, but even Britain sometimes reacted to what it considered a US double standard of morality. The United States was opposed to other countries' spheres of interest, but retained the right to have its own. The fact that the United States was in favor of such regional arrangements did not necessarily mean that the Latin American countries opposed them. On the contrary, most of them showed active support.

The Soviet Union may have shown little interest in Latin America, but the countries in this part of the world were also sceptical towards Moscow and towards communism. In 1953, the Soviet Union had diplomatic relations with only three countries: Mexico, Argentina and Uruguay. In the same year, Moscow made its first trade agreement with such an important country as Argentina.

From a Soviet perspective, Guatemala was the most interesting country at this juncture. After Colonel Arbenz had taken over as president in 1950, Guatemala moved towards the left. In terms of foreign policy, the country took stands in opposition to Washington on several occasions. Land reforms were initiated, at the expense of the United Fruit Company, which had excellent contacts within the Eisenhower administration. However, the Communist party was weak, and the increasing criticism of the United States had not resulted in the establishment of diplomatic relations with the Soviet Union.

Arbenz wanted to acquire weapons, in part to prevent attempts to overthrow his government. The United States would not sell him weapons, and he turned to Moscow. The Kremlin responded in the affirmative and tried to send supplies to Guatemala in complete secrecy. Washington had probably already decided to get rid of Arbenz by that time. The Central Intelligence Agency (CIA) was to carry out a coup in cooperation with opposition groups in Guatemala.

The coup was successful, mainly due to the fact that those responsible for it had the support of the army and the traditional upper-class in the country. Guatemala got a new military regime as one among many throughout Latin America. The Soviet Union could do little but protest against US intervention in a foreign country.

Washington considered Latin America a safe area in terms of the cold war; so safe that Latin America received only very limited economic support. From 1945 to 1960, the United States gave three times as much assistance to the Be-Ne-Lux countries as to all of Latin America.

At the close of the 1950s, it was obvious that changes were underway.

Granted, the situation was 'normal' in Guatemala, and the Soviet Union had not given military help to any country in the western hemisphere since then. On the other hand, Soviet trade and other forms of contact increased rapidly. However, the anti-American sentiment that could now be perceived arose for the most part from local conditions. When Vice-President Nixon toured some Latin American countries in 1958, he was met by protests and riots in several of them.

Washington realized that a more active policy had to be implemented. Latin America could no longer be taken for granted. The Inter-American Development Bank was established. Economic assistance was increased. There were also hints that Washington was less interested in maintaining reactionary military dictatorships. The attitude towards Batista's government on Cuba was one example. When Fidel Castro assumed power in January 1959, he was considered an improvement compared to the previous regime. However, that would not last for long.

At first, the Soviet Union made no firm commitments towards Castro. Relations between him and the Cuban Communists were not very good. However, the policy of nationalization and comprehensive land reforms soon resulted in a deterioration of relations with the United States. The Communists gained more influence. From the turn of the year 1959-60, it was obvious that Moscow was beginning to have high expectations for Castro.

Anastas Mikojan's visit to Cuba in February 1960 was the first unmistakable sign that Moscow was prepared to take on far-reaching commitments. An agreement was reached that the Soviet Union would buy Cuban sugar. Havana received a loan amounting to 100 million dollars to purchase industrial equipment from the USSR. In May, the two countries established diplomatic relations. When the United States began drastic cut-backs of its import of sugar from Cuba, the Soviet Union promised to buy what the United States no longer wanted. Cuba received more and more Soviet weapons. In late 1961, the first references cropped up in Moscow that Cuba could become a 'socialist' country, but not until 1963 was the establishment of socialism perceived as accomplished.

The Kennedy administration accelerated the re-evaluation of Latin America policies that had begun during the final years of the Eisenhower administration. Economic assistance was increased, and Washington stressed the need for social and economic reforms. These elements were bound together in the Alliance for Progress. However, the break with the past proved not as great as it first appeared.

As far as Cuba was concerned, Kennedy continued Eisenhower's policies for the most part. The plans for a US-backed invasion were taken over by the new administration. The invasion took place in the Bay of Pigs in April 1961. Kennedy expected the Cuban population to turn against Castro, somewhat like Guatemala seven years earlier. That did not happen. Castro's support was far more solid and better organized than Arbenz's had been. Naturally, the invasion served to strengthen further the bonds between Cuba and the Soviet Union.

In the spring of 1962, the Soviet Union must have decided to install the intermediate-range missiles on Cuba that in October would cause a most serious crisis. The Soviet decision was probably made on the basis of strategic considerations. The primary objective was to achieve parity with the United States in a simple manner. (This will be dealt with on page 160.) Castro probably saw the entire situation in a more local perspective, with emphasis on preventing new attempted invasions and on strengthening Cuba in relation to the United States in general. Washington responded by establishing a blockade around the island to prevent new supplies, and threatened to invade if the missiles that were already on Cuba were not withdrawn. The Soviet Union backed off. The retreat was made easier by the American promise not to invade the island in the future and private assurances that US intermediate-range missiles would be withdrawn from Turkey.

The Cuban crisis illustrated in two ways that the cold war concerned the entire world. In the first place, a conflict between the United States and the Soviet Union could result in a catastrophe for humanity. In the second place, Cuba, which traditionally had been the best example of a country dominated by the United States, had now become closely linked to the Soviet Union. The cold war had also reached Latin America. It had become global.

The United States, the Soviet Union, and the Third World: A Comparison

US involvement around the world had been considerable as far back as the first years after WW II. It had increased greatly during the post-war period, but US expansion gradually became less striking than Soviet expansion. The Soviet Union was far from a global power in 1945, but had become one by the beginning of the 1960s.

The Soviet Union undoubtedly had greater influence in more geographic areas in the mid-60s than had been the case 20 years earlier. Khrushchev had become a central actor in Asia, in the Middle East, in Africa, and even in Latin America. Stalin's possibilities of influencing developments in most of these regions had been small.

Even so, there was little doubt that in most areas the United States was still superior to the Soviet Union. The United States had a large lead in terms of strategic weapons. The same was true of their ability to exercise power in various parts of the world. Only after the defeat on Cuba did the Soviet Union in earnest concentrate on becoming equal to the United States strategically and on acquiring more resources for so-called power projection in remote areas.

In the economic sphere, it was even less possible for the Soviet Union to compete with the United States. The Soviet Union had experienced substantial economic growth in the 1950s. The material basis for a more global policy had improved, but in 1960 the Soviet gross national product was still less than half that of the United States. The United States had a much wider range of instruments to use in relation to the Third World.

From 1954 to 1965, Moscow gave 7.9 billion dollars in economic and military assistance to the Third World (at least agreements were made to give this amount). This was a dramatic change in relation to the complete lack of such assistance under Stalin. The priority the various countries were given was evident by the fact that 5 or 6 countries received two-thirds of this entire amount. They were Afghanistan, India, Indonesia, Iran and the United Arab Republic. India and the United Arab Republic alone received about 40 percent. Compared with US assistance, this was modest nevertheless, for the United States gave more just to India and Pakistan than the Soviet Union gave to the entire Third World.

Many of Moscow's greatest successes had been transformed to disappointments in a somewhat longer perspective. This was particularly true in relation to China, but also in relation to countries outside what had once been the communist bloc. Even progressive regimes had an unfortunate tendency to suppress the local Communist parties. Even more important was the fact that during a period of some three years the Soviet Union's best friends disappeared in four important countries: Ben Bella in Algeria was deposed in 1965; Sukarno in Indonesia gradually lost his grip in the years 1965-68, and in 1965 one of the leading Communist parties in the non-communist world was crushed and several hundred thousand persons killed; Nkrumah in Ghana was deposed in 1966; Keita in Mali met the same fate in 1968.

The United States had to tolerate Cuba as a constant thorn in the flesh. This was a new experience. Power and impotence were intermingled in a complex mixture. The US capacity to influence events in various places around the world was limited, but was still much greater than that of the Soviet Union. Even Britain and France intervened to protect their friends in Africa and Asia (Britain in Oman, Jordan, Kuwait, Malaysia and East Africa; France in several African ex-colonies). The Soviet Union had to sit and watch while radical regimes in the Third World were deposed.

There was a long way to go yet before the Soviet Union was the United States' equal in power and influence. But equality was undoubtedly what Moscow wanted.

4. Detente between East and West, 1962–1975

The first 15 to 20 years after the Second World War were characterized by the spread of the cold war to ever new parts of the globe. Until 1948-49 the situation in Europe was the focal point. Most of the conflicts after this time took place outside Europe. The most important ones, as we have seen, were the Korean war, the Vietnam war, the Congo crisis, the Cuban crisis, and the conflicts in the Middle East.

This geographic expansion did not necessarily mean a steady increase in the temperature between East and West. The period from 1945 to 1962 did not represent a constant rise in the level of tension between the power blocs. There were interim periods with signs of an easing of tensions. This is not easily quantifiable, but it can roughly be said that tension increased from 1945 to 1952, although there were fluctuations during this period as well. The following years, until 1956, showed improved relations between East and West. Although the temperature then rose somewhat, the tension level of the first post-war years was not reached again until the Cuban crisis of 1962.

After the Cuban crisis, the world entered an extended period of detente until the mid-1970s. Contact between the power blocs increased, and several important sources of conflict found at least a temporary solution. Most importantly, the situation in the central region, Europe, was normalized in a manner that was acceptable to both sides. In a sense, detente in Europe overshadowed the continuing conflicts in other parts of the world.

Signs of Detente during the 1950s

Improved relations were evident in several areas. In July 1953 a cease-fire was declared in Korea. In the following year the peace agreement for Indo-China was concluded. In 1955 the Austrian question was resolved. The Soviet Union agreed to withdraw its troops, and Austria became a neutral country. The Soviet Union also withdrew from Porkkala in Finland. There were signs of rapprochement between the USSR and West Germany. The German Chancellor and 'arch-revanchist' Konrad Adenauer was invited to Moscow, diplomatic relations were established, and the German war prisoners sent home. In the following year diplomatic relations were established between the Soviet Union and Japan. Moscow even hinted at the possibility of a solution for the Kurile Islands, although this issue was not resolved.

The last summit between the leaders of the great powers had taken place in Potsdam in 1945. In 1955 they met again, in Geneva: Eisenhower, Bulganin—Khrushchev, Anthony Eden, and Edgar Faure. No concrete results were reached, but the meeting demonstrated the altered climate between East and West, the 'spirit of Geneva'. Four years would pass before Eisenhower and Khrushchev would meet again, to generate the 'spirit of Camp David'.

Trade between East and West increased, the Soviet Union joined the Olympic summer games in 1952 and the winter games in 1956, and tourists began to make holes in the renowned 'Iron Curtain', which divided Europe. Negotiations on arms control were carried out with greater enthusiasm and realism than formerly. The central issue was a ban on the testing of nuclear weapons. Considerable progress was made at the end of the 1950s, although a final agreement was not reached until 1963.

There were many reasons for the improved climate. One important factor was the fact that the major powers began to accept the existing situation in Europe for the most part. Europe was still by far the most important region for both the Soviet Union and the United States, although conflicts outside Europe naturally influenced these relations as well. The Western powers still advocated reunification of Germany, but it became increasingly evident that they were actually satisfied with a divided Germany in which the largest part was incorporated in NATO, as West Germany was in 1955. From the same year the Soviet Union openly supported the policy of a divided Germany.

The situation in Western Europe became stable. There was no longer any danger of communism being victorious. The establishment of NATO and the high rate of economic growth had provided an increased feeling of security. US talk of 'liberation' and 'roll-back' contributed to new uncertainty in relation to Eastern Europe, especially in the first years after Eisenhower assumed office in 1953. However, it soon became clear that this policy was mostly rhetoric. Neither during the revolt in East Berlin in 1953 nor in Hungary in 1956 did the Eisenhower administration have plans of intervening (see pages 213–215). After Hungary, US propaganda was altered so that the inhabitants of Eastern Europe would not have unrealistic expectations as to what policy the United States actually pursued.

The death of Stalin in March 1953 led to comprehensive changes in Soviet policy. None of the new leaders could expect to attain Stalin's authority. The grip had to be relaxed somewhat. These new signals could be registered in a number of areas in addition to those already mentioned. The boundary claims in relation to Turkey were abandoned; relations were normalized with Greece, with Yugoslavia and with Israel— once more. The Soviet attitude towards the non-aligned countries of the Third World became more positive.

Ideologically, the new tone was most clearly expressed at the Twentieth Party Congress in 1956. Stalin was denounced. The possibilities of peaceful co-existence between capitalist and communist nations that had been suggested previously were now emphasized. In the opinion of the Kremlin, the forces for peace under Soviet leadership had become so strong that no new conflict between East and West need arise. The transition from capitalism to socialism could also take place by parliamentary means. Revolution was no longer necessary. Communism would still conquer the world, but through peaceful competition.

On the part of the United States, the Eisenhower administration represented a mixture of desire for detente combined with a powerful anti-communist rhetoric, both at home and abroad. The rhetoric gradually weakened and the desire for detente grew stronger. For various reasons, primarily economic, Eisenhower advocated a reduction in the defense budget. On several occasions he expressed a strong desire to limit the level of armaments in the world. With his desire to keep the United States out of major armed conflicts, he contributed to decreasing the level of tension in the cold war. However, the President had no strong desire to break with previous policies. He helped extend the pact system to new parts of the world, and there were strong anti-communist forces at work within the administration. The most central figure was Secretary of State John Foster Dulles. Dulles and Adenauer were the two Western leaders who were most sceptical about increased contact between East and West.

During the 1950s the world witnessed only the beginnings of an easing of tensions. Much of the impetus for detente disappeared already in 1956 with the uprising in Hungary and the manner in which the Soviet Union quelled it, and through the Suez conflict (see pages 88–89), although this was as much a conflict within the Western bloc as between East and West.

Tension in Europe increased once more. Except for the status of Austria, none of the central conflicts had actually been resolved. The question of Germany, and of Berlin in particular, was the most crucial in this context.

In November 1958, Khrushchev insisted that the situation in Berlin had to be changed. Moscow undoubtedly favored the integration of West Berlin into East Germany, but was willing to accept so-called free city status. The ties to West Germany were to be loosened in any case. An agreement to this effect would have to be reached within six months. If this was not achieved, the Soviet Union would transfer its occupation rights in East Berlin to the East Germans. Control of the traffic to West Berlin would also be their responsibility. As it had not proven possible to attain a peace treaty for a unified Germany, Khrushchev soon threatened to sign a separate peace treaty with East Germany.

The deadline was postponed, but tension in Europe increased. In a sense, it culminated with the erection of the Berlin wall in August 1961. The flow of refugees from the east had been steadily growing. In 1959, 140 000 persons had left East Germany, in 1960 almost 200 000 and during the first half of 1961 over 100 000 persons. Tanks were driven up on both sides of the dividing line, but the Western powers made no attempt to stop the building of the wall.

The new conflicts outside Europe, such as the Congo crisis in 1960, also contributed to sustaining the level of tension. The Cuban crisis in the autumn of 1962 was in many ways the most dangerous of the entire post-war period. The world seemed even closer to a major war then than during the Berlin conflict in 1948 and the outbreak of the Korean war in 1950.

The Policy of Detente, 1962–1975

The resolution of the Cuban crisis would have great significance for the international political climate. It resulted in a long period of relative detente, a detente that would culminate 10 to 13 years later. Once more it must be emphasized that there was not a constant evolution of steadily improving relations between East and West. There were many interruptions along this path. However, the main tendency was clear.

101

It was paradoxical that the most serious crisis of the post-war period should result in a period of detente. However, the background was simple enough. Moscow and Washington, and the rest of the world for that matter, had seen into the abyss a war would represent. As Khrushchev expressed it, 'the smell of fire hung in the air'. Both sides were interested in preventing a similar crisis in the future.

The interest in arms limitation and confidence-building measures between East and West increased. As Kennedy observed, with reference to this type of measure: 'Perhaps now, as we step back from danger, we can together make real progress in this vital field.'

Agreements and Contact between East and West

The Cuban crisis had demonstrated the need for the possibility of swift contact between the leaders in Washington and Moscow. A hot line was installed to make this possible. It would have a useful function in crises when time was of the essence.

An important new agreement was the test ban treaty of 1963. Negotiations had been carried out ever since 1955. Considerable progress was made, but the new climate after Cuba caused the final breakthrough. The treaty banned all tests in the atmosphere, in outer space, and under water. It had proved impossible to attain agreement as to a control system for underground testing. Thus ever new weapons could be developed, even though there was an end to the radioactive fallout from the US, British and Soviet tests.

Arms control continued to be both a result of and a part of further easing of tensions. An agreement that the Antarctic was to be used for peaceful purposes only had been signed as early as in 1959. In 1967, the superpowers agreed to ban nuclear weapons in space. A separate agreement that same year prohibited nuclear weapons in Latin America. The non-proliferation treaty was signed in 1968. The nuclear nations promised to refrain from transferring nuclear weapons to countries not having them, and they in turn promised not to accept or develop such weapons. However, here as on previous occasions, many of the countries which would be most affected by the treaties refused to agree to them. Thus France and China signed neither the test ban treaty nor the non-proliferation treaty.

The most important of the arms limiting measures was SALT I, the Strategic Arms Limitation Treaty of 1972. SALT consisted of two parts.

One of them was a treaty on anti-ballistic missiles (ABM) which restricted the United States and the Soviet Union to two such deployments each. By this agreement, the two superpowers refrained from developing defenses against weapons. The ABM treaty was of unlimited duration. The other part was a five-year agreement that placed a ceiling on the number of stategic weapon launchers the two powers could have. The Soviet Union was granted a larger number than the United States, 2 400 as compared to 1 700. This was to compensate both for the US lead in terms of multiple independently-targetable re-entry vehicles (MIRVs) and for the fact that bombers, where the United States also had the lead, were not included.

In 1974, Washington and Moscow agreed to limit the number of ABM deployments to one apiece. (In practice, the United States did not develop its system.) That same year, agreement was reached on the guidelines for a new SALT treaty, SALT II. Both countries agreed to a ceiling of 2 400 weapon launchers, of which not more than 1 320 could be equipped with more than one warhead. Bombers were now included. The disparity in the number of launchers in favor of the Soviet Union, which had been sharply criticized in the Senate, had now been amended. On the other hand, the US lead in MIRV technology was in the process of being reduced.

The central element in the policy of detente was normalization in Europe. As we shall see, the geographic expansion of the cold war did not cease in the early 1960s. It continued, not least in the course of the 1970s. However, for a few years at the end of the 60s and the beginning of the 70s this expansion was overshadowed by the easing of tension in the area which was still most important, in Europe.

The question of Germany and Berlin was decisive. The breakthrough came in West Germany with the broad coalition between Kiesinger's Christian Democrats (CDU) and Brandt's Social Democrats (SPD) from 1966 to 1969 and especially with the Social Democratic—Free Democratic government under the leadership of Willy Brandt after 1969. The German *Ostpolitik* could not be pursued without a certain amount of support from the Western allies, but Washington and several other Western capitals were in doubt about some aspects of this policy. The initiative for *Ostpolitik* came from the West German government itself.

At first, Bonn tried to extend relations with the countries of Eastern Europe. However, with the exception of Romania, their success was limited, and the Soviet invasion of Czechoslovakia in 1968 served to emphasize the fact that an eastern policy could not be pursued without the cooperation of Moscow. Priorities were changed. Relations with the Soviet Union became primary in importance.

On 12 August 1970, the Soviet Union and West Germany signed the Moscow treaty. Each side promised not to use violence to alter the existing boundaries in Europe, including the boundaries between Poland and East Germany and between East and West Germany. This was a major concession on the part of the West Germans, as Bonn had consistently maintained that these boundaries were temporary. In theory, they could still be changed, but in practice the agreement meant acceptance of the division of Europe and of Germany. On the other hand, this was merely an acknowledgement of the situation as it had been during the entire post-war period.

This agreement with the Soviet Union laid the foundation for similar agreements with Poland and East Germany. Through the subsequent recognition of East Germany, one of the basic principles of West German post-war policy was abandoned.

However, West Germany achieved return favors for these concessions. The most important one was the Four Power agreement on Berlin in 1971. Although neither East nor West abandoned its formal position with regard to Berlin, this agreement meant that many questions that previously had caused conflict were now regulated. Access to West Berlin from West Germany was approved and West Berlin's ties to West Germany recognized, with certain limitations that were to preserve the city's special status. The access of the inhabitants of West Berlin to East Berlin and East Germany was improved. The wall between East and West Berlin remained. This was probably politically necessary if the question of Berlin was to be resolved. It consolidated East Germany's position and created more stable relations in the area at least in the long run.

West Germany also achieved other advantages by means of its *Ostpolitik*. Although there were slight variations from year to year, all in all West Germany became the Soviet Union's largest Western trade partner. The same was true for most of the countries of Eastern Europe. Trade between East and West Germany was particularly important. The human gains were substantial: the emigration of Germans from Poland and the Soviet Union increased and contact over the border between East and West was facilitated considerably with regard to both personal visits and telephone calls. No other Western country experienced such great benefits from detente as West Germany did. That contributed to the gradual demise of Christian Democratic opposition to *Ostpolitik*.

During the period of detente, summits between East and West became increasingly common. Kennedy and Khrushchev met only once, in Vienna in 1961. The same was true of Johnson and Kosygin, in Glassboro in 1967. In the 1970s summits became annual events. The greatest success was Nixon's visit to Moscow in 1972, where SALT I and a number of other agreements were signed, among them one called 'The basic principles of mutual relations between the United States of America and the Union of Soviet Socialist Republics'. That agreement, and a similar one the following year, 'The agreement on the prevention of nuclear war', were to draw up the rules for mutual contact and prevent future conflicts between the two superpowers. Nixon and Brezhnev met again in both 1973 and 1974, Ford and Brezhnev in Vladivostok in November 1974. That would prove to be the last meeting for some years, except for the important summit in Helsinki in 1975.

Brezhnev and Kosygin's meetings with the leaders of France and West Germany were almost equally frequent. However, Moscow's relations with Britain were more strained, partly because the British expelled 105 Soviet citizens in 1971 for espionage. After Labour had assumed power again in 1974, Britain was more on the same terms as the other Western countries.

Detente in Europe culminated symbolically with the Conference on Security and Cooperation in Helsinki in August 1975. The final act from the conference represented a superstructure for the agreements West Germany had made. From a Soviet perspective, confirming the status quo in this manner was of primary importance. The act also established certain principles for economic and cultural cooperation, principles which were generally acceptable to the United States, Canada, and all 34 European countries which participated at the conference. The participants also promised to promote basic human rights, and contact across national borders was to be made easier. Here the Soviet Union and the Eastern European countries had made promises they could hardly keep.

Reasons for Detente

There were many reasons why detente went as far as it did. Several factors have already been touched upon. In the first place, the Cuban crisis disclosed the need to prevent a direct conflict between the two superpowers. No one could be interested in doing anything that would result in war between them. In the second place, the situation in Europe during the post-war period had become solidified to such a degree that all parties were finally ready to let the status quo be the basis for a formalization of conditions there.

The policy of detente also had many other explanations. It gave the Soviet Union a number of advantages. Not only did Moscow manage to establish the inviolability of the boundaries in Eastern Europe and at least indirectly attain acceptance of its sphere of interest there; the Soviet Union was also directly granted superpower status on a level with the United States for the first time. This was evident through the many summits and the agreements between the United States and the Soviet Union, especially the SALT treaty, and was also expressed openly by the Americans. For the Soviet leaders it followed naturally that the two superpowers should refrain from interfering in each other's domestic affairs. Nixon and Ford acknowledged this principle for the most part. When the Soviet author Alexander Solzhenitzyn was expelled from the Soviet Union, he was not received in the White House even though many in Congress wanted him to be.

Superpower status meant a lot. What greater honor could be imagined than the capitalist leaders themselves admitting that the Soviet Union was the equal of the United States? That meant legitimacy within the Soviet Union and in Soviet-controlled areas, and could give strength abroad, not only in relation to the Western countries, but throughout the world.

In fact, the Soviet Union could measure up to the United States in one sphere only—in military terms. Of course the hope was to attain the level of the capitalist superpower economically as well. Khrushchev had had high hopes of this. In 1959, for instance, he had promised that Soviet living standards should reach the US level within twelve years. They did not. The Soviet gross national product remained less than half the size of the US GNP until 1980. The difference in productivity was greatest in the field where Khrushchev had promised the most, within agriculture.

The growth in Soviet production was declining. In the 1950s it had been approx. 6 percent annually. In 1962–63 it was probably around 3 percent. Later it rose again somewhat, but the Soviet Union was facing serious problems. Economically, too, the policy of detente could be highly advantageous for the USSR.

In the first place, trade in general, and imports of Western technology in particular, would bring in important impulses for growth. As other methods for stimulating the economy, such as Prime Minister Kosygin's proposal for greater decentralization, were not carried out, this type of import became even more significant. In addition, Soviet crops often failed. Grain imports, from the United States in particular, were necessary. At the Twenty-third Party Congress in 1966, the importance of greater international trade was stressed by many participants. It was 'discovered' that Lenin had touched on the law of comparative advantage as a guideline for such trade.

In the second place, it was advantageous to get some control over defense expenditures. Khrushchev had introduced substantial reductions in the armed forces several times in order to meet the lack of money and labor in other sectors. Just before his fall in 1964, the Soviet leader suggested that Soviet defense was then at a 'suitable level'. By then the trend had already been reversed. Greater emphasis was to be placed on defense (see pages 163–168). Brezhnev-Kosygin continued this policy, but that did not reduce the need to place certain limitations on armaments. With arms limitations, the Kremlin could more easily realize the demand for equality with the United States at the same time as it was to maintain non-military investments and consumption.

In the United States, Kennedy had increased defense expenditures considerably, and the US lead over the Soviet Union was great as far as strategic weapons were concerned (see pages 159–163). Washington had come out of the Cuban crisis strengthened. That made it relatively easy for Kennedy to advocate a re-evaluation of relations with the Soviet Union, as he did in his speech at American University on 10 June 1963. With the ambitions Kennedy and not least Lyndon Johnson had on the domestic scene, freeing funds from the defense budget was desirable. Now poverty was to be eradicated by means of sweeping social policy measures. After the former increase, the defense budget was actually reduced in the mid-60s (until the war in Vietnam reversed this trend).

The fact that the Soviet Union gradually became the equal of the United States in the military sphere could cause problems for Washington, but it had its advantages as well. Equality contributed to establishing favorable conditions for arms limitations, especially the SALT I treaty. The Soviet Union was not willing to make agreements on any other basis than equality. The United States was aware that the pace of Soviet strategic armament was greater than its own and that it could thus be beneficial to place a ceiling on Moscow's build-up. The development of technologically highly sophisticated satellites made it possible to use them for the verification the United States so firmly insisted on. Thus the Soviet resistance against the demand for inspection on Soviet soil could be circumvented.

The Vietnam war would gradually influence the US attitude towards detente. Some Americans became more hostile towards the Soviet Union because of the country's support of North Vietnam. On the other hand, the growing opposition to the war meant that in many ways increased detente was to be desired. This could weaken the opposition against the Vietnam war and increase the possibilities that Moscow would help Washington to achieve a favorable agreement with Hanoi in order to end the war. Finally, the protest movement contributed to the growth of new attitudes towards the Soviet Union and towards the defense budget. If the United States was 'guilty' in the Vietnam war, perhaps the United States would also have to bear a large share of the responsibility for the cold war and the global arms race.

The policy of detente also represented economic advantages for the United States, although the Americans were more reserved than the Western Europeans about exploiting the opportunities that presented themselves. Congress was rather lukewarm about terminating the many trade restrictions that had been built up during the 1940s and 1950s. The American trade union movement, with its strong anti-communist streak, was opposed to nearly any increase in contact with the Soviet Union and Eastern Europe.

Even so, there was little point in the United States being so reserved while the Western European countries and Japan traded with the Soviet Union and Eastern Europe. The restrictions punished the United States itself more than anyone else. In addition, the United States had a deficit balance of payments and from 1971 a deficit on the trade balance as well. From 1970–71, trade with the Eastern countries began to take on a certain significance for the United States. Big business entered into the contracts it had long been interested in, the farmers increased their grain deliveries substantially, and credits were given to further stimulate trade. Before 1971, US exports to the Soviet Union had seldom exceeded 100 million dollars a year. In 1976 they had reached 2.5 billion dollars. Most of this increase was due to the grain trade. Apart from in agriculture, West Germany, France, and Japan had a higher level of exports to the Soviet Union than the United States had. The United States imported much less from the Soviet Union than it exported.

Total Soviet Foreign Trade

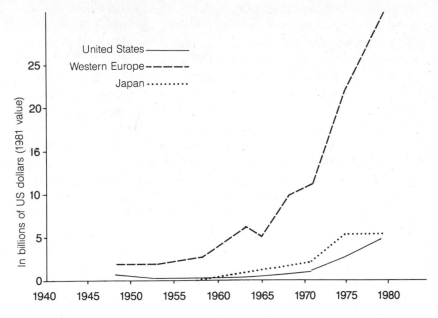

Source: United Nations Statistical Yearbook, 1949—80/81

Western Europe's political contacts with the Soviet Union and Eastern Europe stimulated political changes on the part of the United States as well. De Gaulle's overtures to the east in 1963-64 had little influence, because France was relatively isolated. Things were different when West Germany began to pursue an active policy towards the east. Brandt stressed that *Ostpolitik* was a central aspect of his foreign policy. The United States had to march somewhat in step with its Western European allies. However, the degree of conflict can easily be exaggerated, for to a great extent US and European attitudes coincided. Even early in the 1960s the United States had been more eager for overtures to the east than West Germany was, and the desire for detente increased further in the 1970s on the part of the United States as well, although the changes here were less dramatic than in West Germany.

Towards the close of the 1960s, Moscow's policy was more accommodating towards Western Europe in general and France in particular than

109

towards the United States. Western Europe's increasing independence probably led the Kremlin to hope that it could drive a wedge between the Europeans and the Americans. On the part of the Soviet Union, detente was to serve such a purpose as well. However, the United States could not be excluded from the process. The resolution of central problems such as the Berlin question required US participation. The Europeans refused to take part in a European security conference without US participation. Besides, the United States held the key to agreements on arms limitation and acknowledged superpower status for the Soviet Union.

It was no coincidence that Richard Nixon was the US President who carried detente the furthest. As has been said, he was the first American President who didn't have to worry about Richard Nixon. During the 1940s and 1950s, Nixon had established himself as one of the toughest anti-communists among leading US politicians. Against that background, it was difficult for the conservatives to accuse the President of being 'soft' on communism when he changed the course of US policy. Nor could those who were on the left of the political spectrum easily accuse Nixon of going too far in cooperation with Moscow.

The anti-communist tradition had shown itself most clearly in the US relationship to China. Mention of China was taboo in Washington. The meetings that took place between the two countries' ambassadors in Warsaw from 1955 were the only contact of any significance that existed between them. Nixon had been among those who were most critical of China. During the election campaign of 1960, he had declared that the Chinese Communists 'don't just want Quemoy and Matsu. They don't just want Formosa. They want the world.'

The growing conflict between the Soviet Union and China only gradually altered the picture. When Washington began to realize towards the end of the Kennedy administration how deep the breach between China and the Soviet Union actually was, China was considered an even greater danger than the Soviet Union. The war in Vietnam became a war against the Chinese pattern for liberation of the Third World. Neither the Kennedy nor the Johnson administration had anything but the bare minimum of contact with China.

It is possible that at first the breach between the two communist countries slowed down rather than hastened the process of detente. In the ideological competition with Peking, the Soviet leaders could easily become vulnerable if they showed too great an interest in cooperation with the capitalist superpower. This cooperation could also take place at

China's expense. Seen from a Chinese perspective, the test ban was thus a subtle attempt to prevent China from getting its own nuclear weapons. The Chinese reaction resembled the French reaction in the West. China's ideological criticism of the Soviet Union made it even more difficult for the Chinese than for the Soviets to make overtures towards the United States.

As the conflict between the two communist giants became more intense, the perspective changed. The breach between the Soviet Union and China became one of the most important factors behind the policy of detente. The Cultural Revolution and the border skirmishes made it clear that these two countries had a greater clash of interests between them than each one had with the United States on its own (see pages 218–219). The fear of a confrontation with China and the United States at the same time was bound to make Moscow interested in improving relations with Washington. The Soviet Union even had feelers out to inquire as to how the Nixon administration would respond to a first strike against the Chinese nuclear arsenal before it had become too large and could represent a threat to the Soviet Union.

In 1969, when the Cultural Revolution was waning, the Chinese leaders made their first overtures towards improving relations with the United States. Nixon and Kissinger were prepared to respond. The time was ripe for a total restructuring of US policy towards China. The breakthrough came with Kissinger's secret visit to China in 1971 and Nixon's grander tour the following year. The change in course was effected without noticeable domestic political dispute. Nixon was the right man once more to unite the country behind a new policy. It is possible that the changes caused greater problems on the Chinese side. At least Mao told Nixon in 1972 that Vice-Chairman Lin Piao's attempt to seize power in 1969 had been a reaction against the overtures towards the capitalist superpower.

Washington did not play the so-called 'China card' very directly. That might have contributed to bringing the two communist countries closer together again, or it could have intensified the breach to a dangerous level. But as Kissinger expressed it 'we could not "exploit" that rivalry; it exploited itself'.

Both Moscow and Peking had to see to it that the other part did not achieve excessive gains in Washington. The Soviet desire for detente with the United States must have been stimulated by that fact. In many ways the years from 1970 to 1972 represented a climax for detente. It was certainly no coincidence that relations between the United States and the Soviet Union were at their best precisely during the years when rapprochement between the United States and China was in its most dramatic stage.

Detente and Geographic Expansion of the East–West Conflict

Geographically, the policy of detente meant detente first and foremost in Europe. There were also unmistakable signs that the two superpowers had acquired a greater interest in respecting each other's influence in other regions. However, detente did not mean the end of further geographic expansion of the cold war by any means. Rivalry in the Middle East increased, and the Vietnam war culminated just as detente reached its climax. This war was the most expensive, in both human and material terms, of any conflict in the post-war period. Only the Korean war could to some extent be compared to Vietnam.

Respect for each other's vital regions

The most evident signs of restraint were to be found in the respective vital regions, Latin America for the United States and Eastern Europe for the Soviet Union. As far as Latin America was concerned, the Cuban crisis had strongly emphasized both US strength and the superpower's willingness to use force to protect its interests. Nor can the huge Soviet subsidies of the Cuban economy have been alluring for the Kremlin. In many ways, one Cuba in the western hemisphere was enough.

Castro was eager to spread the Cuban revolution to other countries in Latin America. He supported various guerilla movements and criticized even the Soviet Union and the local communist parties for passivity in the struggle against reactionary regimes. In 1968, however, Cuba's policy showed a change of course. The guerilla strategy seemed to have proven bankrupt, and the island's economic dependence on the Soviet Union had become so great that the country began to pursue a course that was openly pro-Soviet.

Moscow had little sympathy for the guerilla strategy and placed priority on ordinary diplomatic relations with the countries in the region. However, economic assistance to Latin America was very limited, except for Cuba and to a much lesser degree Chile and Argentina. The only country except Cuba that received Soviet military assistance was the relatively radical government of Peru in the early 1970s.

In 1965, the United States intervened in the Dominican Republic with 20 000 men in order to prevent the radical Juan Bosch from assuming power. Bosch was said to be supported by communists and could allegedly represent the danger of a new Cuba. The Soviet reaction was not much stronger than that of many of the United States' allies. Moscow raised the issue in the UN Security Council and denounced the US intervention, but even the language used was moderate.

In many ways, policy towards Allende's popular front government in Chile (1970–73) also demonstrated Soviet restraint in the US vital region. Allende did not request military assistance, so Moscow did not have to take a stand on that issue. Economic support was given, but its extent was far from overwhelming. In June 1972 Santiago was granted trade credits for a possible total value of 260 million dollars. The Soviet Union also expressed its willingness to import copper from Chile when other importers withdrew because of the dispute concerning compensation for the nationalized American copper mines. It appears that Allende hoped for an additional 500 million dollars at the end of the year. He received only 30 to 50 million. The fall of Allende in 1973 was due mainly to local conditions, but also the US policy of destabilization. His fall caused a limited reaction in the Soviet Union. Declarations of sympathy were moderate in tone, but the Kremlin broke off diplomatic and trade relations with the new military regime.

In Western Europe, another vital region for the US, Soviet policy towards Portugal after the revolution in 1974 remains somewhat more obscure. Moscow gave economic support to the pro-Soviet communist party and obviously hoped that radicalization of the country would strengthen the position of both the party and the Soviet Union. But it was probably a question of exploiting the local situation rather than challenging the Western position, unless the Western powers more or less voluntarily let themselves be out-maneuvered. After the pendulum had swung quite a way to the left for a while, it swung back towards the political center. Local forces determined the course of development in Portugal as in most other places.

If Soviet policy was relatively restrained, especially in Latin America, the same can be said about US policy towards the vital region of the Soviet Union, Eastern Europe. Washington tried to strengthen relations with the more independent countries, especially Romania and to a certain extent Poland, but US moderation was clearly illustrated in Czechoslovakia. In the first place, the Western powers were on the whole cautious about giving support to the liberalization policies of the Dubcek government (see pages 230–231), because this could only increase Moscow's scepticism about developments in the country. In the second place, the Soviet invasion in August 1968 produced fairly limited reactions. President Johnson reluctantly cancelled a planned summit meeting, and negotiations on the SALT treaty were thus drawn out. The United States and the other Western powers, with the partial exception of Britain, were still intent on continuing the policy of detente after a reasonable interval to underscore their disapproval of the invasion. Johnson revived his proposal for a summit as early as in November, but by then it was already clear that Nixon would be the new president. The summit meeting had to wait.

There was a growing sentiment in the United States that the country had assumed excessive commitments and that a reduction was necessary. The United States could not bear the primary responsibility for any regime that was threatened by some type of aggression. This attitude represented first and foremost the fear of a new Vietnam and was in no way intended to increase Soviet influence. Nevertheless, it limited Washington's possibilities of assuming large-scale involvement. This attitude was most clearly presented in the so-called Nixon Doctrine of November 1969. In his speech on Guam, Nixon maintained that the United States would stand by its treaties and protect vital regions against aggression by major powers. 'In cases involving other types of aggression we shall furnish military and economic assistance when requested in accordance with our treaty commitments. But we shall look to the nation directly threatened to assume the primary responsibility of providing the manpower for its defense.' US forces on the Asian mainland were reduced considerably, not only in Vietnam, but in most countries where US troops were stationed.

The Grey Zones between East and West

The two superpowers were prepared to exercise moderation, particularly in each others' vital regions. The existence of a number of 'grey zones' where the superpowers and others competed to gain influence represented a problem. Almost all of them were in the Third World, where many countries were characterized by little domestic stability, and there was

114

always a danger of the superpowers being drawn into local conflicts. Circumstances beyond the control of Washington and Moscow might cause a clash between them. In addition, there were numerous instances in which the two were actively engaged in trying to strengthen their influence.

A local conflict that had a degree of influence on superpower relations was the conflict between India and Pakistan. The antagonism went back to the period before independence in 1947 and flared up from time to time, in part because of the situation in Kashmir. Even though the United States and the Soviet Union would have liked to have good relations with both India and Pakistan, the United States was linked to Pakistan through SEATO and CENTO, while the Soviet Union tried to establish close relations with India in particular. However, in 1966 Prime Minister Kosygin acted as a mediator after the war over Kashmir. Although the conflict was not resolved, a cease-fire was effected.

In the early 1970s the Soviet Union oriented itself more and more towards India, because of Pakistan's good relations with China and the danger of a civil war in which India would support the independence of East Pakistan. The 1971 cooperation and friendship agreement between the Soviet Union and India gave New Dehli the backing against China that was needed for the Indians to intervene on the side of East Pakistan. The subsequent war ended with victory for India and the establishment of the new country of Bangladesh. The United States sent a fleet to the region, primarily to prevent the spread of the war to West Pakistan. If any such danger existed, it was averted. All in all, the policy of detente did not suffer much damage from this conflict.

The Middle East, 1967–1975

The threat to detente was greater in the Middle East. Soviet influence was on the increase, in part as a result of US ties with Israel. The Soviet Union gave substantial military and economic assistance to countries such as Egypt, Syria and Iraq. The Soviets had also built up a fleet in the Mediterranean that could underscore Soviet diplomacy.

There is little reason to believe that the Soviet Union wanted war in the Middle East in 1967. On the other hand, Moscow did not want to weaken its relations with the radical Arab countries. The escalation began when the Soviet Union—probably to help the Syrian government—spread rumors that Israel was preparing an attack on Syria. In

The Middle East—the Six Day War
5–10 June 1967

Positions of the UN forces–withdrawn
21 May 1967
☆ Airports bombed by Israeli planes 5 June
→ Advances by Israeli armored troops
Israel's enemies during the Six Day War
Members of the Arab League
Areas occupied by Israel in the Six Day War

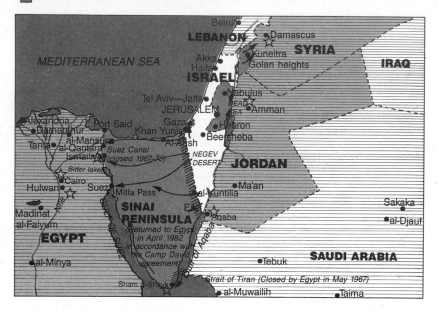

order to prevent such an attack, Egypt mobilized forces in Sinai. Nasser demanded that the UN forces there be withdrawn. Events began to acquire a momentum of their own that probably exceeded both what Moscow desired and what Nasser originally seems to have planned. Egypt blockaded the Strait of Tiran, which gave Israel access to the Red Sea and the Indian Ocean. Verbal hostility escalated dramatically; troops were concentrated along the Israeli borders. Israel chose to strike first. In the course of six days Egypt, Jordan and Syria were defeated.

In the short term, the war represented a defeat for the Soviet Union. Moscow did not send military supplies of any magnitude to help the Arabs. Nor was the Soviet fleet in the Mediterranean engaged in the action. The Soviet Union had to accept a cease-fire without Israeli withdrawal to the pre-war boundaries. Moreover, Moscow accepted UN

116

Resolution 242, which entailed recognition of Israel in return for Israeli withdrawal from 'territories occupied in the recent conflict'.

In a somewhat longer perspective, the Soviet Union was able not only to re-establish, but even to reinforce its position. Moscow provided diplomatic support and the Arab countries were again built up militarily. Nevertheless, success and defeat shifted rapidly. In 1971, the Soviet Union and Egypt signed a friendship and cooperation agreement. Twenty thousand Soviet soldiers were stationed in Egypt, and Soviet bases were established. In the following year the soldiers were sent home and the Soviet Union suffered one of its worst set-backs. One of the reasons for the reversal was that Sadat, who had taken over after the death of Nasser in 1970, was not promised the necessary support in the event of a new war with Israel. When Sadat did not receive the welcome he had hoped for in the West, he turned to the Soviet Union once more. Moscow now wanted to recover what it had lost and sent large supplies of weapons.

Soviet policy was more active in 1973 than in 1967. The Soviet Union probably still did not want war but did nothing to prevent it. Information as to Arab intentions was not given to the United States, although many leaders in Washington claimed that this was required by the 1972 agreement on 'The basic principles of mutual relations between the Soviet Union and the United States'. After war had broken out, the Soviet Union advocated an immediate cease-fire. That would have benefited the attacking Arabs considerably. When the fortunes of war were reversed, the Soviet Union gave substantial military assistance. The Arab countries which were not involved in the conflict were encouraged to assist their brethren. When Israel did not respect the cease-fire agreement that the United States and the Soviet Union brought about, the Soviet Union threatened to intervene directly on the side of the Arabs. It is not known how genuine this threat was, but Soviet troops were placed on the alert. The United States, which had increased its assistance to Israel, also placed troops on the alert. The danger of a conflict between the United States and the Soviet Union in the Middle East increased, but passed when the Israelis halted their advance before the Egyptians were defeated entirely.

The Middle East conflict of 1973 was a strain on the policy of detente. The Soviet Union was opposed to the area being considered a Western sphere of influence. Moscow had just as much right to influence there as Washington had. The Western powers reacted against the increasing

Soviet involvement. Many policy-makers asked whether no price was too high for the Kremlin to increase its influence in the Middle East.

Even so, many Arabs were disappointed with the insufficient Soviet support. After the 1973 war, Egypt returned to a pro-Western course. The war had given Sadat the backing that was needed to promote a diplomatic solution. The key to such a solution was in Washington, as only the United States could pressure Israel to make concessions. In 1976 Sadat terminated the cooperation agreement of 1971. The last Soviet base rights vanished. The Soviet military presence that had been so great in 1972 was reduced to nothing.

The Vietnam War

According to most criteria, the Vietnam war was the most comprehensive conflict after the Second World War. It was certainly the most lasting. After France's defeat in 1954, the United States took over as North Vietnam's chief enemy. This new war lasted for about 20 years. It exceeded all other wars in use of fire power. By 1970, with much of the bombing yet to come, more bombs had been dropped in Vietnam than the sum total of all other targets in human history. The Vietnam war was also the most expensive economically. US expenses alone have been estimated at 150 billion dollars. There are no reliable estimates as to how much it cost the communist side. The number of American casualties was about 58 000 (as compared to approx. 33 500 during the Korean war). However, the total number of civilian and military deaths did not exceed the 3.5 to 4 million killed during the Korean war.

US involvement was escalated gradually. From 1954 to 1961, military, political and economic assistance was given to the Diem regime in South Vietnam, but the extent was fairly moderate. In November 1961 there were still 'only' 948 military advisers in the country. The years from 1962 to 1965 were an interim period in which the US role was expanded considerably, but it was still subject to clear limitations. The number of military personnel rose to 12 000 by the end of 1962 and to 75 000 in the middle of 1965. Their functions were increased, although they still primarily lent support to South Vietnamese combat troops.

From 1965 to 1968, most of the restrictions on the US warfare disappeared. In March 1965 the first combat troops were landed. The first bombing raids over North Vietnam had taken place as early as in 1964. From February 1965 they became a regular element of the war, although all in all more bombs were dropped in the south than in the north. At the end of 1968 the number of US soldiers had reached 540 000.

There were many reasons for US policy. Vietnam was one of many places where Washington tried to contain 'communist aggression' in the post-war period. From this perspective, there was nothing unusual about Vietnam. The policy of containment was generally accepted in the United States, and at least until 1965 there was little reaction against the way the war was carried out. To the extent the official stance was criticized, most of the criticism came from the right, in the form of demands for more intensive warfare.

Behind the policy of containment was the belief that a communist victory in one area would result in further expansion. This was the domino theory. Once again this was a belief that was widely held. This is how President Johnson's leading advisers summed up their view in 1965:

> ... Thailand could not be held if South Vietnam were taken over, and ... the effects on Japan and India could be most serious ... the effect in Europe might also be most serious, and ... de Gaulle would find many takers for his argument that the US could not be counted on to defend Europe .... South Vietnam was *a crucial test* of the ability of the free world and the US to counter the Communist tactic of 'wars of national liberation' and ... a US defeat would necessarily lead to worldwide questioning whether US commitments could be relied on.

These general explanations of the US involvement can be sub-divided. During the first years after WW II, the primary objective was to strengthen France in Western Europe (se page 68). Then defense against 'world communism' became the primary motivation. When the breach between the Soviet Union and China was perceived in earnest by Washington in 1962—63, the war was justified as a defense against the 'Chinese' pattern for wars of national liberation. A defeat for the United States would mean new guerilla thrusts in other parts of the world, whereas a victory would frighten other movements from taking such a course of action. From the mid-60s, the fact that the United States had already invested so much prestige became a primary element preventing a re-evaluation of US policy.

US economic interests in Indo-China were small. In the abundance ofsources available, there are few indications that they had much significance for the judgements of the leading politicians. Most of the referen-

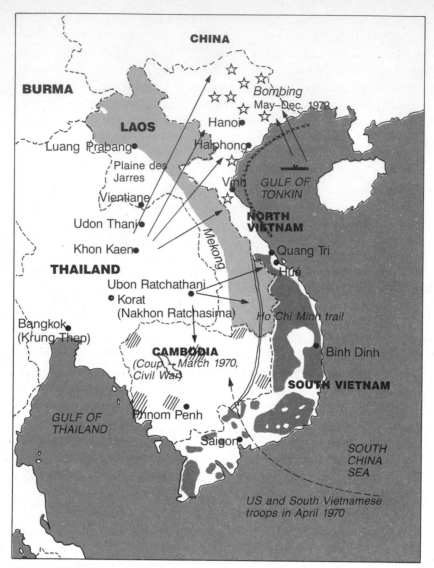

THE VIETNAM WAR
1969–73
Cease-fire and the United States out of
Vietnam in January 1973. But warfare continued

Areas controlled by the Viet Cong (FNL) in 1973
Areas controlled by Pathet Lao
xxxxx American blockade, May–December 1972
///// FNL bases in Cambodia

ces to the significance of the natural resources in the area are to be found in the Eisenhower period. On the other hand, the domino theory virtually abolished the distinction between strategic, political and economic considerations. For any of these dimensions, a defeat for the United States would have highly negative consequences.

There were instances in which the United States had not been particularly active in trying to prevent communist expansion, such as in China in 1945–49. This example could not have encouraged moderation in American warfare. The fall of China had resulted in bitter strife within the United States and had undoubtedly been an important factor behind McCarthyism in the 1950s. The Democrats had struggled with the problem ever since. They were not about to be blamed for the fall of Indo-China.

The differences between China in the 1940s and Vietnam in the 1960s were interesting. The material resources of the United States had increased tremendously. The Americans' belief in themselves as the world's leading nation had increased at an even faster pace. The situation in Europe had stabilized, so that efforts could be concentrated on the new type of conflicts arising in Asia and Africa. Vietnam appeared to be a problem that would be much easier to handle than China had been. There was no reason not to believe that Washington could take on Hanoi. The danger of Peking or Moscow intervening was considered minimal as long as the United States did not invade North Vietnam and observed certain self-imposed limitations with regard to bombing it.

However, the relative position of the United States was weakened in many ways, and time would show that the American capacity to exert influence in Vietnam was much less than nearly everyone had assumed.

Until 1964–65, Soviet involvement in Vietnam was very limited. In 1957 the Soviet Union had advocated that both North and South Vietnam become members of the UN. Economic and military assistance to North Vietnam was moderate and was actually reduced in 1964. This was possibly a reflection of increasing Chinese influence in Hanoi. The Cuban crisis and the conflict between China and India probably also curbed Soviet interest in new major commitments.

But as the war in Vietnam increased in intensity, the Soviet Union became more active. The Kremlin could not entrust Peking with the defense against 'capitalist aggression'. The conflict in Indo-China tied up large US resources. That was advantageous for the Soviet Union in many different ways, ranging from the reaction against the war in US and

European public opinion, to reduced appropriations to the sections of US defense that were not involved in Vietnam. In any case, Soviet economic and military assistance increased rapidly. In 1964 it had probably amounted to about 40 million dollars. In the years from 1967 to 1972 it was about one billion dollars annually. Soviet support clearly exceeded Chinese support, although Hanoi was fairly successful at playing these two countries off against each other in order to achieve maximum gains. This policy continued after Ho Chi Minh's death in 1969.

In June 1962, Secretary of Defense Robert McNamara declared that: 'Every quantitative measurement we have shows we're winning this war.' However, there was a lot that was not quantifiable. Morale was much higher on the side of North Vietnam and the Viet Cong than on the side of the United States and the South Vietnamese government. To a certain extent it appeared that US involvement was counter-productive. The more the Americans fought, the less motivated the South Vietnamese were to bear their part of the burden. To an ever-increasing extent, the South Vietnamese governments were considered US-dominated and thus forced upon the country by foreigners. Moreover, governments came and went every few months after the fall of President Diem in 1963, until the generals, first Ky and then Thieu, managed to achieve a degree of stability after 1965.

The extensive US bombing probably contributed to the relative stability in the south after 1965, but it could not prevent an escalation of the war on the part of North Vietnam. Official US estimates showed that the influx of troops from the north increased from 35 000 in 1965 to 90 000 in 1967. The bombing seems to have had little negative effect on Hanoi's willingness to carry on the war, and probably contributed first and foremost to drawing the North Vietnamese closer together.

The US warfare in general, and the bombing in particular, led to widespread reactions in many countries, including among Americans themselves. The protests spread from the universities to large segments of US society. US objectives in Indo-China seemed unclear for increasing numbers of people. The means were all the clearer and were portrayed in detail daily in the first televised war. The fact that the massive effort did not result in any visible success further strengthened the opposition to the war, especially after the Tet offensive of North Vietnam and the Viet Cong in 1968.

Johnson decided not to run for re-election. Nixon had no alternative when he assumed the office of president: the ground forces had to be reduced in number. By the turn of the year 1970–71 they had been reduced to 280 000. In other ways the war was intensified. The air force and the navy were used even more actively than formerly, and the South Vietnamese government received even more support. Geographically, the war was extended in 1970 by the US-Vietnamese invasion of Cambodia, in the following year by the invasion of Laos. The bombing of North Vietnam was at its most intense in 1972.

In January 1973 a cease-fire was established. The US troops were to be withdrawn, while the North Vietnamese were allowed to remain in South Vietnam. Hanoi did have to agree to let Thieu remain in power in Saigon for the time being, but negotiations were to be initiated concerning the establishment of a government comprised of the two competing local factions as well as the political forces that represented views between these two factions. In the polarization of the war there were not many who still took a middle stance. Nor could water and fire be unified. Nothing ever came of a political solution for South Vietnam.

The cease-fire collapsed. The US forces had not been able to win militarily, but had prevented a North Vietnamese victory. Public opinion and attitudes in Congress now made it impossible for the Ford administration to continue the bombing raids. A well-equipped South Vietnamese force consisting of one million men proved insufficient to resist the North Vietnamese offensive which came in 1974–75. The Viet Cong had suffered great losses, particularly during the Tet offensive, and the North Vietnamese played an ever increasing role in the south. The Thieu regime collapsed in the course of a few months. The military dispositions of the regime were unwise, the political support slight, economic chaos reigned, and the Americans could no longer do much to influence the result. On 30 April 1975 the communist forces conquered Saigon, or Ho Chi Minh City as it was now called. The Khmer Rouge had then already been victorious in Cambodia. Just after the fall of Saigon the communists gained complete control in Laos. The Vietnam war was over.

However, even the war in Vietnam had little influence on relations between the United States and the Soviet Union—how little was most clearly illustrated by Nixon's visit to Moscow in May 1972. Just two weeks prior to his visit, the United States mined seven North Vietnamese ports and escalated the bombing. The White House expected these dramatic measures to result in a postponement of the summit with Brezhnev. This did not happen. Moscow was prepared to carry out the scheduled talks, which would actually represent one of the zeniths of the policy of detente. No one can say with any certainty whether this policy could have been carried even further if it had not been for Vietnam, but at least Vietnam did not prevent detente in any way.

The Vietnam war also illustrated how limited the influence of the superpowers could be. Even a total expenditure of 150 billion dollars and the employment of more than 500 000 US soldiers could not prevent the events in Vietnam from resulting in victory for North Vietnam and the Viet Cong, a victory that could not be explained by foreign support. Soviet assistance did not amount to more than approximately one-thirtieth the American assistance.

5. Renewed tension between East and West, 1975–1986

The policy of detente had primarily meant detente in Europe. Here the status quo was acceptable to both power blocs. Detente also contributed to regulating the arms race through certain limitation agreements.

After 1975 this policy lost its momentum. Relations between East and West, particularly between the United States and the Soviet Union, soon became so poor that many people felt the cold war had returned, or not only that: more and more people claimed that it had never actually ceased.

Few new agreements on arms limitations were reached. SALT II was signed but not ratified by the United States. The intensity of the arms race increased (see pages 170–175).

It became evident that the point of departure for detente had differed in the two blocs. The Soviet Union combined cooperation in certain areas with conflict in others. Moscow was prepared to accept the status quo in Europe, but normalization here went hand in hand with more active policies in other regions of the world: in southern Africa, the Horn of Africa, Indo-China, and Afghanistan. The United States had had higher expectations for detente. There disappointment over new conflicts gave new fuel to those who opposed cooperation with the Soviet Union—a sentiment that had always existed in parts of the population. Vietnam faded somewhat into the background. The United States' need for self-assertion increased, and this need was further stimulated by various setbacks around the world.

In a sense, detente in Europe had overshadowed conflicts in other regions. Now detente was almost taken for granted in this part of the world, while the many conflicts outside Europe assumed greater significance than previously. The United States and the Soviet Union were determined to pursue more active policies, even in the adversary's backyard. Washington considered the end of liberalization in Poland a greater setback than the Soviet invasion of Czechoslovakia. Cuba, with the assistance of the Soviet Union, began once more to support revolutionary movements in several Central American countries.

The Soviet Union: A New Globalism

It is important to point out what detente was not. Moscow stressed that while the policy of detente was necessary, not least to avoid another major war, the ideological differences between communism and capitalism would still remain. Both at home and abroad, the Kremlin emphasized that there could be no question of ideological co-existence. The struggle between ideologies would continue until communism had won its final victory throughout the entire world. Anything else was inconceivable from a communist ideological point of departure.

Even when detente was at its peak, *Pravda* wrote: 'Only those politically naive can argue that what we are witnessing is some understanding between capitalism and socialism, its costs to be borne by the Third World. The Soviet Union will continue to rebuff any aggressive attempts by the forces of imperialism and render extensive help to the patriots of Angola ... Mozambique, Zimbabwe, South Africa ..' And at the Twenty-fifth Party Congress in 1976 Brezhnev claimed that 'detente does not in the slightest way abolish, and cannot abolish or change the laws of the class struggle. We do not conceal the fact that we see detente as a way to create more favorable conditions for peaceful socialist and communist construction.'

According to the Soviets, the policy of detente meant that the Soviet Union would be recognized as a superpower on a level with the United States. No major international question was to be resolved without Soviet participation. Moscow's train of thought showed clear tendencies towards superpower hegemony. The United States had long had both the will and the capacity to use military force almost anywhere in the world. After 1945 the United States had intervened a total of more than 200 times to promote its policies. Such intervention took place close to home, such as in Guatemala, Cuba, and the Dominican Republic, as well as in more distant parts, such as Berlin, the Middle East, the Congo, Vietnam and Quemoy-Matsu. Not all US interventions had been equally successful, but the Soviet Union had experienced defeat even more frequently when it occasionally ventured far from its borders.

During the 1960s and 1970s, Moscow strengthened its capacity to pursue a more global policy. This was not a sudden change, but a gradual increase throughout the two decades. In the strategic sphere, the Soviet Union achieved approximate parity with the United States around 1970. The overall level of defense was increased. An important aspect of this increase was the improved facility for so-called power projection. The air force gained the capacity to undertake large transfers over long distances, and the navy was strengthened extensively. After Khrushchev had first reduced the conventional surface fleet, it was expanded once more. By the mid-60s the Soviet navy had established a fairly permanent presence in the Mediterranean, a few years later in the Indian Ocean and the Caribbean Sea. At the end of the decade there were several instances in which it was employed to support foreign policy objectives (Yemen, 1967 and Ghana, 1969). The Soviet Union obtained bunkering rights in Africa, in the Middle East and on Cuba, a fact that further increased the possibilities of pursuing this type of policy.

The Soviet Union also became more active in the export of armaments. Traditionally, US weapon exports had been much greater than those of the Soviet Union. This trend changed from the mid-70s, and in the early 1980s the Soviet Union was responsible for slightly more than 30 percent of the world's weapon exports, whereas the US share was slightly less than 30 percent. The major importers of Soviet equipment were Syria, Libya, Iraq, India, and Vietnam. On the whole, Moscow placed greater emphasis on military assistance than on economic assistance. For the years 1976–80, military transfers to the Third World were four times as great as economic transfers. On the part of the United States, the economic share remained somewhat greater than the military share.

The Soviet military build-up reflected first and foremost the fact that Moscow placed high priority on defense, more so than the United States did during this period (see pages 163–168). This took place without any corresponding shift in the relative economic strengths of the two superpowers, although the rate of growth in the Soviet Union seems to have been higher than in the United States at the end of the 1960s. According to rough Western estimates, the Soviet gross national product equalled approximately 44 percent of the US GNP in 1960. In 1970 this figure had risen to 49 percent, and to 50 percent in 1980.

All in all, the Soviet Union was still clearly inferior to the United States in terms of its capacity for power projection in the Third World.

The United States, the Soviet Union and the World's Total GNP

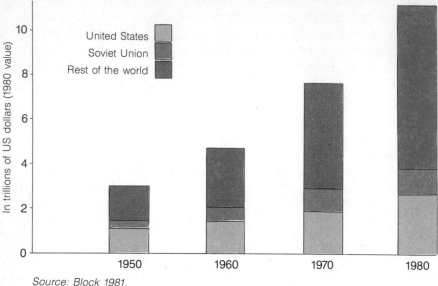

Source: Block 1981.

What was new was that the Soviet Union had at least achieved the capacity to pursue a more ambitious course of policy than previously. In step with its increasing capacity, its will had also grown stronger, although Soviet expansion seems to have been more a response to opportunities that were created locally in various parts of the world than the expression of a 'grand design' behind Moscow's policy.

After the fall of Ben Bella in Algeria, Nkrumah in Ghana, and Keita in Mali in the years 1965–1968, Soviet presence in Africa was minimal for a long time. On the whole, Brezhnev's first years were somewhat characterized by a reaction against the policies Khrushchev had pursued. Now the limited resources were to be concentrated on key countries, such as Algeria and Morocco, or on the few more progressive regimes that existed, such as in Guinea and Congo-Brazzaville. Africa's share of Moscow's economic assistance to the Third World sank from 47 percent of the total amount during the decade 1954–64 to only 13 percent in the years 1965–74. For North Africa, this figure declined from 34 to 9 percent and for Africa south of the Sahara from 13 to 4 percent. In 1971 most of the Soviet advisers were sent home from Sudan, in the following year from Egypt.

However, new opportunities for Soviet policy in Africa presented themselves in the mid-70s. In 1974 the Salazar-Caetano regime in Portugal collapsed. Thus the Portugese colonial empire moved quickly towards its end. In Guinea-Bissau and in Mozambique, unified independence movements had achieved substantial results even before the revolution in Portugal and were ready to assume power.

In Angola, however, there were several rival liberation movements, and they had only liberated small parts of the country. The three combatants, the MPLA, the FNLA, and UNITA, had all received assistance from abroad for many years. The Soviet Union supported the MPLA, the United States and China the FNLA. Supplies from abroad continued after an agreement was reached in January 1975 for a coalition government. The first Cuban advisers arrived to support the MPLA, while Zaire and South Africa supported the FNLA. The antagonism between the three groups, particularly between the MPLA, on the one hand, and FNLA-UNITA, on the other, was great, and the attempt at cooperation soon disintegrated. Warfare escalated, and the assistance from abroad increased. Portugal would withdraw in November 1975, and what mattered for each faction was to achieve the best possible point of departure for seizing power then.

There is little doubt that Soviet support to its faction was more comprehensive than US support to its faction. In December 1975 the Senate stopped the assistance the United States had given FNLA-UNITA. The US fleet was not sent to the region to neutralize the Soviet presence if necessary. Cuban intervention began somewhat earlier and became considerably more extensive on the whole than that of South Africa. Cuba would send a total of about 20 000 men to Angola. Even so, the South African intervention proved to be most significant for the attitude of black Africa, in disfavor of UNITA-FNLA. Even though the MPLA was victorious, warfare continued in parts of Angola.

Cuba had long had advisers in various African countries. It had proved difficult to spread the revolution to Latin America, so Castro concentrated all the more on Africa. However, before Angola Cuba's contribution had been limited to a relatively moderate number of advisers. Even though there were slight differences between Soviet and Cuban policies in Africa, the two countries had mutual interests for the most part. Both financially and in terms of transport, the Cubans were dependent on Soviet assistance for their presence in Angola and several other places in Africa. Obvious reasons of language, race and great power politics made Cuban troops highly preferable to Soviet troops.

On the Horn of Africa, the Soviet Union had signed a friendship and cooperation agreement with Somalia in 1974, and acquired an important navy base in Berbera. After Emperor Haile Selassie's fall in 1974, and particularly after Haile Mengistu had taken over the leadership of the revolutionary council in 1977, Ethiopia changed to a more pro-Soviet course of policy. The Kremlin wanted to have its cake and eat it too, but as Somalia and Ethiopia were at war over the Ogaden province, it was difficult to support both sides at the same time. The Soviet plans for a socialist federation of Ethiopia, Somalia, Eritrea and Djibouti were rejected.

For the Soviets it was not so much a question of shaping events. At this stage they had more than enough to do reacting to the changing local situation. Somalia terminated its agreement with the Soviet Union. The Soviet Union then concentrated its efforts on Ethiopia, the larger and more influential of the two countries. Once more, Cuba and the Soviet Union intervened, with about 17 000 men. In November 1978 the Soviet Union and Ethiopia signed a friendship and cooperation agreement. Soviet weapon assistance has been estimated at about one billion dollars in a single year.

Again the US reaction was modest, in part because of its Vietnam complex, in part because Somalia's claim on Ogaden was not recognized by the African countries. However, the United States gradually drifted towards Somalia. When the fortunes of war turned in the favor of Ethiopia, the United States supported Somalia directly, and Ethiopia and the Soviet Union were warned not to invade Somalia. They did not do so.

In South Yemen, too, the Soviet Union had gained a foothold after the British withdrew in 1967. In February 1979, North Yemen was invaded by troops from South Yemen. The Soviet Union had given substantial military assistance to the South, but tried to maintain good relations with the North as well. Now Washington was prepared to send supplies and advisers. The United States cooperated with Saudi Arabia. Even radical Arab countries spoke out against the invasion. A cease-fire was declared and the troops from South Yemen withdrawn, although guerilla combat continued until 1982.

In Indo-China, the Soviet Union cooperated with Vietnam. After their victory over the US-backed Thieu government in 1975, the (North) Vietnamese became increasingly more dependent on Moscow. To a great extent this was because Hanoi's relations with Peking became very strained owing to border disputes and differing policies in relation to Cambodia. When the Vietnamese invaded Cambodia in January 1979 and deposed the Pol Pot regime, they could count on Soviet support. Thus what was probably the most brutal regime the world had experienced after 1945 had fallen. However, Vietnam's intervention was such a clear example of encroachment on another country that the new government won only modest international support. Once more there were many in the West who spoke of Soviet-backed expansion. After Teng Hsiao-p'ing had first proclaimed his intentions in Washington, China responded in February 1979 by sending troops into Vietnam. The Soviet Union sent warnings to China, although a direct invasion does not seem to have been planned. The war went badly for the Chinese, and they withdrew from Vietnam after a brief campaign.

The clearest example of Moscow's expansive role was the invasion of Afghanistan in December 1979. The Soviet Union had traditionally had close relations with the changing Afghan governments. Relations with Afghanistan and Finland were considered exemplary for relations with non-communist countries. In April 1978, a pro-communist government assumed power in Afghanistan. The Soviet role in this coup was unclear. The Afghan Communist party was divided into rival factions. A second coup followed. Many of the reforms that were instituted were moderate in a Western context: land reforms, general access to education, a reduction in marriage taxes. In Afghanistan, however, they were radical.

The combination of a rapidly growing Soviet influence, political repression and opposition to the reforms mentioned led to a large-scale guerilla war against the Marxist government. There was a very real danger of its collapse despite the 10 000 Soviet advisers/troops that were already in the country. In December 1979 Moscow intervened. The total number of troops rose to 90 000 men. With the possible exception of the events in Eastern Europe in the wake of WW II, this was the most direct Soviet intervention anywhere. The reaction was sharp, not only in the United States and many other Western countries, but also in non-aligned countries, particularly the Islamic countries.

Soviet policy in Latin America had also become more active. In 1983 Moscow had diplomatic relations with 19 countries, as compared to only four 25 years earlier. Trade with this part of the world had increased considerably, although it was still relatively limited, with the partial exception of Argentina. The increased Soviet presence was due not only to an altered Soviet stance, but also to a widespread desire in Latin America itself for improved contacts to the east.

In addition to Cuba, the Soviet Union had particularly close relations with Nicaragua after the Sandinista government assumed power in 1979, and with Grenada, from 1979 as well. They were both referred to in Moscow as 'people's democracies' and received military and economic assistance from Cuba and the Soviet Union. Even so, the Kremlin seemed determined to avoid more comprehensive commitments towards governments which were under such strong pressure from the United States.

The Soviet Union wanted both continued detente with the United States and increased influence around the world. The Soviet leaders had not concealed their intentions, even their duty, to support 'wars of national liberation'. Why should such assistance endanger detente? After all, the Soviet Union had been willing to continue detente even when the Vietnam war was at its peak.

However, it is likely that the leaders in the Kremlin gradually began to feel that they had less to gain by the policy of detente than they had hoped. SALT II was in difficulties. In December 1979 NATO decided to deploy US intermediate-range missiles in Western Europe in response to the Soviet SS-20 missiles if a solution was not reached through negotiations (see pages 173–174).

The Soviet Union received less economic and technological help from the United States than they had expected. On the other hand, Washington showed an ever-increasing willingness to grant China advantages in the economic and even in the semi-military sphere (see pages 224–226). In 1971-72 the US opening to China had contributed to accelerating detente. Now the consequences seemed to be the opposite. This difference could possibly be explained by two considerations. In the first place, Moscow's fears as to how far US rapprochement would go were greatest at the time of the sensational events of 1971–72. In the second place, the overtures towards China at that time were accompanied by a strong desire in Washington for detente with the Soviet Union. This was much less the case at the time of the transition from the 1970s to the 1980s.

If the advantages of detente were smaller, it is possible that the gains from a more aggressive policy in Africa and Asia were greater than the leaders in the Kremlin may have expected. In Africa in particular the Soviet Union had attained a position at the beginning of the 1980s that few would have considered possible ten years earlier.

The United States: Reaction to Detente

On the part of the United States, the policy of detente was viewed with high expectations. US-Soviet relations had moved from confrontation to negotiation. The rhetorical descriptions of the new relations could reach great heights. At the signing of SALT I in 1972, President Nixon declared: 'The historians of some future age will write of year 1972 ... that this was the year when America helped to lead the world out of the lowlands of constant war to the high plateau of peace.' Even when the President wanted to caution against excessive expectations in relation to detente, his choice of words could indicate the opposite. In his speech to Congress after returning from the SALT conference, he said that 'we did not bring back from Moscow the promise of instant peace, but we do bring back the beginning of a process that can lead to lasting peace', This type of statement was partly a result of genuine optimism and partly an attempt to upstage the sceptics, not least in Congress, who would oppose some of the many agreements that had been signed by the United States and the Soviet Union.

Some segments of public opinion swung from the one extreme to the other. Whereas the Soviet Union had previously been considered practically the embodiment of evil, the policy of detente was now to usher in peace and cooperation. Gallup polls showed that confidence in the Soviet Union was greater in 1973 than at any time after the outbreak of the cold war. Forty-five percent of the respondents had a positive perception of Soviet intentions, whereas the corresponding figure as late as in 1967 had been 19 and in the 1950s as low as 3 percent.

Much of the public had difficulty in accepting the fact that relations with the Soviet Union were to consist of cooperation in some areas and conflict in others. It had to be one or the other. In the short term, this meant that the possibilities for agreement were exaggerated. In a somewhat longer perspective, this type of attitude paved the way for a strong reaction when the disappointments set in.

Despite the optimism that existed during the period of detente, even in 1972–73 a greater share of the population had little or no confidence in the Soviet Union than those who had a more positive perception. The trade union movement was basically on the sceptical side. Senator Henry Jackson was the chief spokesman for the sceptics in Congress. He got Congress to pass an amendment to SALT I establishing that in future agreements there would have to be equality between the United States and the Soviet Union with respect to the number of weapon launchers (despite the lead the United States had in terms of multiple warheads).

Thus Jackson enjoyed some support in terms of his scepticism towards arms control. He gained even more widespread support when he tried to bring about freer emigration from the Soviet Union. In October 1972 he presented a proposal that the 'most favored nation clause' for liberalizing trade between the United States and the Soviet Union, as agreed on by Nixon and Brezhnev, should only be ratified by Congress if Moscow allowed free emigration. It was particularly Jews who wanted to leave the Soviet Union. Jackson's proposal soon acquired a majority, as both conservatives and liberals could support it. The Nixon administration was sceptical about interfering directly in the Soviet Union's domestic affairs. However, there were few who were in favor of the most favored nation clause. Parts of big business and the farmers were those who showed the greatest interest. Moreover, the administration's authority in relation to Congress was weakened considerably by the Vietnam war and the Watergate scandal.

The Soviet Union was willing to make certain concessions in relation to Jewish emigration, but Kissinger's negotiations to reach a compromise between Jackson and Moscow failed. Not only did nothing come of the most favored nation clause, but Congress voted that the Soviet Union should not be able to borrow more than 300 million dollars during the course of the three-year period the trade agreement lasted.

Trade between the United States and the Soviet Union increased nevertheless, but most of the increase was due to Soviet imports of large quantities of grain. Here many Americans felt that they as capitalists had been outsmarted at their own game by the fantastic bargain the Soviet Union had made in 1972, the so-called 'great grain robbery'. Moreover, the emigration of Jews began to decline. Fluctuations in Jewish emigration often reflected the extent of Moscow's interest in improving relations with the United States.

The Nixon administration's foreign policy was continued to a great extent during Ford's short presidency (August 1974–January 1976). Kissinger represented the continuity, although an increasing opposition to the policy of detente was noticeable. The reaction came from at least two different quarters. On the part of the conservatives, it found expression in Ronald Reagan's campaign to become the Republican presidential candidate in 1976. Reagan felt that detente had benefited the Soviet Union alone. Even though Reagan lost to Ford, he received widespread support, and it was illustrative that the word detente now dropped out of the Republican vocabulary.

The other reaction was among liberals. Most of the people who were left of center claimed that the policy of detente was beneficial. However, as practiced by the Republicans it had its drawbacks. Too little emphasis was placed on relations with Japan and the allies in Western Europe, as these countries themselves claimed. Moreover, Nixon and Kissinger's policies were not sufficiently in accordance with American ideals, in the sense that their policies ostensibly lacked a moral dimension. Where, for instance, were human rights in all these pragmatic policies towards the Soviet Union? The need for a moral awakening was strengthened by the crises the United States had experienced during the Vietnam war and Watergate.

The United States would try both methods of approach. In 1976 the relatively liberal Jimmy Carter won the presidential election. Carter wanted to retain much of Nixon and Kissinger's foreign policy, more than he admitted publicly, but new elements were also to be introduced. However, there was less agreement within the Carter administration than in any other administration after WW II. One wing was associated with UN Ambassador Andrew Young, emphasizing human rights, cooperation with the Third World, and less emphasis on East-West issues. A second wing was linked to national security adviser Zbigniew Brzezinski, representing in part a continuation of Kissinger's policies, but with a sharper tone towards the Soviet Union, even more cooperation with China and emphasis on US self-assertion. A third wing was associated with Secretary of State Cyrus Vance, representing a pragmatic course. Each issue should be considered in isolation, caution was to be exercised in any change of course, and moralism and grand design could both easily lead the United States astray.

Each of these factions represented elements in Carter's own thinking. The new president lacked foreign policy experience and a dominant overall perspective. It was equally significant that these factions represented various attitudes in the United States as a whole. They had been there during the entire post-war period, but the conflict between them had never been as great as it was now. The United States was in a period of transition. Realism existed side by side with idealism, anti-communism with the desire for detente, great power politics with an aversion against such politics.

The Soviet reaction to Carter was reserved at first but gradually became openly more sceptical. The administration exhibited a willingness to follow up the SALT negotiations, but confused the Soviets by proposing much greater reductions in the weapons arsenals than had been the premise at Vladivostok in 1974. When a new SALT agreement was finally signed in 1979, it was doubtful whether the Senate would ratify it with the necessary two-thirds majority.

Carter placed greater emphasis on the issue of human rights than previous presidents had, but here, too, there was considerable wavering. Washington stressed that it was not only concerned about such conditions in communist countries, and a harder line was undoubtedly pursued towards rightist dictatorships, for instance in Latin America. But the administration's attitude towards countries such as Iran and South Korea showed that this dimension had to be balanced against other considerations. Moscow considered support to champions of human rights to be interference in domestic affairs, and disagreement on this account contributed to poorer relations, although the Carter administration gradually pursued a more cautious policy towards the Soviet Union in terms of human rights.

In the Middle East the United States first based its efforts for achieving a comprehensive peace treaty on cooperation with the Soviet Union. However, as soon as the United States and the Soviet Union had reached agreement on a joint outline in October 1977, the Carter administration—under pressure from the Congress, from Israel, and more indirectly from President Sadat in Egypt as well—dropped the entire scheme and staked everything on following up Sadat's dramatic journey to Jerusalem in November 1977. Egypt and Israel reached a peace agreement in September 1978 following Carter's personal participation (the Camp David agreement). The Soviet Union became even more determined to win influence in the radical Arab countries and to cooperate with the Palestine Liberation Organization, the PLO.

The United States brought up Soviet-Cuban policies in Africa in several talks with Soviet leaders, but its relatively mild criticism could hardly have a deterrent effect on Moscow. This was the case in regard to both Angola and Ethiopia—Somalia. In North Yemen and to some extent in the question of Shaba in 1977–78, where the United States' assisted France, Belgium and Marocco in repelling an Angola-backed invasion of the Katanga province in Zaire, Washington intervened more actively and was successful.

Despite the high-flown phrases of 'The basic principles of mutual relations', the United States, as well as the Soviet Union and most other great powers throughout history, was still attempting to obtain advantages at the expense of its adversary. Washington had sought such advantages in its policies towards China, Vietnam, the Middle East, and Chile. Both superpowers pursued detente in such a way that they could improve their position vis-à-vis the other. The Soviet Union probably saw detente as a way of managing the decline of the United States. The Americans saw it, in Henry Kissinger's words, as a way of 'managing the emergence of Soviet power'.

Yet, considering the general attitude of the United States after the Second World War, it was surprising how little the country did to limit the increasing Soviet influence, particularly in Africa. Kissinger argued that Soviet intervention in Angola was 'the first time since the aftermath of World War II that the Soviets have moved militarily at long distances to impose a regime of their choice. It is the first time that the US has failed to respond to Soviet military moves outside their immediate orbit.'

The limited US reaction was first and foremost an aftermath of the Vietnam conflict. But especially to the Carter administration it was also partly a way of expressing the conviction that the East—West dimension was subordinate to local conditions in the countries in question. There was no reason for particular concern about Soviet policies. Moscow's gains did not need to be particularly long-lived. The close partners of the Soviet Union one year—such as Egypt, Sudan and Somalia—could become the most bitter enemies of the Soviet Union the next year.

Likewise, the coup in Afghanistan in April 1978 gave rise to few reactions. The US response to the Soviet invasion in December 1979 would be all the stronger. SALT II was put on ice. Carter proposed major increases in the defense budget, the grain trade was limited, exports of high technology halted, the Olympic games in Moscow boycotted. It was not possible to trust the Soviets. The level of distrust in public opinion rose to old heights once more. Only 13 percent now had a positive opinion of the Soviet Union. Although reactions in Western Europe were more cautious, the events in Afghanistan sharpened attitudes towards the Soviet Union there as well.

The invasion in Afghanistan came on top of other humiliations the United States had experienced. The allies in Western Europe had become less willing to follow US leadership. The United States' economic dependence on the outside world increased, with increased oil imports and higher oil prices as the most obvious manifestation of this fact. Of utmost importance, however, were the events in Iran. The rule of the Shah had disintegrated at the turn of the year 1978–79; in November 1979 US embassy personnel were taken hostage by Iranian students and held in confinement for more than a year. A feeling spread that it was time the United States again let its voice be heard, whether in the face of communists, ayatollahs or lukewarm allies.

The experiences of Vietnam faded somewhat into the background. The United States was prepared to assume new commitments in vital threatened areas. The clearest manifestation of this attitude was the so-called Carter Doctrine of January 1980. The president stressed that 'any attempt by any outside force to gain control of the Persian Gulf region will be regarded as an assault on the vital interests of the United States. It will be repelled by the use of any means necessary, including military force.'

The combination of an anti-Soviet and a nationalistic wave would contribute to Ronald Reagan's victory over Jimmy Carter in the presidential election of 1980, although domestic affairs were more important than foreign policy for most voters. Moscow had come to despair of Carter's vacillation and his gradually more antagonistic attitude to such an extent that even the leaders in the Kremlin apparently preferred Reagan to Carter. Reagan's harsh criticism of the Soviet Union was attributed to the election campaign. Perhaps he could even become a new Nixon with Kissinger at his side, a president who cooperated with the Soviet Union, but who had such an anti-communist point of departure that opposition to this policy would be moderated.

If that was the analysis of the Kremlin, it was wrong. Reagan's anti-communism was firmly established, whereas Nixon's had been more situational. Reagan had always opposed detente. In his opinion, it was based on the dangerous illusion that the United States and the Soviet Union had significant mutual interests. Attitudes in the United States were different than they had been during and after the Vietnam war 8 to 10 years earlier. Scepticism towards the Soviet Union was growing in all segments of the population; the need for an increase in the defense budget was generally accepted. The United States had to act as the leader of the 'free world' once more and dispel the doubt as to its own role the Vietnam war had caused. Finally, the international situation was rather different in 1980 from what it had been at the outset of the 1970s.

Even in Reagan's policies there were certain changes which showed that as president he would not be quite the same as in a position of opposition. US relations with Taiwan were not strengthened to the degree he had advocated (see page 226). SALT II was respected, even though it had been denounced during the election campaign as 'totally flawed'. Negotiations with Moscow on arms limitations—START, as SALT was now called, and the INF negotiations on intermediate-range weapons in Europe—were begun before the United States had acquired the desired position of strength.

Even so, it was surprising how small the changes were. To a great extent Reagan pursued the policies that he had said he would promote and that he had represented throughout the 1970s. The defense budget would be dramatically increased (see pages 171–174). The verbal attacks on the Soviet Union were many and harsh. No US president after the Second World War had publicly so strongly cast doubt on the legitimacy of the Soviet system. Reagan claimed that 'The march of freedom and democracy will leave Marxism-Leninism on the ash heap of history as it has left other tyrannies which stifle the freedom and muzzle the self-expression of the people'.

The Reagan administration found ever new evidence that its analysis of Soviet intentions was correct. The war in Afghanistan continued. There were no signs that the Soviet Union intended to withdraw. In December 1981, a state of emergency was declared in Poland. Even though the Soviet Union did not intervene directly, most leaders in Washington felt that Moscow was behind the tough policies in Poland (see pages 232–233). In September 1983, a South Korean passenger plane was shot down over Soviet territory, and all 269 on board perished. This was considered new evidence of the true nature of the Soviet regime. Confidence in the Soviet Union was weakened further. Only nine percent of the US population had a somewhat positive perception of the Soviet Union.

In Reagan's opinion, the United States had ceased to lead the free world. This would now be changed. However, it became evident that the United States and Western Europe had different perceptions of what results had been achieved by the policy of detente. The Europeans felt that it had had many positive effects and that it ought to continue, though perhaps in a modified form. The United States felt that detente had failed and ought to be abandoned. The Europeans insisted that they should have a say in the formulation of Western policies to an entirely different degree than previously. The United States could no longer decide more or less on its own, whether in terms of nuclear strategy, negotiations on arms limitation, or limitations on Western trade with the Soviet Union (see pages 198–202).

The European perspective was greatly affected by the fact that the policy of detente had produced more beneficial results in Europe than in the rest of the world. But even in Europe this policy had lost its momentum, and tension increased once more. This was in part a result of the events in Poland, but even more so of the developments with regard to intermediate-range weapons and the generally deteriorating relations between East and West.

Even so, the greatest conflicts were linked to areas outside of Europe. Reagan was convinced that most of the unrest in the world could be attributed to the Soviet Union. Communist expansion was to be opposed, in Central America, in the Middle East, and everywhere else, whether the Soviet Union was directly behind it or tried to use others as its instrument.

In Central America, the large landowners, the army and the church had traditionally dominated. In the course of the 1970s this alliance began to crack. The church became more liberal, and new ideas also penetrated parts of the officer corps. In Nicaragua, the Somoza family's power base had become so narrow that the regime collapsed in 1979. The new Sandinista government was at first a broad coalition, but then it too began to lose some of its popular support.

The Carter administration swung from half-hearted support of the Sandinistas to a more sceptical attitude. Under Reagan the objective was openly to undermine and preferably overthrow the government as an element in 'the defense of the Western hemisphere against Soviet—Cuban expansion'.

In El Salvador the United States defended the existing government, whereas in Nicaragua it now supported the political and military opposition. US aid increased steadily in an attempt to bring the situation under control, with only limited success. The fear of a new Vietnam placed clear limitations on the willingness of Congress and public opinion to send military personnel to the region, although the United States built up bases in the neighboring country of Honduras. The US invasion of Grenada in the autumn of 1983 was also defended as necessary to halt Soviet-Cuban expansion. The Marxist government on the island was deposed and the Cuban advisers sent home, but the invasion was denounced even by most of the United States' allies.

The Middle East was the other area that became a focal point of attention. In 1975 civil war had broken out in Lebanon, and the Syrian troops that advanced across the border the following year had remained. Israel intervened in Lebanon twice, first in 1979 and again in 1982. After the second invasion US troops were employed as part of an international peace-keeping force that was to oversee conditions in the chaotic city of Beirut. Gradually the troops were drawn in on the side of the Christian-Falangist government in the ongoing civil war. Thus they became an instrument directed against the Syrian influence. Washington saw Moscow behind Syria, as there were 7 000 Soviet advisers in Syria.

But in Lebanon the domestic situation was so chaotic, the objective of the US presence so unclear, the losses so great, and the opposition to the United States so strong that Reagan was forced to withdraw the troops early in 1984. This action showed that the President could act pragmatically despite his harsh, uncompromising verbal stance.

New signs?

The Reagan administration expected the Soviet Union to yield if only the United States conducted itself firmly enough. For instance, when it became evident that Washington would deploy new intermediate-range missiles in Western Europe, Moscow would make the concessions that were necessary to attain a negotiated solution.

The Kremlin was willing to make some concessions, but not as many as the White House wanted. Instead, verbal attacks on the Reagan administration were increased. Jurij Andropov, who had assumed leadership after the death of Brezhnev in November 1982, said in September 1983 that 'if anyone had any illusions about a possible evolution for the better in the policy of the present American Administration, such illusions have been completely dispelled by the latest developments'. In December 1983, deployment of intermediate-range missiles was begun in the West. This resulted in Moscow breaking off the arms limitation negotiations between East and West (see page 174). In February 1984 Andropov died and Konstantin Chernenko replaced him. This change meant little for the climate between the two power blocs. Relations between the United States and the Soviet Union were worse than at any time since the Cuban crisis in 1962.

In the autumn of 1984, however, there were signs that the frigid climate was in the process of thawing somewhat. For the first time, Reagan met with a representative of the top Soviet leadership, Foreign Minister Gromyko. The rhetoric used about the other side was modified in both Washington and Moscow. That in itself was significant, considering the sharp verbal attacks that had dominated previously. Both sides regained a greater interest for talks and other forms of contact. In November 1985 Reagan met in Geneva with Mikhail Gorbachev, who had taken over as Soviet party leader upon Chernenko's death in March 1985. This was the first US—Soviet summit since Carter and Brezhnev met in 1979. Although the summit did not produce any substantial results, the East-West atmosphere improved somewhat. In October 1986 they met again, this time in Reykjavik. The Reykjavik meeting was prepared at short notice. The discussions on nuclear arms control were the most far-reaching ever, but led to no new agreements (see pages 174–175).

Reagan's attitude towards the Soviet Union was more conciliatory now than during the first years of his presidency. He wanted to show the American voters and history that his administration not only stood for firmness but was also capable of establishing normal relations with the Kremlin. US public opinion wanted both strength in relation to the Soviet Union and 'peace' with arms control. Reagan had clearly given priority to the first consideration during his first administration. A more open attitude towards the Soviet Union would also improve US relations with the Western Europeans. In the November 1984 election he won a great personal victory. The US economy was also doing well. Now he could argue that the United States had become so strong that negotiations with Moscow could be carried out from an advantageous position. To use a Soviet term, 'the correlation of forces' had changed in Washington's favor.

On the Soviet side, Gorbachev was a more forceful and skilled leader than the rapid succession of old men who had led the Soviet Union in the early 1980s. Gorbachev had to give priority to the domestic situation and particularly to the stagnant Soviet economy. It became evident that the productivity and technology gap between the United States and the Soviet Union was now growing, not diminishing. Two-thirds of a century after the Bolshevik revolution, Soviet leaders still had rather limited evidence to support their thesis that the communist system was inherently superior to the capitalist system.

The economic problems probably made Moscow more interested in improving relations with Washington. Vast resources had to be invested to turn the Soviet economy around. The import of Western technology could provide a most necessary stimulus in some fields. The Soviet leaders also clearly feared a renewed arms race with the United States. Reagan's Strategic Defense Initiative (see pages 172–174) represented a challenge both to the Soviet position as the military equal of the United States and to the Soviet economy.

All along the Kremlin had argued in favor of maintaining detente. From the Soviet perspective detente had been killed by hostile forces in the United States, who had used Soviet actions simply as a pretext to weaken a policy they had always been against. On the other hand, the Soviet expansion in Africa and Asia and the economic problems in the Soviet Union and in Eastern Europe all made a certain retrenchment desirable. The new leadership appeared to shun international crisis and confrontation.

The change in the international climate was certainly one of style, but it was also one of substance. Again and again Gorbachev stressed the common interest in avoiding a nuclear war. Even the ideological conflict between capitalism and communism had to be subordinated to this objective. The costs of the arms race and the global commitments of the Soviet union had to be reduced. Afghanistan represented the most troublesome problem. Reagan went from condemnation of the 'evil empire' to praising the new Soviet leadership. With Reagan pursuing such a policy it became rather difficult for the American right to oppose the new course.

6. The Arms Race, 1945–1986

Perspective and motivating forces

The development of destructive weapons has been a part of life since time immemorial. But the arms race after 1945 was still unique in many ways.

One of the greatest changes in the post-war period was to be found in the level of military expenditure. The absolute and probably even the relative figures have never been higher in peacetime.

During the Second World War, the Soviet Union and Britain used about 60 percent and the United States between 30 and 40 percent of its national product at the most for warfare and weapon production. After 1945, this figure never exceeded 14 percent on the part of the United States. Nor for the Soviet Union could expenditure after the war compare with that during the war. However, compared to any other peacetime period in recent history the world was spending more now on arms. As a percentage of world output, total expenditures came to 6–8 percent. In the years preceding World War I and during the inter-war years, the corresponding figure was some 3–3.5 percent. In the 1980s, total world military expenditures approximately equalled the income of the poorer half of the world's population. The two superpowers spent roughly half of that total.

Changes in two other dimensions should also be noted. In the first place, an entirely new range of weapons was developed — the nuclear weapons. These weapons had a destructive capability that was unique. Humanity could fear its own demise if a new major war broke out. Nuclear weapons and the new launchers, long-range bombers and missiles, united the world. A future war would affect everyone, military or civilian, belligerent or neutral.

In the second place, the pace of new invention was faster than it had ever been. Armament still had a quantitative dimension, but the qualitative aspect would play an increasingly greater role. Ever new weapon systems were developed. Each side was constantly preparing for the new weapons that the other could possibly develop not only tomorrow, but 10 to 15 or 20 years into the future.

To simplify, it can be said that there are two main interpretations of the motivating forces behind the arms race. The first one places greatest emphasis on the foreign policy environment. The arms race between East and West, like previous arms races, arises from international anarchy. Distrust and fear cause nations to try to protect themselves by armament. The competing sides then impel each other on through a pattern of action and reaction. Initiatives by one side result in counter-measures on the other side, which again lead to new measures, and so on. Thus the arms spiral continues.

The other interpretation places greatest emphasis on internal causes. Armament is pursued to satisfy various pressure groups. The military establishment seldom or never gets enough weapons. The weapons industry endeavors to earn profits and secure employment. These groups in turn receive support from politicians. According to this theory, there are actually two parallel arms races, one in the West and one in the East.

There are also combinations of these two main views. They provide the basis for the present discussion. Primary emphasis will be placed on the foreign policy anarchy and the pattern of action and reaction. However, a number of other factors also contributed, most often strengthening but occasionally weakening this primary pattern. Economic trends, prevailing economic theories and the priority given to defense within the total national economy were significant. The same was true of technological developments and the influence of scientists, the military and the weapons industry. The relative importance of the various factors could vary considerably from case to case. It also makes a difference whether one concentrates on overall indicators such as total defense spending or on the history of individual weapon projects. Here the emphasis will be on the former aspect.

Hiroshima, atomic weapons and conventional forces, 1945–1949

When Franklin Roosevelt decided in the autumn of 1941 that the United States should substantially increase its level of research on nuclear weapons, two considerations seem to have been crucial. The first one was the international situation, or more specifically the fear that Germany would be the first country to acquire such weapons. The decision was made before the United States had entered the war. The second consideration was technological: the probability that an atomic bomb could be produced. In the summer of 1941, the British had reached the conclusion that not only could such weapons be constructed, but that they could be developed within a two-year period. As would frequently prove to be the case, the possibility of developing a weapon very often meant that the decision to develop it would be made.

Research concerning the US motive for dropping atomic bombs over Hiroshima and Nagasaki in August 1945 has been intense. Today there is a high degree of consensus that the primary motive was to defeat Japan as quickly as possible. In order to achieve this objective, the weapons that were available were employed. It was not a major decision for Truman and his advisers to determine that the bomb should be used. They almost took it for granted. The more quickly the war was brought to an end, the fewer lives would be lost, particularly on the US side.

An important decision seldom has a single motive, nor was that the case in this instance. A number of leading politicians, including President Truman, Secretary of State Byrnes, and Secretary of War Stimson, all felt that demonstrating the bomb in the war would prove clearly advantageous in relation to the Soviet Union as well. Perhaps a rapid end to the war could reduce the role the Soviet Union would play in Asia, although it was difficult to renege on the concessions that had been made to Stalin at Yalta, concessions that were particularly unfavorable for China. Even more important was the consideration that the bomb would underscore the power of the United States and thus, presumably, get the Soviet leaders to show greater consideration for US interests in international politics.

Domestic policy considerations also favored the use of the bomb. Many policy-makers feared that the administration would suffer a political defeat when it one day became known that millions of dollars had been spent developing a weapon that then was not used to hasten Japan's capitulation. Finally, some people, particularly a number of the scientists who were engaged in the Manhattan Project, as the bomb project was called, felt that only a realistic use of the new weapon could force the revolution in attitudes that was needed to avoid a new major war in the future.

After the war, a few initiatives were taken in an attempt to ensure that the new source of energy came under the control of the UN and that it was exploited for peaceful purposes. The Baruch plan was the most important initiative on the part of the United States. According to this plan, an international authority was to control all aspects of development, from mining to the finished weapon. The United States declared that it was willing in principle to relinquish its atomic weapons.

This plan was not acceptable to the Soviet Union. The United States was to relinquish its atomic weapons only as the final step in a number of measures. The Americans would still retain their monopoly on the know-how of atomic bomb production. Finally, a comprehensive international control system would violate the Soviet policy of seclusion from the rest of the world.

It was equally obvious that the United States could not accept the Soviet plan. It quite simply prohibited the use of atomic weapons under any circumstances and called for the destruction of all such weapons within three months. No international system of control was to be established. Each country was to promise to adopt stiff punishments for any breach of agreement within its own boundaries.

The role of the atomic bomb in US strategy during the first years after WW II can easily be exaggerated. Everyone was aware that it was a weapon of entirely new dimensions. Even so, military planning did not presume that the bomb would immediately revolutionize warfare.

In the first place, US war plans until 1948–49 were based on the assumption that a war with the Soviet Union could extend over a long period of time. Because of its conventional superiority the Red Army would probably conquer most of the European continent. The atomic bomb would be a part of the US general mobilization strategy. Only after a considerable build-up in a number of areas could the United States expect to repulse a Soviet offensive. In principle, atomic bombs would function as conventional bombs, but with a much greater explosive force.

In the second place, the United States only had a few atomic weapons, and those they had were unwieldy. After Nagasaki Washington seems to have had only one for a time. By the end of 1948 the country still had only 50, and none of them was ready for immediate use. Moreover, the navy and the army were reluctant to place primary emphasis on a weapon that would be under the control of the air force.

Gradually, however, politicians began to do just that. A primary reason was that atomic weapons were so cheap compared to conventional forces.

The greatest military significance of the atomic bomb probably lay in its deterrent effect. Washington and most of the capitals of Western

Europe considered the chances of a Soviet attack small, partly because of the US atomic monopoly. When the Atlantic treaty was signed, the implicit atomic guarantee, combined with the US troops in Europe as a sort of trigger mechanism, was the very foundation of the US contribution, at least in the short term.

The political advantages of the new weapon soon proved to be much smaller than the leaders in Washington had hoped. Threatening the Soviet Union directly with the atomic bomb was politically impossible, so what was needed was that the Soviet Union itself should feel the need to take into consideration the reality the bomb represented in terms of power politics. However, the Truman administration soon concluded that it was difficult to perceive any such moderation.

Outwardly the Kremlin played down the significance of atomic weapons. Stalin ostensibly placed little emphasis on the information he received when Truman, in general terms and very briefly, told him about the bomb at the Potsdam conference in July 1945. Molotov practically laughed it off at the meetings of foreign ministers in London and Moscow later in 1945. Soviet military journals did not have a single article on the new weapon until 1953.

Stalin's military conservatism was one reason for this attitude. However, of more significance was the fact that the Soviet leaders must have felt almost obliged to dismiss the significance of a weapon that only the adversary had and not they themselves. Admitting the revolutionary effect of this weapon would be admitting Soviet inferiority at the same time.

Under the official surface, however, the Soviets worked energetically on developing their own atomic weapons. These efforts had begun in earnest in 1942. The Soviet Union, like the United States, wanted to develop the weapons it was possible to develop. It merely appeared that Stalin made light of the information Truman gave him in Potsdam. In reality, this information, combined with what Moscow knew through Soviet espionage and finally from the bombs over Hiroshima and Nagasaki, led to a strong escalation of Soviet research. Developments in one country influenced others. The Soviet Union also stepped up its efforts in missile research, a field on which it concentrated more than the United States did.

In most areas the Americans had the lead over the Soviets. Only in terms of conventional forces could the Soviet Union be said to be stronger than the United States. The Soviet Union was long assumed to have had 4 to 5 million men under arms when demobilization after WW II was completed. These figures were probably too high. Khrushchev later claimed that 2.8 million was the correct figure, but even this was considerably higher than the corresponding figure for the US side. US forces totalled approx. 1.4 million from 1947 to 1950. The leaders in Washington complained about the rapid demobilization, but it was considered political suicide for the Truman administration to try to stem the process.

The US Turnabout, 1949–1953

In August 1949 the US atomic monopoly came to an end. The Soviet Union detonated its first atomic bomb, earlier than most experts had expected. At first, Truman actually doubted whether it could be true that the Soviet Union had carried out such a test. When it became evident that this was the case, the mood reversed. After having underestimated Soviet nuclear strength, Washington now overestimated it.

The United States decided to increase its production of atomic weapons, a decision that was not particularly controversial. On the other hand, there was considerable discussion about the step that was taken in January 1950: production of an even more powerful weapon, the hydrogen bomb. Whereas several of his advisers were in doubt or opposed to the new weapon, at least at that time, Truman felt that the decision was relatively easy. The United States had to keep ahead of the Soviet Union at all times in the nuclear field.

Uncertainty spread in Washington. The Soviet Union had been underestimated militarily. Politically, Mao's victory in China represented a major defeat for the United States. In January 1950, Klaus Fuchs, a British scientist who had cooperated with the Americans in atomic matters, was arrested for espionage. In February Senator Joseph McCarthy made his first vigorous attacks on ostensible communist sympathizers in the State Department.

In this atmosphere, the State Department and the Department of Defense carried out one of the formative studies for US foreign policy after WW II, NSC 68, which was completed on 7 April, 1950. Its main author was Paul Nitze. What was new was not the fact that the US leaders were sceptical as to Soviet political intentions, but that Soviet military strength was evaluated as much greater than previously. The threat from Moscow was considered much more direct now. The United States was still superior to the Soviet Union in nuclear terms, but NSC 68 assumed that with a rapid build-up the Soviet Union would have 200 long-range atomic charges in 1954. Then even continued US superiority would be much less reassuring.

The solution was to be found in large-scale rearmament on the part of the United States, in both conventional and nuclear terms. The nuclear part of the program was already being implemented. The men behind NSC 68 had not suggested specific sums for the implementation of their proposals, but a defense budget of about 40 billion dollars seemed realistic. This was far too high for Truman, for after all it meant nearly trebling what he had previously considered a maximum figure.

The outbreak of the Korean war was highly significant for further developments. On 30 September Truman approved NSC 68. In the course of 2 or 3 years the defense budget was increased to more than 50 billion dollars. Little was now to be heard about the United States 'bleeding to death' if more than 15 billion dollars was used for defense, as had earlier been claimed. Rearmament was effected so rapidly that the three services could not possibly use all the appropriations. Even so, they would not agree to a reduction.

The United States sent four new divisions to Western Europe, to the great embitterment of the right wing of the Republican party. Although Western Europe received substantial support for its military rearmament, the Europeans, too, would have to increase their defense budgets dramatically. The most ambitious conventional plans were drawn up at NATO's Lisbon conference in February 1952, where the alliance committed itself to having 50 divisions in 1952, 75 in 1953 and 96 in 1954.

West Germany was included in the defense of Europe. This was decided in principle as early as in September 1950. The reluctance most of the Western European governments felt about German rearmament faded alongside the increased threat from the Soviet Union. Only with a German contribution was it possible to plan a forward defense along the East—West border, and not, as previously, a defense strategy based on the loss of the area east of the Rhine.

In order to safeguard against a new German national army and to increase the efficiency of the individual countries' defense build-up, the Western powers aimed at a high degree of military cooperation. NATO evolved from a treaty into an organization. The alliance acquired a joint staff that was to make preparations for complete integration in the event of war. General Dwight D. Eisenhower was the first Supreme Commander. He would be succeeded by a series of other US generals. The Europeans in particular considered it advantageous to have a US Supreme Commander. That would tie the United States more closely to Western Europe.

A number of important changes took place outside Europe as well (see pages 78–79). All in all, John Lewis Gaddis thus seems to be right when he claims that at least in the military field, the greatest change in US post-war policy came with NSC 68 and the outbreak of the Korean war.

In order to explain this shift, it is reasonable to point out the primacy of foreign policy. The strained international situation before, and especially after, the outbreak of the Korean war was the most important single factor. However, other considerations also had an effect. The mentality of budget policy was in the process of changing. Within the Truman administration, Keynesian expansionism gained a foothold in earnest. A higher level of government activity was to result in increased production without necessarily entailing higher inflation.

The military services had long pressed for increased defense expenditures, although without the support of Secretary of Defense Louis Johnson in the years 1949-50. A number of scientists spoke out in favor of the development of new weapons, although many were opposed to the hydrogen bomb. This bureaucratic pressure had some effect. But only when the president and the leading decision-makers changed their views—and this in turn to a great extent as a reflection of the Korean war and the international situation—did this pressure achieve decisive influence in Washington.

New Directions in US and Soviet Defense Policies

The 'New Look'

When Eisenhower assumed office in January 1953, major changes in US defense policy ensued. Nuclear weapons acquired an even more central position, while conventional forces were given a lower priority. The new president felt that the build-up under Truman had been far too expensive. Not until 1958 did Eisenhower's defense budget reach the same level as Truman's last defense budget in 1953. The share of the gross national product that went to defense declined from 13.8 percent in 1953 to 9.1 in 1960.

The central premise of the 'New Look', as the new strategy was called, was that the Soviet Union was never to rest assured that nuclear weapons would not be employed. Eisenhower and Secretary of State Dulles did not state explicitly when they would be employed, but the option was to remain open to respond to even a minor conventional attack with nuclear weapons. Whereas Truman's policy of containment had had as its point of departure the premise that Soviet aggression should be answered in the region where the attack had taken place, the 'New Look' meant that the US response could possibly come in an entirely different area and with completely different means.

What was it that made a former army general promote a strategy that in many ways gave his own service lowest priority? For the air force was again the focal point. The air force's share of total defense expenditures rose from 26 percent in 1950 to 47 percent in 1957. The navy's share remained relatively constant, while the army's declined in step with the increase for the air force. In 1957 it had dropped to 22 percent.

The 'New Look' was in part a reaction to the Korean war. The United States had been drawn into a lengthy conventional war that had ended as a draw. The threat of massive retaliation was to get the Soviet Union to refrain from similar aggression. If a war broke out nonetheless, it was to be decided swiftly in favor of the United States.

Strong economic considerations spoke in favor of the 'New Look'. Eisenhower and the Republicans had a different view of the federal government's responsibilities from the one that had developed particularly towards the end of the Truman administration. Washington was to limit its expenditures, including defense expenditure. Eisenhower was firmly convinced that large expenditures, with the taxes they entailed, could destroy the capitalist system. Moreover, his administration based itself on the assumption that the threat the Soviet Union represented was lasting, without any specific critical point, whereas NSC 68 had singled out 1954 as a particularly dangerous year. As a former general and army commander, Eisenhower knew better than most people where cuts could be made in the defense budget, and he could do it without anyone daring to accuse him of making the United States vulnerable in relation to the Soviet Union.

Technological developments were also significant for the 'New Look'. Deployment of so-called tactical nuclear weapons started in 1953. These new, smaller weapons would be more versatile and thus ostensibly more credible than strategic weapons, in that they could more easily be employed in the event of a Soviet attack. Eisenhower himself expressed it as follows: 'Where these things are used strictly on military targets and for strictly military purposes, I see no reason why they shouldn't be used just exactly as you would use a bullet or anything else.'

In practice, the British had chosen a similar strategy. The Conservatives had assumed power in 1951, and their strategic thinking was similar to that of the Republicans on the other side of the Atlantic in many ways. However, the British Labour party, like the Democrats in the United States, placed somewhat greater emphasis on conventional forces.

Even so, the most important factor for the introduction of the 'New Look' was the simple fact that the concentration on conventional weapons that had been so clearly stated previously—most recently at the Lisbon meeting in 1952—had proved unrealistic. Truman's last defense budget pointed towards many of the same conclusions that Eisenhower reached, placing greater emphasis on nuclear weapons and the air force. Instead of 96 divisions, NATO had 25 in 1954, with an additional 25 in reserve. Finally, the international climate had become somewhat less strained from 1952-53 onwards. That made it easier to be in favor of reductions in the defense budget.

As long as the United States was clearly superior, there seemed to be little reason to doubt the country's willingness to use nuclear weapons in the event of a Soviet attack. But as the Soviet Union developed atomic and hydrogen weapons with suitable means of delivery, many people began to question the credibility of US nuclear policy. This doubt came from some so-called strategic thinkers in the West, thinkers who partly reflected developments in weapons technology but who also influenced them in turn. Their views were supported by those for whom such criticism was politically or militarily advantageous. In US politics that meant the Democrats, and within the military establishment primarily circles within the army and to some extent the navy.

The attitude of the Eisenhower administration changed somewhat in the course of the 1950s. Tactical nuclear weapons played an ever increasing role, although calculations showed that even they would cause destruction to such a degree that the discussion of credibility soon spread to concern them as well.

Even so, US nuclear superiority was so great in the 1950s that the 'New Look' could be sustained. A certain degree of unpredictability was a deliberate aspect of this strategy. This uncertainty could be exploited politically by Washington more or less directly threatening to go to war to attain specific objectives. This was what Dulles liked to call 'brinkmanship'. He emphasized his conviction that 'the ability to go to the verge without getting into the war is the necessary art'.

On at least three or four occasions the Eisenhower administration threatened to employ nuclear weapons. In April 1953, Dulles warned Peking through diplomatic channels that such weapons could be employed if a peaceful solution was not reached in Korea. This threat probably contributed to the difficult question of repatriation of war prisoners being brought closer to a solution 11 days later.

In 1954, Washington threatened to use nuclear weapons in Vietnam to prevent Chinese intervention. It is unlikely that the Chinese had any plans of intervening at all. In the following year, the use of atomic weapons on the Chinese mainland to prevent a Chinese landing on Quemoy and Matsu was discussed fairly openly. When the Chinese pressure decreased, these plans were put aside. It is difficult to make any conclusive judgement concerning the question of Chinese motivation in this case. In 1958 the Chinese began to shell the islands once more, without achieving much.

Even with Eisenhower's reduced defense budget, close ties existed between the various branches of the military, leading politicians, and large companies linked to the arms industry. On several occasions, most emphatically in his farewell address, the President himself gave a warning about the strength of the combination formed by this military-industrial complex.

There was undoubtedly strong pressure to put into production the many new weapons the researchers first developed, the companies then wanted to manufacture, and the military so strongly wanted to acquire. Those who had a vested interest in a new weapons system had a natural tendency to depict the situation in black and white. If 'their' system was not developed, the adversary could gain a lead that at worst would result in defeat in the event of war. One service was unwilling to see its weapons in relation to those a different service had. Rival groups were to be found even within a single service. With regard to strategic weapons, some members of the air force campaigned for bombers, others for missiles. The fact that the navy got its first submarine with long-range missiles in 1960 did not result in a reduced need for planes and missiles within the air force. The exact opposite tended to be the result.

However, the extent of technological-military pressure can be exaggerated. For there were counter forces at work. Overall economic goals could, as in the Eisenhower years, reduce the appropriations that were made available to the military. Many officers were technologically conservative, precisely owing to bureaucratic considerations. Thus leading circles in the air force were actually quite sceptical about intercontinental ballistic missiles (ICBMs) for a long time. The air force had always been based on manned planes and ought to be so in the future as well. In 1955, the civilian leadership, with the support of a minority within the air force, more or less had to compel the air force to give top priority to the development of ICBMs. But then of course the air force was to have both planes and missiles. In the navy, too, certain vested interests showed reluctance to accept the development of the new Polaris submarines. However, the opposition within the navy towards Polaris was less than the air force's towards ICBMs, not least because the missile era had already begun to establish itself.

The 'New Look' in the Soviet Union

Developments in the Soviet Union were also determined both by the international situation, including US military dispositions, and by domestic factors within the Soviet Union. The possibility of carrying out detailed analyses is limited by the lack of information about the various weapons systems and even about such things as the actual size of the defense budget. Roughly, however, developments on the Soviet side followed those in the United States. The early 1950s were characterized by rearmament, emphasizing both nuclear weapons and conventional forces. From the middle of the decade the conventional forces were reduced substantially and nuclear weapons granted priority.

Outwardly, Stalin continued to claim until his death that the areas in which the Soviet Union was strong were the ones that meant anything. Domestically, he pressed for the development of atomic and hydrogen weapons with the accompanying means of delivery. In August 1953 the Soviet Union detonated its first hydrogen bomb, less than a year after the United States. It appears that mass production of Soviet intermediate-range missiles began in 1955. The Soviet Union could also compete with the United States in terms of intermediate-range bombers. This was all the result of decisions that must have been taken during the Stalin period.

Despite this build-up, developments were much less dramatic than assumed in NSC 68. This was particularly true in the strategic field. The estimates that the Soviet Union would have 200 long-range atomic charges in 1954 proved to be considerably exaggerated. Not until the mid-50s did the Soviet Union develop a bomber that could reach the United States and return. After this plane had taken part in the May Day parade in Moscow in 1955, rumors sprang up concerning a bomber gap in the Soviet favor. They proved to be wrong. The Soviet Union concentrated on the production of intermediate-range planes aimed at Europe rather than on long-range planes intended for use against the United States. The technology was less complicated and the costs were smaller.

The United States remained far ahead of the Soviet Union in the strategic field. In 1956, the Strategic Air Command (SAC) had at least 540 planes with an intercontinental range. As late as in 1960 the Soviet Union probably had only 135 such planes, while US intelligence sources had considered it likely that they would have three times that number. In addition, the US planes were considerably more advanced technologically than the Soviet planes.

Soviet conventional forces grew from approximately 2.8 million men in 1948 to approximately 5.7 million in 1955. The United States had 2.9 million men under arms in 1955. Although the Red Army had not reached the number of divisions Western intelligence operated with, the Soviet Union and the Eastern European countries remained superior to NATO in conventional terms.

In 1955 West Germany joined NATO. That increased Western conventional strength rather dramatically. The fear of a strong Germany once more was genuine in the Soviet Union and a not unexpected result of the fact that the country had suffered tremendous losses during WW II. The creation of the Warsaw Pact was partially a response to this fact, although to a great extent the Pact represented a formalization of relations that already existed in Eastern Europe.

In August 1957 the Soviet Union carried out its first test of an intercontinental missile. Then in October the Soviets launched Sputnik I, the first satellite. Sputnik in particular came as a shock to the United States. This shock was even greater than when the Soviet Union developed its first atomic bomb in 1949. The launch struck at the belief in US technological superiority.

Khrushchev now adopted a public strategy that was the opposite of the one Stalin had pursued. Nuclear weapons were given primary importance. Khrushchev loudly proclaimed Soviet superiority in the intercontinental sphere. That obviously did not reduce the level of concern in the

United States. Many Washington policy-makers chose to take the Soviet leader literally when he stated for instance that the Soviet Union had enough nuclear weapons to wipe any aggressor off the face of the earth.

Like Eisenhower, Khrushchev placed great emphasis on expanding the sectors of the air force that were based on nuclear weapons. Missiles were given higher priority than planes, although in this matter he met resistance from much of the air force, as was the case in the United States as well. In 1959 the strategic missile forces were established as a separate military service. The Soviet Union was far behind the United States in the development of nuclear submarines.

In the light of the new weapons, an economic change of priorities within the Soviet Union and the incipient detente in the mid-50s, Khrushchev began to reduce the level of conventional defense. Defense expenditures sank towards the end of the 1950s. The conventional navy was reduced substantially, especially the surface fleet. The armed forces were reduced. Cut-backs were effected in three stages. From 1955 to 1957 the armed forces were reduced from 5.7 to 3.9 million men. In 1958–59 the number was reduced by another 300 000. In January 1960 Khrushchev announced a new cut-back, to 2.4 million. It was only halfway achieved by the time of the Berlin crisis in 1961, and it is unclear how much ever came of the second half of this reduction. By way of comparison, US forces under the 'New Look' were reduced from 3.5 million men in 1953 to 2.4 million in 1960.

The smaller nuclear nations

Nuclear developments illustrated the prominent leadership of the two superpowers. Here, even more than in most other fields, the United States and the Soviet Union were the primary actors. In 1986 these two countries had 96 percent of the world's nuclear weapons. Even so, they did not have an absolute monopoly.

The United States and Britain had cooperated closely in the development of the atomic bomb during WW II. During the initial stages in particular the British contribution had been highly significant. But the agreements made in 1943 and 1944 by Roosevelt and Churchill concerning continued cooperation after the war were soon set aside when the war was over. This was due partly to the fact that the agreements were not known outside a very narrow circle, and partly to the fact that the

157

politicians in Washington, and especially in the Senate, were firmly determined to safeguard the US monopoly, even in relation to Britain. The US Atomic Energy Act of 1946 was an expression of this view.

In January 1947 the British government decided to develop atomic weapons on its own. This decision seems to have been based on three considerations. In the first place, atomic weapons could come to play an important strategic role. They represented a qualitative new step in weapons development, and it was essential that Britain take part. In the second place, there was the question of Britain's political role. Even though it would inevitably be diminished compared to the period between the wars, atomic weapons would strengthen the position of the United Kingdom in relation to both the Soviet Union and the United States. Finally, London hoped that having its own nuclear force would open the way to cooperation with Washington at a later date. This could be significant not only in the nuclear sphere, important as that was, but also far beyond that.

The first British detonation took place in October 1952. It contributed to moderating the US attitude to some extent, but it was the test of a hydrogen bomb in May 1957 that truly liberalized Washington's policy.

With regard to delivery systems, London became entirely dependent on US assistance from the late 1950s. When the Americans stopped development of the planned Skybolt missile in 1962, and Britain was thus left without the launcher the country had based itself on, Kennedy promised Prime Minister Harold Macmillan in December 1962 that Britain would get the new Polaris missile instead. The British nuclear submarines were to be placed under NATO joint command, but could be withdrawn if the British felt that their 'supreme national interests' were at stake. France would receive a similar offer.

France had enjoyed a relatively strong position in the field of nuclear physics during the period between the wars. However, the country's position in international politics was even more weakened than that of Britain after WW II. It is difficult to single out any specific time when the decision was made to develop a separate French atomic force. Technology, economics and politics were closely intertwined.

To a great extent the French process rested on the same basis as the British. Strategic considerations were significant, as were political considerations. The Suez incident in 1956 was important because it convinced French decision-makers that something had to be done to strengthen France's position. Relations with Germany and Britain were also of significance. France wanted to counterbalance the Germans' rapidly growing role in the military field. If London was capable of producing nuclear weapons, Paris ought to be so as well.

De Gaulle first increased the pace of development of the French atomic force and then made it far more independent of NATO than previous French governments had intended. He was also much more concerned about a problem that would gradually interest increasing numbers of people: Could one truly trust the United States to use nuclear weapons to defend Western Europe when the Soviet Union had achieved the possibility of striking the United States directly? The first French test detonation took place in 1960.

The French President was not interested in the US Polaris offer. He preferred to continue work on a separate French nuclear force. Moreover, the agreement between Kennedy and Macmillan probably contributed to de Gaulle's rejection of British membership in the EEC in 1963. In de Gaulle's eyes, the British had once more demonstrated their dependence on the United States.

The number of nuclear powers has grown more slowly than most observers expected just two or three decades ago. In 1957 the Soviet Union promised to help China develop nuclear weapons. However, two years later Moscow backed out of this agreement, a fact that contributed strongly to the growing antagonism between the two communist countries (see pages 218–219). It is not clear how much help the Chinese actually received from the Soviet Union during the two years this cooperation lasted. In 1964, the first Chinese nuclear test detonation took place. China was clearly far behind Britain and France in terms of both nuclear technology and delivery systems. A decade passed before the nuclear club gained a new member. In 1974, India carried out what the government called a 'peaceful nuclear explosion'. New Delhi is thus capable of producing nuclear bombs for military use. Israel probably also possesses nuclear weapons. A large number of other countries also have the necessary technological prerequisites.

Kennedy, McNamara and Flexible Response

The Eisenhower administration stuck to a relatively low defense budget until the very last. The necessary condition for achieving this was an emphasis on strategic deterrence entailing a willingness to employ nuclear weapons, especially tactical ones. Soviet development of intercontinental missiles further accelerated this concentration on nuclear weapons. As the Pentagon had to contribute more in the nuclear sphere, this took place at the expense of the conventional forces once more.

When John F. Kennedy assumed the presidency in 1961, he planned to make major changes in US defense policy. The defense budget would have to be increased substantially, and, as under NSC 68, emphasis was to be placed on both strategic armament and conventional forces. In the former field especially a dramatic effort was needed. In the light of the launching of Sputnik and Khrushchev's declarations of Soviet superiority, the belief had spread that there was a missile gap in favor of the Soviets. Kennedy made much of this in his election campaign, promising to overtake the Soviet lead.

Eisenhower had not believed in the alleged missile gap. In part, he wanted to shelter the administration from accusations of negligence. In part, he relied on intelligence reports showing that the Soviet Union deployed far fewer missiles than Moscow's own statements would indicate. Information from the U-2 spy plane was important in this context. The Kremlin chose to develop a new and better missile rather than rely on the first, relatively primitive ICBMs.

Kennedy and Robert McNamara, his dynamic Secretary of Defense, increased the pace of production of ICBMs, based on the promises Kennedy had made during his election campaign. However, quite early in 1961 it became evident that the talk of a Soviet lead had been misleading, as pictures from new satellites showed. The decision to increase production had already been made. The Kennedy administration felt that it could not reverse its decision without seriously undermining public confidence. The result was that at the end of 1963 the Soviet Union still had less than 100 ICBMs. The United States had by then acquired at least 550.

This was probably an important reason for the Soviet attempt to deploy intermediate-range missiles on Cuba in 1962. Khrushchev's bluff had been called. The Soviet Union had never had the strength he had tried to give the impression of. Instead the United States now had a great, rapidly growing lead. The cheapest and fastest way for Moscow to counterbalance this lead was to install shorter-range missiles on Cuba. Deployment would not give the Soviet Union any superiority at first, but of course the number of missiles could later be increased (see page 95).

The foundation for subsequent US strategy was laid under McNamara. Quantitative growth was comprehensive and continued even after Kennedy's death in 1963. McNamara set the ceilings on US strategic weapons that have applied right up to the present: 1056 ICBMS and 656 submarine-launched ballistic missiles (SLBMs). These levels were reached in 1967.

It was more a question of expanding existing weapon systems than of developing new ones. McNamara stopped the plans for a new bomber, the B-70. He considered planes the least important part of the US triad of strategic weapons. As far as missiles were concerned, Minuteman II and III were developed, but they were not dramatically innovative. Skybolt was stopped. The greatest change occurred in terms of submarines, with the major emphasis that was now placed on Polaris and later on Poseidon. With their survival capacity in the event of war, submarines were McNamara's favorites. The most important entirely new program was multiple independently-targetable re-entry vehicles (MIRVs). McNamara was sceptical about anti-ballistic missiles. He felt that offensive weapons would be superior to defensive weapons. However, political and military pressure got him to support a limited program of development and deployment. With regard to the strategic doctrine, key concepts such as mutual assured destruction (MAD), damage limitation, counterforce-countercity and flexible response were all developed in the early 1960s.

However, conflicting interests created problems for McNamara, as they had done for most of the preceding Secretaries of Defense. Tension developed, for instance, between the strategies of complete avoidance of war—which was a primary objective of MAD—and of limiting a war to military targets if it should arise. Moscow denounced the belief in a limited nuclear war. Western Europeans feared that deterrence would be reduced if the United States was no longer willing to meet Soviet aggression with an unlimited reponse. Other critics expressed their fear that a strategy based on striking military targets would result in a race to strike first.

The result, at least verbally, was to push the strategy of damage limitation into the background and again stress that a nuclear war could not be limited. Thus there was little purpose in distinguishing between military and civilian targets. However, the concrete US war plans appear to have followed the verbal fluctuations only to a slight degree. Both civilian and military targets were considered, in a number of different possible combinations, under both Eisenhower and Kennedy.

Eisenhower's policy of massive retaliation had built on the principle that local aggression could be met with a nuclear response. But the Vietnam war showed even in the 1950s that it was easier said than done to use or even threaten to use nuclear weapons in limited conflicts. There was no getting past the fact that even tactical nuclear weapons would mean a dramatic escalation. Nuclear weapons could have a deterrent effect with regard to large-scale aggression, but in limited local conflicts they almost seemed irrelevant.

In the autumn of 1959, Senator John F. Kennedy had criticized Eisenhower's reduction of the conventional forces and claimed that '... we have been preparing primarily to fight the one kind of war we least want to fight and are least likely to fight. We have been driving ourselves into a corner where the only choice is all or nothing at all, world devastation or submission.'

To put it briefly, flexible response meant that if possible the enemy should be met with the same means he himself had employed. The United States had to improve its ability to fight wars without resorting to nuclear weapons. Thus the conventional forces had to be built up. If the Soviet Union, contrary to all expectations, instigated a comprehensive attack, and the West was in the process of being defeated, the premise was now as previously that NATO would be the first to use nuclear weapons. But if that occurred it would be at a later time than under Eisenhower's insufficient conventional readiness.

In 1967, flexible response was adopted as NATO strategy. This resulted in a certain, but fairly limited, degree of reinforcement of conventional defense. Western Europe was not willing to make much of an effort in this field (see page 193). The United States built up its forces in the course of the 1960s, from 2.4 million men in 1960 to 3.4 million in 1969, but the Vietnam war made the practical consquences small in Western Europe. On the other hand, the Kennedy administration came to represent a dramatic increase in the number of tactical nuclear weapons in Europe, paradoxically enough. This was due partly to the fact that changes were not made in plans that were already being realized, and partly to the fact that the conventional build-up was smaller than had been planned at first.

As far as the size of the defense budget was concerned, substantial growth took place in nominal figures, from 45.9 billion dollars in 1960 to 81.2 billion in 1969. However, the share of the gross national product that went to defense declined, mostly because the 1960s were a period of flourishing growth in the US economy.

Whereas it can roughly be said that Eisenhower had taken as his point of departure the amount he felt was available for defense on an economic and political basis, after which he worked out a doctrine that fitted this amount and let the services decide rather freely within this framework, McNamara worked in the opposite direction. He began with a doctrine, found out how much it would require in weapons and appropriations, and then tried to ensure that the three services followed up through coordination rather than each of them planning their own war against the Soviet Union. McNamara's strategy was apparently logical and coherent, but it was also considerably more expensive than Eisenhower's, without anyone being able to claim that the latter had endangered the security of the United States.

The most concrete inheritance from McNamara was the quantitative growth, partly in the defense budget as a whole, but most particularly in the number of ICBMs and SLBMs. What was the cause of this growth? As we have seen, to a great extent it was determined by foreign policy interpretations—or rather misinterpretations—of Soviet strength at the time Kennedy assumed office. The program that was initiated on an erroneous basis was continued, even after the true strength of the Soviet Union had been disclosed.

This quantitative growth was also strongly related to new attitudes in domestic policy, particularly the attitude towards government activity. Kennedy and Johnson promoted a far higher level of activity than Eisenhower had done. They were willing to use larger amounts of tax money in many areas, including defense. It was paradoxical that although the Republicans in general were even more sceptical towards the Soviet Union than the Democrats, the latter were willing to spend more on defense because of their attitude towards the role of the government in economic policy.

The Soviet Build-up

Developments in the strategic sphere brought the Soviet Union on a level with and in certain areas even beyond the United States in the course of the 1960s and 1970s.

In the Soviet Union, as in the United States, least emphasis was placed on bombers. 'Backfire', in the 1970s, was the first new type of plane with possible intercontinental range. There was actually a slight decrease in the total number of planes. Thus the Soviet Union continued to lag behind the United States in this regard. In 1985, the United States had 2 520 airborne nuclear warheads, as compared to the Soviet Union's 680.

The changes were greater with regard to strategic submarines. In this field, too, the Soviet Union continued to lag behind the United States, but they applied considerable efforts to reducing this gap. In 1967—68, the Soviet Union developed a submarine that could compare with the US Polaris to some extent. In 1973–74 they developed an even newer model. Although the Soviets now began to retire their old submarines so that the total number no longer increased, the Soviet Union soon had more strategic submarines than the United States. However, the United States' new Poseidon and Trident were technologically superior to the Soviet submarines, and because the United States had much more advanced MIRV technology, especially at sea, it kept its lead in terms of the number of nuclear warheads. In 1985, the United States had 5 536 nuclear warheads as compared to the Soviet Union's 3 123.

Whereas the Americans had a fair balance among the elements of the so-called triad, especially between the navy's submarine-based missiles and the air force's land-based missiles, the Soviets concentrated primarily on land-based missiles. This difference can be explained to a great extent by tradition and geographic conditions. The Soviet concentration was both quantitative and qualitative. The Soviet Union's arsenal increased from approx. 100 ICBMs in 1963 to approx. 1 400 in 1970, outstripping the United States in numbers.

On the whole the Soviet missiles were larger than the US missiles. This compensated for the greater accuracy of the US weapons. But the Soviets gradually approached the US level of accuracy. The lead the United States had long enjoyed in terms of MIRV technology was also diminishing, particularly as far as land-based missiles were concerned. In 1985 the Soviet Union had 1 398 land-based missiles with 6 420 warheads. The corresponding figures for the United States were 1 018 and 2 118.

From the time the United States had withdrawn its intermediate-range missiles from Western Europe in the early 1960s, the Soviet Union had enjoyed a clear lead in terms of intermediate-range weapons. At the end of the 1970s, Moscow deployed modern SS-20 missiles, partially to replace the old SS-4 and SS-5. This emphasized a new Soviet superiority in relation to NATO. Roughly one-third of the rapidly increasing number of SS-20s were aimed primarily at China and other targets in Asia.

In a number of other areas as well a considerable build-up took place. The Soviet navy expanded rapidly during the 1960s and 1970s. Whereas Khrushchev had made drastic cut-backs in the number of conventional surface vessels, this policy was reversed from the mid-60s. Now the Soviet Union was not only to have a modern submarine fleet—for that had been the assumption all along—but a modern surface fleet as well. The Soviet navy gradually appeared on all the oceans of the world (see pages 126–127). The merchant fleet was doubled from 1964 to 1969.

In the mid-60s the Soviet Union began to build up its conventional forces again in earnest. This could partly be seen as a reflection of the US strategy of flexible response. In part it must be linked to the tense situation along the Chinese border. The build-up was concentrated in that region. The number of Soviet troops in Eastern Europe remained constant at approx. 500 000.

It is difficult to state conclusively when the Soviet build-up began and even more difficult to analyze Soviet motives. Political scientist David Holloway claims that it probably started as early as in 1959–60. In any case, most of the new projects must have been initiated under Khrushchev. For a long time, he had hoped to balance the nuclear build-up with reductions in the conventional forces. That proved not possible in the 1960s. The pace was possibly stepped up even further under Brezhnev, when greater emphasis was again placed on conventional forces.

If the build-up was begun in 1959–60, it was stimulated by developments in US policy under McNamara and by the defeat on Cuba. The Soviet Union considered itself one of the two superpowers and wanted the rest of the world to share that view. Superpower status had to be secured primarily on a military basis for want of other alternatives. Khrushchev attempted to build up the needed strength in the cheapest possible way. The very cheapest way was by exaggerating Soviet military strength. After this had been exposed as a bluff and had only strengthened the US military lead, he had attempted to deploy intermediate-range missiles on Cuba. When that, too, failed, there was only one option left: to build up the necessary strength, especially in the form of intercontinental missiles.

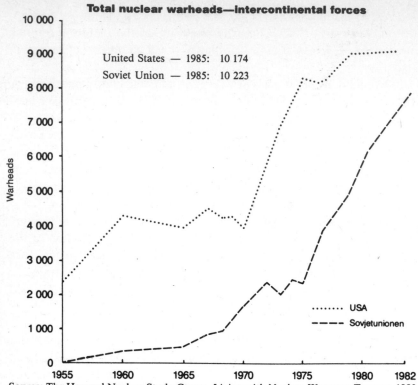

Total nuclear warheads—intercontinental forces

United States — 1985: 10 174
Soviet Union — 1985: 10 223

.... USA
— — — Sovjetunionen

Source: The Harvard Nuclear Study Group, *Living with Nuclear Weapons,* Toronto, 1983, p. 74; *The Economist,* October 11, 1985, p. 50.

Total strategic nuclear delivery vehicles

United States — 1985: 1 914
Soviet Union — 1985: 2 574

.... USA
— — — Sovjetunionen

Source: The Harvard Nuclear Study Group, *Living with Nuclear Weapons, p. 75; The Economist,* October 11, 1985, p. 50.

An overview of the strategic arsenals (1982)

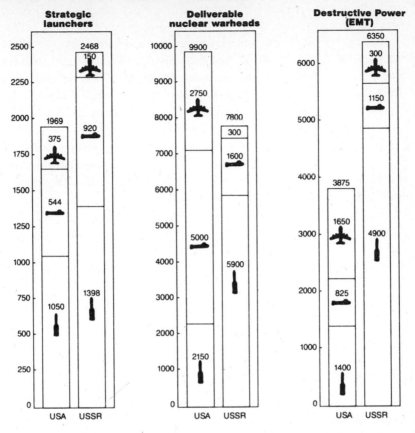

Strategic launchers	Deliverable nuclear warheads	Destructive Power (EMT)

Source: The Harvard Nuclear Study Group, *Living with Nuclear Weapons, p. 120.*

In the short term, at least, the Soviet objective must have been to attain military equality with the United States. In the early 1960s such a goal was still a long way off. To aim for superiority must have seemed rather illusory. The costs would be enormous. Equality would give the Soviet Union greater freedom of action without threatening international stability. In the course of the 1970s the SALT negotiations probably reinforced this course of policy. By approving the SALT agreements, the Soviet Union imposed limitations on itself that were more in line with a policy of equality than of superiority. (Agreements on arms limitations are discussed on pages 102–103.) Yet during the 1960s and 1970s Soviet military leaders frequently issued statements indicating that superiority was the objective.

In the early 1970s, the increase in the number of intercontinental missiles leveled off. It was true that old missiles were replaced with new ones, and the Soviet Union gradually mastered MIRV technology. In 1985 the Soviet Union probably had even more strategic warheads than the United States did, but considering the vast arsenals of both sides even this did not introduce any dramatic new elements into the situation. The Americans had a tendency to place primary emphasis on land-based missiles in comparing their strength with that of the Soviet Union. That veiled the fact that for the United States this component of the triad was less important than for the Soviet Union.

During the 60s and the first half of the 70s, the annual growth of the Soviet defense budget was four or five percent. In itself this growth was not extraordinarily high. What was more important was that it was sustained over such a long period. It probably declined towards the end of the 70s. At least the CIA has estimated that the annual growth since 1976 has been about two percent.

The US Reaction

The First Phase: Prior to 1973–74

For a long time, the US reaction to the Soviet build-up was limited. Early in the 1960s the United States had substantially increased its lead in the strategic sphere. Washington's first appraisal was that the Soviet Union would develop only the minimum force needed to deter the United States and to maintain its superpower status. When Secretary of Defense McNamara felt that the Soviet Union had reached that level in the mid-60s, he began to claim that there was no sign the Soviet Union aimed at developing a force equal to that of the United States.

The Soviet build-up was also underestimated, at least during the 1960s, by the US intelligence sources that were responsible for predicting these developments. This underestimation may be largely considered an over-reaction to the many erroneous statements from the late 1950s concerning the missile gap that it was later known had never existed.

Moreover, part of the reason the number of Soviet missiles increased so rapidly was that Moscow did not retire old missiles to the same extent

Washington did. The fact that the Soviet Union developed missiles that were considerably heavier than the US missiles was mainly interpreted as evidence that the Soviet Union had to make up for their lacking accuracy with more blast effect. All in all, McNamara saw little reason to react as long as the United States was certain the country could survive a Soviet first strike and still have the capacity for adequate retaliation. This capacity in itself would deter the Soviet Union from considering such a first strike.

In many ways, Nixon and Kissinger evidenced the same reaction to the Soviet build-up as McNamara had had. The United States continued to retire old ICBMs and bombers. A total of approx. 1 000 ICBMs and 300 B-52 bombers were withdrawn during the period from the early 1960s until the mid-70s. The relative strengths would have been quite different if these had been retained. The share of the defense budget that was used for strategic weapons continued to decline. Many people had the feeling that the stockpiles of nuclear weapons were now so large that further increases would have little significance. As Kissinger exclaimed, in what has become an almost classic quote, in reponse to opposition to the SALT I agreement in Washington:

> And one of the questions which we have to ask ourselves as a country is what in the name of God is strategic superiority? What is the significance of it, politically, militarily, operationally, at these levels of numbers? What do you do with it?

The Nixon administration shifted from talking of the need for US superiority to the use of expressions such as 'parity' and 'sufficiency'. Why have more weapons than necessary? It was easy to air such thoughts when the United States was still believed to have a slight lead in the strategic race. When the United States also had a more than sufficient defense capacity and when Soviet intentions were judged more optimistically than at any previous time during the cold war, there was little reason to react to the Soviet build-up. After all, the policy of detente reached its peak in the early 1970s.

The new arms limitation measures made it less necessary and politically more difficult to initiate a new round of armament in the United States. The Vietnam war heightened scepticism towards the defense budget in public opinion. Beginning in the late 1960s and continuing until the mid-70s, a clear majority felt that the defense budget was too

169

large. This influenced not only members of Congress, but also the Johnson and Nixon administrations.

Even so, weapons development continued in the United States. During the SALT I negotiations the US military establishment insisted that MIRV technology was not to be included, and their wishes were observed. Thus even though the SALT agreement limited the number of missiles on each side, it could not prevent an explosion in the number of warheads on those same missiles. Later in the 1970s the United States insisted on keeping the MX missile out of a new agreement. The same was true of most aspects of the new cruise missile technology.

The Second Phase: the years up to 1986

The United States allowed the Soviet Union to reach its level in the strategic sphere and even to surpass it in certain limited areas. However, the Soviet build-up gradually led to major changes in US policy. First the existing strategic doctrine was altered, then the defense budget was increased substantially.

A new strategy was introduced as early as in 1973-74 and was associated with the name of Secretary of Defense James Schlesinger. Schlesinger's point of departure was that it was no longer credible that the United States would start a full-scale nuclear war to defend anything other than extremely vital interests. In his opinion, MAD had been based on a US superiority that no longer existed. The country needed a strategy for the flexible use of nuclear weapons, in part to limit the destruction in the event of war. Military targets were assigned top priority, and strikes against large cities and other civilian targets were ranked correspondingly lower.

This was a return to thoughts McNamara had presented in his early phase as Secretary of Defense. He had later abandoned them, but his retreat was more evident on the verbal level than in relation to the targets US strategic weapons were actually aimed at. Schlesinger did away with this contradiction. Moreover, military technology had become more advanced. The accuracy of the weapons increased the possibilities for a selective choice of targets.

However, the problems of this strategy were the same ones McNamara had encountered. Many people felt that preventing war now came second to being able to fight a limited war. The Soviet Union still did not express

170

any conviction that such limitations were possible. The Western Europeans remained sceptical, if not to the same degree as previously.

For a long time Carter and Secretary of Defense Harold Brown were hesitant about various aspects of Schlesinger's strategy, but in practice they accepted the major components of his scheme. Schlesinger had concentrated primarily on military targets. Brown would include economic and political targets to a greater extent. The Carter administration's view was established in Presidential directive 59 in 1980.

The idea of a flexible use of nuclear weapons gained further momentum under Reagan and Weinberger. The result was that the US and Soviet doctrines converged. The United States, which had placed strong emphasis on deterrence, placed greater priority on analyses of how a nuclear war should be conducted and possibly even won. Soviet military leaders had long placed relatively little emphasis on deterrence, as interpreted in the West, and stressed that the Soviet Union would be capable of winning even a nuclear war. However, a number of statements by top politicians now concluded that in a nuclear war there would be no victor.

In nominal figures, The US defense budget increased throughout most of the 1960s and the 1970s. This was a reflection of the Vietnam war and rising inflation, for apart from expenditures for the war in Vietnam there was no real growth. The share of the federal budget that was used for defense was halved in the course of these two decades. This was first and foremost a result of major increases within health and social services, education, etc. Defense expenditure as a percentage of the gross national product decreased as well. In 1960 this percentage had been 9.1. In 1978 it reached its lowest level since 1950, 5.0 percent, or less than half of the corresponding Soviet figure. On the other hand, the US national product was twice the size of the Soviet GNP.

From 1975-76, the policy of detente was subject to strong pressure (see chapter 5). Even so, it took time before the political reversal resulted in significant increases in arms expenditure. When Carter was elected president in 1976, he promised to cut back the defense budget. Nothing came of this. The budget increased, and towards the end of his four-year term there were substantial increases. Public opinion was now in favor of the United States again building up a stronger defense.

The high growth rate in the defense budget at the end of Carter's term was accelerated further under Reagan. He proposed 14 percent real growth for 1982, and subsequently 7 percent annually, as compared to the 5 percent Carter had recommended for 1982-86. Even though Congress reduced this increase somewhat, most of it remained.

In his second term, however, Reagan was able to get only very small increases from Congress, since public support for dramatic defense outlays quickly dwindled after the rapid growth of the first Reagan years.

In the perspective of party politics, Reagan's defense policy was an innovation. Republicans had traditionally placed priority on keeping down expenditures, including defense expenditure. Only in that way could government activity be reduced, allowing for tax cuts. Reagan was highly in favor of reducing government activity, but made one major exception for defense. Contrary to the pattern from earlier in the postwar period, it was now a Republican president who went furthest not only in general anti-communism, but also in armament to strengthen the United States in the contest against the Soviet Union.

New weapon systems were to be developed, while production of those Carter had already approved was to be escalated. In terms of aircraft, the decision to cancel the B-1 was reversed, at the same time that the new Stealth plane was also to be produced. In terms of missiles, the MX was retained, although the Reagan administration had great problems deciding how it should be deployed. In addition, the Midgetman, a new single warhead missile, was to be developed. In terms of submarines, the pace of production of the new Trident was stepped up. Carter's decision not to assemble the neutron bomb was reversed, although it proved impossible to deploy the new weapon in Western Europe because of the opposition there. The build-up was almost as pronounced in conventional terms. The navy and the air force in particular were strengthened.

The foundation was laid for a new round in the arms race. Cruise missiles became more advanced. They were so small and easy to hide that they could undermine the possibilities of further arms limitation. The first anti-satellite weapons were produced, first in the Soviet Union, then in the United States.

Most important were the attempts to develop a defense against the opponent's missiles, based partly on laser and particle beam weapons. The Soviet Union was also doing research in this field, but Reagan's speech to the nation on 23 March 1983 signalled a dramatic acceleration of the US effort to develop 'a program to counter the awesome Soviet missile threat with measures that are defensive ... I am directing a comprehensive and intensive effort to define a long-term research and development program to begin to achieve our ultimate goal of eliminating the threat posed by strategic nuclear missiles.' It was far from clear how effective such a defense system could be, but in any case these were qualitatively new questions. The development represented a clear threat to the most important arms limitation measure, the ABM treaty of 1972.

The Reagan administration justified the large increases in the defense budget by stating that they were necessary in order to eliminate the lead the Soviet Union had supposedly taken. Accordingly, Washington's primary objective in future negotiations on arms control would be to achieve substantial reductions in the areas where Soviet strength was the greatest. Western reductions were to be much smaller than Soviet reductions. Several statements by the administration could be interpreted to mean that equality should preferably be combined with an 'extra margin for safety.' The need felt by many policy-makers in Washington to carry out negotiations from a position of strength could also suggest that the objective was more than mere equality with the Soviet Union. Reagan's view of relations between East and West (see pages 138–139) opened the way for development of virtually all the new weapons technology was capable of producing.

US armament frightened not only the adversary, but also allied countries and US citizens, a paradox that had appeared on several occasions during the post-war period. The reactions in the early 1980s were stronger than at any previous time. The protests appeared first and most strongly in many Western European countries, then in the United States itself. They were directed against many different aspects of the military build-up: armaments in general, the new strategic doctrines with less emphasis on deterrence and more emphasis on how nuclear weapons could be used in a war, and the proliferation of new weapons.

However, the most important single factor in Western Europe was NATO's decision in December 1979 to deploy 572 cruise and Pershing II missiles in Western Europe. They were to be a response to the Soviet SS-20 build-up. The German chancellor, Helmut Schmidt, had been among the first to warn against this build-up. Moscow on its part claimed that the SS-20 merely compensated for British and French nuclear weapons as well as US bombers in Europe. However, there was little doubt that the Soviet Union had a growing lead in terms of intermediate-range weapons in Europe.

The NATO decision was also intended to link the United States more closely to Western Europe. The theory was that the United States would have to build up an escalation ladder. A step was needed between the tactical and strategic nuclear weapons. Such an intermediate weapon could make the defense of Europe more credible than the other weapons alone could do. However, in large segments of public opinion the deployment decision was interpreted as a sign that the United States was preparing to fight a limited nuclear war, but not on American soil. This fear was reinforced by confusing statements, not least by President Reagan himself, on how nuclear weapons could possibly be employed in a war.

During the 1970s, the importance of Western Europe within NATO had grown (see pages 196–202). This fact, combined with the intensity of the points of view that surfaced in most of the European NATO countries and the opposition within the United States, forced the Reagan administration to place greater emphasis on arms control than could have been expected given Reagan's ideology and former statements. After a time, negotiations were entered into with the Soviet Union regarding limitations on both strategic weapons and the intermediate-range missiles that had caused such uneasiness in Western Europe.

There was little progress to be seen. In December 1983, deployment of the cruise and Pershing II missiles began. Negotiations broke down altogether (see page 141).

However, in late 1984 it was evident that both the United States and the Soviet Union again acquired a greater interest in new contacts. The Soviet Union abandoned its demand that the US intermediate-range missiles had to be withdrawn from Western Europe before negotiations could be reopened. An accelerated arms race would have to be relatively more expensive for the Soviet Union than for the considerably richer and technologically more advanced United States. The Soviet leaders clearly feared a new round of armaments, particularly Reagan's Strategic Defense Initiative ('Star Wars'). Reagan, on his part, wanted to show the American voters, Western Europe and future historians that he cared about 'peace' as well as 'strength.'

Arms control negotiations were resumed in March 1985. They showed little progress and the 1985 Geneva summit between Reagan and Gorbachev did not speed matters up to any great extent. The October 1986 Reykjavik meeting, on the other hand, saw the most dramatic nuclear arms control discussions, certainly since the Baruch plan. Reagan and Gorbachev appeared close to tentative agreements on deep cuts in and even the potential elimination of all strategic weapons. The meeting collapsed, however, over the Strategic Defense Initiative. Gorbachev insisted that potential agreements be linked to a 10-year ban on all SDI research outside the laboratory, a demand Reagan was unwilling to accede to. And disagreement soon arose as to exactly what had really taken place in Iceland. It remained unclear whether the summit represented an attempt at the most sweeping kind of nuclear reductions or, more likely, was meant primarily for tactical-political consumption.

The pace of weapon developments remained high. Soon after the Reykjavik meeting the Reagan administration exceeded the number of strategic weapons permitted under SALT II. The ABM treaty was also in trouble, owing to both SDI and the new radar facilities developed particularly in the Soviet Union. On the other hand, the political climate undoubtedly improved and an agreement on the elimination of intermediate range weapons seemed likely once the Soviet Union abandoned the linkage between these weapons on the one hand and SDI and the British and French nuclear weapons on the other.

7. Developments within the Western Camp, 1945–1986

After the Second World War the United States attained a dominant position in world politics. The greatest difference in relation to the period between the wars was the new role the country would play in Western Europe and Japan. The US influence was based on many different elements: the United States' economic strength at a time when economic needs were acute; the country's military strength, combined with a growing interest—especially in Western Europe—for military guarantees in relation to the Soviet Union; the pervasive cultural and political influence of the United States; and US participation in the occupation of vital countries such as West Germany, Japan and Italy.

Relations between the United States, Western Europe and Japan gradually changed in character. US economic assistance ceased, the extent of US economic superiority declined, and cooperation now intermingled with competition in an uneasy mix. The need for military guarantees also decreased somewhat in the light of detente in the 1960s and 1970s, although the changes were considerably smaller in the military than in the economic sphere. Occupation came to an end, and West Germany and Japan in particular became central actors in international politics. Japan would become the stronger of the two economically, but West Germany played a more active role politically and militarily nonetheless. Economic and political integration in Western Europe strengthened Europe in relation to the United States. The basis of cooperation within the Western bloc had to be redefined, but it would prove difficult to find a systemic replacement for US hegemony.

Expansion by Invitation, 1945–1950

The main features of relations between the United States and Western Europe were established in the years before 1950. The United States had great power and strong interests in many different parts of the world. It was only natural that Washington wanted to promote these interests. But the situation in Western Europe in particular could be described as expansion by invitation.

There was a widespread fear in Western Europe that the United States would revert to the policy of the period between the wars. The politicians of the day knew little of what the future would bring. However, they well remembered how the United States had retreated into 'splendid isolation' after the First World War. Most Europeans wanted to prevent history from repeating itself.

The British government was the most prominent example of this. Although London overestimated the position of the United Kingdom, both Churchill's coalition government during the war and Attlee's Labour Party government after the war were actively engaged in linking the United States more closely to Western Europe. They favored obtaining both economic and military support from the United States, for that was the only possible source of substantial assistance. Britain no longer had the resources to play such a central role as formerly, neither in the world economy nor in the global or even European balance of power. Good relations with the United States could compensate to some extent for this decline.

The British were thus highly disappointed at the US reductions in Lend-Lease assistance in May and September of 1945. The Attlee government had hoped for an even larger and even cheaper loan than the 3.75 billion dollars on fairly favorable terms the two countries agreed on in December 1945. When the US and British zones in Germany were unified in 1946-47, the British were strongly in favor of the Americans paying a larger share of the joint expenses. Both the Churchill and the Attlee government wanted to maintain the Anglo-American combined boards that had been established during the war, the most important of which was the Combined Chiefs of Staff. The British also wanted to continue cooperation on nuclear weapons. For London, a final objective was to bind the US occupation forces to Western Europe for as long as possible.

In 1946, Congress put a halt to the scheme Churchill and Roosevelt had agreed on with regard to nuclear weapons. In a number of other areas, however, cooperation between the United States and Britain continued after the war. The British wanted this to take place relatively openly, but because of political misgivings in Washington most of it was kept secret.

In January—February 1947, the British, led by Foreign Minister Bevin, were actively engaged in efforts to get the United States to assume the role Britain had traditionally played in containing Soviet-Russian influence in South-eastern Europe. The dramatic way in which the British announced their withdrawal from Greece contributed to the willingness with which the United States, through the Truman Doctrine, assumed this responsibility. Bevin also played a significant role in shaping Marshall's speech of 5 June 1947 into what would become the Marshall Plan. Finally, London's role was important for the changes in March—April 1948 that transformed Washington's role from that of an encouraging adviser to a full partner in Atlantic military cooperation (see pages 41–43).

Although relations between the United States and Britain were unique, attitudes similar to those in Britain were to be found in a number of countries. In the economic sphere there was a nearly unanimous desire for help. The countries of Western Europe requested far more than the 7.4 billion dollars they received from the end of the war until July 1947. Under the Marshall Plan the Europeans originally requested 28 billion dollars from the United States. The Truman administration reduced the amount to 17 billion, and Congress finally granted 14 billion. Only Moscow's opposition prevented Finland, Czechoslovakia, and Poland from participating. Spain wanted to be included as well, but Truman was opposed to Franco's participation.

The pattern was largely the same when it came to US military ties to Western Europe. Although there were nuances among the various countries' views, France, Belgium, the Netherlands, and Luxembourg all basically supported the British efforts in 1948 to persuade the United States to increase its commitments. In the short term they wanted to receive as much weapon assistance as possible; in a somewhat longer perspective the objective was a treaty system. Just as there were many countries that wanted to take part in the Marshall Plan, there were also many that wanted to participate in NATO. In addition to the countries mentioned, Italy, Portugal, Iceland, Norway, and Denmark joined, although the last two or three would probably have preferred somewhat looser ties to the alliance than they acquired. Once more there were countries that were not allowed to join. Spain was still barred from membership. Nor did Washington want to include Greece, Turkey and Iran. The Western European NATO countries were all eager to make the US guarantees in the event of a Soviet attack as automatic as possible, whereas the Truman administration, not least out of consideration to Congress, was concerned about incorporating a certain degree of flexibility.

The interest in binding the United States to Western Europe continued after the establishment of NATO. Most countries favored involving the United States directly in the various regional planning groups that were to be established within NATO. After the outbreak of the Korean war the pressure to increase Washington's involvement was further intensified. Four new divisions were sent to Europe. US military assistance was stepped up substantially. Most importantly, a joint command structure was developed (see pages 150–151).

All in all, the countries of Western Europe actively applied pressure to get the United States to play a greater role in European affairs. This was not only the policy of the governments. To the extent satisfctory material on public opinion exists, the public mostly rallied round this policy. But of course there were differences among the countries, and in occupied or more or less authoritarian countries it was hardly meaningful to speak of any public opinion.

The Europeans could not force the Americans to do anything against their own will. Strong forces in the United States supported the policy most of the Western European governments pursued. Even so, the attitudes of the Western Europeans must be said to have contributed to strengthening US involvement. They also had the effect of hastening a clarification of US relations with Europe.

With increased involvement came increased influence; economic assistance was not given without return favors. Under the Marshall Plan, trade within Western Europe had to be liberalized, contact with Eastern Europe limited, and the United States given a certain degree of influence in the formulation of the individual countries' economic policies. Politically, the US influence spanned from opposition to socialization in the Bi-zone in Germany to interference in the Italian elections in 1948. Within NATO, the formulation of the organization's strategy became mainly a US concern. Washington also brought about the rearmament of West Germany after the outbreak of the Korean war.

As soon as US assistance was secured, European criticism of certain aspects of US policy increased. The support was too limited, the return favors too many, US policy too variable, the Americans too moralistic, and so on.

However, the level of both US assistance and US influence can be exaggerated. Marshall funds did not account for more than 10 to 20 percent of the various European countries' capital formation in the years 1948–49 and less than 10 percent in 1950–51. Washington's direct intervention in domestic political affairs was also modest, apart from in the occupied countries and in countries such as Greece and Turkey, where the domestic conditions were rather special.

The main point in the first years after WW II was that the United States and Western Europe to a great extent had corresponding interests. Western Europe faced enormous tasks of reconstruction and needed assistance from abroad. Only the United States could offer assistance of any magnitude. This assistance would be advantageous for the Americans themselves as it would generate large-scale purchasing from the United States. The Truman administration and most of the European governments also had mutual interests in preventing increased Soviet influence in Western Europe. Only the United States could represent a political and military counterweight to the Red Army.

European Integration, 1945–1973

The United States wanted to weave the Western European countries into a comprehensive international network. Economically, what was needed in 1945–46 was to attain their support for the World Bank and the International Monetary Fund. In 1947–48, the Marshall Plan was based on close cooperation across the Atlantic, although the United States did not join the organization that administered the assistance, the Organization for European Economic Cooperation (OEEC). The European economies were also to be made more open through the establishment of the International Trade Organization, which never materialized, and through the General Agreement on Tariffs and Trade (GATT). NATO brought the United States and Western Europe closer together militarily and politically.

At the same time, the Americans encouraged much closer cooperation among the countries of Western Europe. Truman, and to an even greater extent the Eisenhower administration, actively supported the Western European efforts at integration. This was evident on a number of occasions. Washington would have preferred the OEEC to become as binding as possible in the form of a permanent customs union, but the OEEC did not go that far. The Americans showed all the more support for the continental countries when they joined together in supranational organizations.

180

It can roughly be said that there were two main attitudes towards integration in Western Europe during the post-war period, later often called the federalist and confederalist views. The former dominated on the continent and aimed at supranational cooperation within certain sectors, or preferably in general. The latter accepted a certain degree of coordination of policies in the various countries, but without their relinquishing any of their independence and without any sweeping institutionalization. This view dominated in Britain, in the Scandinavian countries, and in politically distinctive countries such as Switzerland and Austria.

The federalist way of thinking was behind the Coal and Steel Community (1950), the proposal for a European army (1950–54), Euratom (1958) and the European Economic Community (EEC) (1958). The confederalist philosophy formed the basis for the OEEC (1948), the European Council (1949) and the European Free Trade Association (EFTA) (1960). Despite these divergent attitudes, historically the extent of cooperation and integration in Western Europe was a new phenomenon. Several factors must be included to explain this development in the 1940s and 1950s.

On the international level, the influence of the United States and the Soviet Union was important, although in different ways. As mentioned, the United States encouraged the Western Europeans to cooperate, and clearly preferred what is here called a federalist approach rather than a confederalist one. The Soviet contribution was based on the fact that European integration was also a means of containing Soviet and communist influence.

The international standing of the United States and the Soviet Union showed that the traditional European powers had become second and third ranking nations. The French and British colonial empires began to disintegrate. Only through European cooperation could Western Europe make its voice heard once more. Later, experiences such as the Suez conflict (see page 190) would explicitly confirm how reduced the role of Britain and France had become, and especially that of France.

A number of political conditions can explain why the continent was dominated by the federalist philosophy, while confederalism was strongest in Northern Europe. In the first place, the experiences of the Second World War had influenced the various countries in different ways. In countries such as Germany and Italy nationalism was discredited for obvious reasons. In France, nationalism was waning, at least in some segments of the population, although de Gaulle did his best to restore the country's self-respect. It was no coincidence that the idea of integration was strong within much of the European resistance movement. Peace was to be secured through an integrated Europe. Small countries such as Belgium, the Netherlands and Luxembourg were naturally in favor of plans that could put an end to the destructive German-French conflicts.

In Northern Europe, on the other hand, WW II had contributed to strengthening nationalism in many ways rather than weakening it. The British were extremely proud of their performance during the war. Many people, both within Britain and outside the country, felt that they had fought the most glorious struggle of all the allied nations. In Norway, too, self-esteem flourished in the wake of the resistance against the Germans and the local Nazis. Sweden had managed to preserve its neutrality once more.

In the second place, the continental countries were strongly under the influence of the Christian Democratic parties, which to a great extent had a shared political and religious perspective that made it easier for them to cooperate. Cooperation was further stimulated by the fact that several of their leading representatives came from border districts that had suffered greatly from the European conflicts: Robert Schuman in France, Konrad Adenauer in West Germany, and Alcide de Gasperi in Italy. The continental Socialists were more divided, although the majority of them also supported the integration efforts. The best-known spokesman for this group was Paul-Henri Spaak in Belgium.

The fact that the Christian Democrats, most of them Catholics, enjoyed such a strong position on the continent, was bound to increase the opposition between these countries and the Northern European countries. In Britain and Scandinavia socialism and Protestantism held a strong position, although that was not a sufficient basis for such close cooperation as on the continent.

In the third place, Britain in particular still had comprehensive political and economic commitments outside Europe that made it difficult to establish close links to the rest of Western Europe. As the British government made clear in its response to the plans for a Coal and Steel Community in 1950: 'A political federation, limited to Western Europe, is not compatible either with our Commonwealth ties, our obligations as a member of the wider Atlantic community, or as a world power.' This type of consideration was decisive for the changing British governments during the course of the 1950s. Norway and Denmark were in turn linked to Britain economically, politically, and militarily. It was nearly inconceivable that they should join European organizations to which Britain did not belong. The same was true of Sweden.

Considerations of economy and communications were also significant for integration in general and for developments on the continent in particular. The countries in the geographic center of Europe cooperated, while what may roughly be called the northern and southern periphery did not take part. Improved communications had made distances shorter. Trade increased, and tourism flourished.

There were clear economies of scale linked to a European market. For many people, the United States was the pattern to be emulated. In the continental countries, leading financial circles were enthusiastic spokesmen for European integration, with the partial exception of France. French industry was relatively protectionistic and afraid of competition, especially from Germany. On the other hand, the French farmers could attain significant advantages. In Britain and Scandinavia this was not the case, in part because the trade patterns were different. Contact with the continent was more limited, whereas there was more trade with other regions.

Finally, there were a number of 'local' conditions on the continent that stimulated the idea of integration. Germany could only achieve sovereignty through integration. No one dared give the Germans entirely free reins. Italy was seeking both political protection against an internal communist threat and economic progress through European cooperation. France could only become a major power again as the spokesman for a fairly unified Western Europe.

France played a central role in the political decision-making process on the continent. Here were both the strongest and most influential adherents of integration (Monnet, Schuman, etc.) and the strongest opponents. The large Communist party received support from de Gaulle's nationalists in their opposition to supranational Western European cooperation. It was these two groups, with scattered support from others, that toppled the plans for a European army in 1954.

After de Gaulle assumed power in 1958, he reconciled himself with French membership in the EEC. He even became interested in using the organization to achieve coordination of the member countries' foreign policies. But foreign policy cooperation, like cooperation in other areas, was to take place between independent countries and not be based on supranational bodies. The so-called Luxembourg compromise of January 1966 was in reality a victory for de Gaulle's view in this matter.

However, in these years nothing much came of the foreign policy cooperation the French President advocated. The main reason was the differing attitudes among the EEC countries towards Britain and the United States. Washington worked actively to do away with the breach between the EEC and EFTA, on the terms of the EEC. Five of the six EEC member countries supported British membership. However, de Gaulle thwarted the British application both in 1963 and in 1967. In his opinion the 'Anglo-Saxon' countries would attain too much influence, at the expense of France in particular.

De Gaulle's successor, Georges Pompidou, admitted the United Kingdom in 1972. Britain was followed by Denmark and Ireland. Following a referendum, Norway chose to remain outside the EEC, or the European Community (EC) as the organization was called from 1967 onwards. Pompidou was generally somewhat less nationalistic than de Gaulle. The growing political independence West Germany exhibited, combined with the country's economic strength, increased France's need to be able to counterbalance the German influence within the EC. Moreover, the then British government under Edward Heath was the most pro-European government Britain had had.

There were several reasons why the British had re-evaluated their stance, from choosing to remain outside the EEC at first, to then applying for membership and finally to working more actively to become a member of the EC. In the long run Britain did not manage to sustain what the British loved to call their 'special relationship' with the United States. Washington did not consider it either desirable or necessary to have a mediator in its contacts with continental Europe, especially not when British influence was dwindling, while French and German influence was growing. London's long-standing relations with the British Commonwealth became less significant as well. The new countries of Africa and Asia were only mildly interested in following Britain's lead in political and economic matters. The Commonwealth became an ever more loosely-knit organization.

Nor could building up EFTA as a counterweight to the EC succeed. EFTA was too randomly composed. The political and economic center of Europe was located on the continent. If Britain was to play a role in world politics once more, and, not least, attain economic growth on a level with the other countries of Europe, membership in the EC seemed to be their only option.

So, in the final analysis Britain's re-evaluation reflected that country's

184

declining position in great power politics, a fact that in turn was largely a product of Britain's relatively weakened economic role. As late as in 1950 the British economy was still the third largest in the world. In the course of the 1950s, first the West German and then the Japanese and the French gross national products surpassed the British. The process of decolonization was another major sign of Britain's decline.

Explanations for the US Stance

It can be argued that in terms of power politics it would have been much better for the United States to establish ties with the European countries individually rather than through European unity. How then can the strong US emphasis on European integration be explained?

In the 1940s and 50s, it was largely assumed in Washington, as in most of the European capitals, that the United States and Western Europe would have similar, if not identical, interests in most matters of any significance. Of greatest importance in this context was their shared attitude towards the Soviet Union and communism. Cooperation in Europe would strengthen the entire 'free world'.

The Americans also considered themselves and their own path of development a natural model for others. In the United States, the growth of a large market had resulted in the highest standard of living in the world. The Europeans would have to be willing to tear down trade barriers if they wanted rapid economic growth. Many Americans even drew a parallel with the United States of some 200 years ago. As originally separate states had grown together into the United States, the same process would take place in Europe.

The problem of Germany also influenced the US stance. It was important that Germany be drawn into international politics, both in the joint front against the Soviet Union and in the reconstruction of and further growth in Western Europe. West Germany would have to become independent but not be granted complete freedom. Integration was to grant Germany equal status with other countries and take into consideration Europe's need for German resources, while minimizing the danger of German nationalism.

The traditional American isolationism had died. However, there were still remnants of isolationist tendencies, especially within the right wing of the Republican party. For instance, former President Herbert Hoover and Senator Robert Taft wanted to reduce the US role in Europe economically and militarily. This could more easily be accomplished if the Europeans cooperated to assume the responsibilities the Americans now had to fulfill against the wishes of the right wing. Although Eisenhower's foreign policy was far from that of Hoover and Taft, he shared their overall view of the need to exercise restraint in the use of US resources.

The general assessment of the Truman and Eisenhower administrations was that supporting European integration was desirable despite the disadvantages this would entail for US trade. It was expected that the combination of common external tariff barriers and the abolition of internal trade restrictions would result in increased inter-European trade, at the partial expense of trade with countries from outside the region. To a great extent, this proved to be the case. From 1958 to 1967, trade among the EEC countries was doubled, measured as a percentage of their total trade.

However, even this type of shift could have positive side effects seen from a US perspective. The alternative could well have been that the United States would have had to continue to subsidize Western Europe by paying these countries' dollar deficits. Washington made it plain as early as in 1947-48 that there was no chance of such a subsidy after the four-year period of the Marshall Plan ended.

Nor did initial US willingness to bear the anticipated economic consequences prevent the Americans from attempting to secure certain economic benefits. European cooperation was first and foremost to be adapted to a wider international framework. But in addition there were a number of conditions, especially in the Marshall Plan, that directly promoted US interests, for instance within agriculture and shipping. Moreover, as time passed it became evident that with the rapid economic growth in Europe, US-European trade increased as well, although this increase was much smaller than for trade within Europe.

Gradually friction developed in relations between the United States and several of the Western European countries. This friction in turn contributed to the United States becoming ever more concerned that cooperation in Europe should not discriminate against US trade interests. The United States was no longer willing to assume an economic burden in order to promote overriding political objectives. Finally, Europe's economic situation was entirely different from what it had been during the reconstruction years just after the Second World War. The breakthrough for a new US policy came in 1971 (see page 196).

186

US–European Relations, 1950–1973

Cooperation prior to 1962

Through its support for European integration, the United States to some extent encouraged arrangements that could limit US influence in Western Europe. The Western Europeans, on the other hand, were still interested in increasing the US presence in many fields, although the main pattern was established by around 1950. This showed that the 1950s were characterized by good relations between these two parts of the world.

For the most part, the United States and Western Europe had a shared assessment of the threat the Soviet Union represented. The Americans needed the Europeans, and the Western Europeans needed the Americans just as much. The US nuclear guarantee and US troops in West Germany were the central elements in NATO's policy of deterrence. US military assistance to Europe was substantial. From 1950 to 1959 it amounted to 13.7 billion dollars.

Western Europe was not only dependent on military support from the United States. Economic assistance was still significant, although it was in the process of being reduced. Washington had insisted at first that Europe should stand on its own feet when the Marshall Plan ended in 1951-52. But assistance was given to some countries even after that, to a total value of approximately three billion dollars from the time the plan ceased until 1960. In addition, most of the Western European countries made active efforts to attract US investment.

In 1961, the OEEC, originally established to administer the Marshall Plan, was restructured as the Organization for Economic Cooperation and Development (OECD). The United States and Canada became full members, and the objective was to link the two sides of the Atlantic more closely together. They were also to cooperate on matters outside the Atlantic region, such as aid to developing countries.

Throughout the post-war period, the Americans had been concerned with reducing trade restrictions in general, especially across the Atlantic. In that way, the disadvantages of remaining outside a common European market could be reduced. Through five rounds of negotiations within GATT, the barriers were reduced. Throughout this process, the initiative was taken by the United States, which made major concessions in order to attain a successful result.

For a long time, US and European politics were dominated by leaders who were marked by the fellowship that was created during WW II and through the establishment of the Marshall Plan and NATO. Close friendships developed between Acheson and Bevin, Eisenhower and Churchill, Dulles and Adenauer. The relationship between the considerably younger Kennedy and Macmillan was also warm, although time would show that to a great extent the close personal ties were linked to one particular generation.

Relations across the Atlantic were probably strengthened by the conservatism that was the strongest political movement in the 1950s, both in the United States and in Western Europe. The elections in Italy in 1948, in Britain in 1950-51, in France in 1951, in the United States in 1952, and in West Germany in 1953 all signaled a period of conservative dominance and a decline for the more radical parties. Even so, in many ways the popularity of the United States in Western Europe reached its peak during Kennedy's brief presidency and subsequently declined.

Even during this period, there were shades of difference in US and Western European attitudes towards the Soviet Union. Thus in 1953 Churchill was more eager than Eisenhower to exploit the possibilities for detente that might present themselves after Stalin's death. Likewise, later in the 1950s the British governments of Anthony Eden and Harold Macmillan tried to ease the strained relations between East and West. From the end of the 1950s and the early 1960s, the Europeans would generally be more interested than the Americans in increasing trade with the Soviet Union and Eastern Europe. West Germany was no exception in this respect.

For the most part the British gave in to the more cautious US policies. In 1962, Washington persuaded Bonn to halt a controversial gas pipeline deal with the Soviet Union.

However, there was no doubt that US relations with the Soviet Union were also strengthened in the course of the 1950s. Perhaps most importantly, attitudes varied considerably both among and within the various countries of Western Europe, so that on many occasions Washington was more willing to negotiate than at least some European capitals were.

The Germans consistently pressed for German reunification as the first item on any East-West agenda. Towards the end of the Eisenhower administration and particularly under Kennedy, the Americans considered the German stance both unrealistic and negative. The fact that the US position was often in the middle, in addition to US military and economic superiority, strengthened the leadership of the country within the Western world.

There were only slight differences between the United States and the European countries with regard to their attitudes towards the Soviet Union. Other issues would cause greater tension across the Atlantic during the 1950s, although there were seldom or never dramatic differences nor a truly unified European perspective.

The most important controversy in Europe was German rearmament. From September 1950 onwards, the United States insisted that West Germany had to find its place within the Western military cooperation. France was naturally highly sceptical, whereas the other NATO countries, more or less reluctantly, were prepared to follow the United States in this matter. When the French government under Prime Minister René Pleven proposed in October 1950 that rearmament should take place within the framework of an integrated European army, the Americans supported this plan. But when France hesitated to ratify the treaty for a European army, Paris was subject to strong pressure from Washington, without that preventing the national assembly from rejecting the proposal in 1954. In 1955, West Germany was granted direct membership in NATO instead.

Differences of opinion between the United States and Western Europe were more numerous with regard to issues outside Europe, but even here most of the differences were limited in scope. Britain, followed by certain other Western European countries, recognized communist China. The United States did not. The Europeans supported the basic outlines of US policy during the Korean war, but the nuances that existed indicated that many Europeans were more cautious: they dissociated themselves from even threats of the use of nuclear weapons and evidenced greater understanding for Chinese wishes. Many European governments were sceptical about the growing US support to Chiang Kai-shek on Taiwan in the course of the 1950s.

During the Indo-China crisis of 1954 as well, most Europeans were more hesitant than the Eisenhower administration, with the partial exception of the French, who wavered between the desire for a military victory, on the one hand, and the need for a complete withdrawal, on the other hand (see pages 80–81). Under Eisenhover and Dulles, the Americans were much sharper in their denunciation of neutral governments, such as that of India, than most Europeans were.

Even so, there were clear instances in which the United States evidenced a more moderate stance towards radical regimes in the Third World than Western Europe did. Most striking was the Suez conflict in 1956, perhaps the most important controversy between Washington, on the one hand, and Paris and London, on the other, during the 1950s. Before the Israeli-British-French invasion of Egypt, the policy of the Americans was rather unclear; after the invasion, Eisenhower applied political and economic pressure to bring it to a halt as quickly as possible. The humiliating British-French retreat undoubtedly contributed to the rise of anti-American sentiments in certain segments of the population, especially in France. (For US-European differences on colonial issues, see also pages 237–238.)

Political and Military Controversy, 1962–1973

In the 1960s it became increasingly more evident that the premise that in many ways had been the foundation for US policy towards Europe— the assumption that the United States and Western Europe had coinciding interests on most of the important issues—could no longer be taken for granted.

Several attempts were made to absorb and adjust to the great changes that had taken place between and within the two regions. Europe would have to attain greater influence, and the growing European cooperation would have to be more firmly incorporated in the Atlantic framework. However, these attempts could not prevent the transatlantic cooperation from beginning to crack.

The first major reform proposal was Kennedy's program for 'Atlantic interdependence', which he proclaimed in a speech on US independence day, 4 July 1962:

> ... I will say here and now, on this Day of Independence, that the United States will be ready for a declaration of interdependence, that we will be prepared to discuss with a United Europe the ways and means of forming a concrete Atlantic partnership, a mutually beneficial partnership between the new union now emerging in Europe and the old Union founded here 173 years ago.

Militarily and politically, little came of Kennedy's Atlantic partnership. There was no unified Europe for the United States to cooperate with.

190

Britain did not join the EEC, an important condition for Kennedy's plan. De Gaulle was preoccupied with limiting French policy towards the United States.

In fact, there were strong elements of French independence even before de Gaulle. During the first post-war years, France had pursued a separate policy in the German question, in which Paris advocated a weakest possible Germany (see pages 51–52). However, the rapidly increasing tension in the cold war and US-British concessions with regard to the Saar region contributed to drawing France into the Western cooperation. As early as in 1948-49, the French government first aired the idea that the Western military alliance should be led by a triumvirate consisting of the United States, Britain, and France. Preparations for an independent French nuclear force were proceeding before de Gaulle assumed power in 1958.

Only gradually did de Gaulle's policies become more independent of US policies. For a long time the French president was at least as harsh in his anti-communism as Washington was. He advocated firm policies both in Berlin and during the Cuban crisis in 1962 and was concerned about combating Soviet influence in Africa, especially in Algeria.

Until 1963, the French showed their independence primarily by emphasizing anew the old triumvirate plans and by withdrawing the French Mediterranean fleet from NATO control. In 1963, the Atlantic fleet was withdrawn from NATO control as well, and in 1966 France withdrew entirely from NATO's military program, although the country remained a member of NATO and kept its troops in West Germany. Criticism of the United States increased sharply, and Britain was kept out of the EEC in part to limit Anglo-American influence in Western Europe. Relations with the Soviet Union and the Eastern European countries were expanded, and France soon became the Western country with the best contacts to the East.

For a long time de Gaulle was isolated in Western Europe in his attitude towards the East-West conflict and the two superpowers. Towards the close of the 1960s, however, the attitudes of the European countries began to change, and the desire for detente with the Soviet Union was more clearly formulated throughout most of Western Europe.

This increased Western European independence can primarily be linked to two circumstances: the Vietnam war and the new German policy towards the Eastern bloc. Criticism of US warfare in Vietnam was harshest in France and in some of the smaller European countries. But even in Britain and West Germany the criticism could be noticed under the official surface of agreement with Washington.

It was even more significant that West Germany abandoned its hard line policy towards the Soviet Union and Eastern Europe. The first signs of a more flexible eastern policy had been apparent before Adenauer's term expired in 1963, but at that time there was much talk of adjusting to new signals from Washington. The breakthrough came in two stages, first under Kiesinger and Brandt's coalition government (1966–69) and then in earnest under Brandt and Scheel in the years following 1969. The German *Ostpolitik* paralleled the general movement towards detente, but even Nixon and Kissinger were uneasy about both the pace and the way in which *Ostpolitik* was practiced (see pages 103–105).

In the military sphere, more and more of the burden of conventional defense was borne by West Germany, with the political consequences this entailed. An imbalance could easily arise between West Germany's military and economic strength, on the one hand, and on the other hand, the fact that the country—in contrast to Britain and France—did not have nuclear weapons.

This was part of the background for plans for a multilateral nuclear force (MLF) within NATO. The initiative originally came from experts on Europe in the US State Department as early as during the Eisenhower administration. The plans were then developed further in a number of variations under Kennedy, and now the West Germans became more and more interested. Even though the United States was still to have control over the nuclear weapons, at least the guidelines for their use were to be drawn up by the member countries, and manning and financing the vessels the force was to consist of was to be multilateral. West Germany was to acquire a say in NATO's nuclear policy, without the country actually having a finger on the button, at least not in the foreseeable future.

However, from the turn of the year 1964–65 the plans for a multilateral nuclear force faded into the background. Secretary of Defense Robert McNamara showed little interest in the idea. Congress grew ever more sceptical. Many policy-makers both in the United States and in Western Europe felt that the entire scheme was too complicated. Britain and France feared that a joint force would entail pressure on their own more independent nuclear forces. The Soviet Union was opposed to anything that could give West Germany a say in nuclear policy.

Instead of MLF, a nuclear planning group was established within

NATO which was to give the Western Europeans greater insight into and perhaps a greater influence on US nuclear planning. It did re-establish a calmer atmosphere concerning the role of nuclear weapons, but the entire process had probably worsened rather than improved the Atlantic climate. Even so, the main differences of opinion regarding MLF were among the European countries, not between the United States, on the one hand, and Western Europe, on the other.

However, when it came to changing NATO's strategy from massive retaliation to flexible response (see page 162), the differences were greatest between the two sides of the Atlantic.

The Western Europeans were actually satisfied with the strategy of massive retaliation. This strategy linked the United States firmly to the countries of Western Europe while demanding little of them. In 1967, flexible response was formally accepted by NATO nonetheless, without any major changes on the part of the Europeans. This was similar to what had happened after the Lisbon meeting in 1952: ambitious plans for contributions to conventional defense, but few concrete results.

Washington applied pressure to get the Europeans to assume a larger share of NATO's defense expenses. In 1960, the United States bore 74 percent of the alliance's total expenditure. Here, too, the Americans accomplished little during the 1960s. The US share was just as high in 1970 as it had been ten years earlier (expenditure in Vietnam not excluded). West Germany, however, increased the compensation paid for the US troops stationed there. Partly to limit US criticism, the European members of NATO (with the exception of France, Iceland, and Portugal) established a EURO-group within the alliance in 1968 for the purpose of strengthening and coordinating the European contribution.

There were strong US reactions against Europe's insufficient willingness to contribute more to its own defense, especially in the Congress. Western Europe had the economic strength to do far more than previously. A large number of US forces were tied up in Vietnam. In 1968, most of a US division was withdrawn from Europe.

The pressure for Western Europe to pay more for NATO defense increased in 1970-71 and culminated in 1973. The Nixon administration found itself in a difficult position between Congress and Western Europe. On this issue, however, the difficulties were solved surprisingly easily, at least for the moment. In part, the Western Europeans assumed more of the cost, so that the US share had declined to 60 percent by 1975. (This decline was partly due to the phase-out of the Vietnam war and a new exchange rate on the dollar.) In part, the West Germans again increased their compensation for the US forces stationed in the country. Finally, Brezhnev helped the situation by agreeing to start negotiations on mutual force reductions in Europe.

Economic Relations, 1962–1973

The controversies between the United States and Europe were due in large part to the changes that had taken place in the relative economic strengths of the two parts of the alliance. Just after WW II, the United States alone was responsible for almost half of the world's production. This share was bound to sink as the razed countries were rebuilt after the war. However, the decline continued even after reconstruction. In 1960 the US share had sunk to 28 percent. From the moment Britain joined the EC, the total GNP of the EC was greater than that of the United States, at least if measured in market prices.

One of the results of these economic realities was that US assistance to Western Europe gradually ceased. The economic assistance had been discontinued at the end of the 1950s. In the course of the 1960s, the program of military assistance was also phased out. The purely economic advantages that Western Europe enjoyed through cooperation with the United States were reduced.

Kennedy's plans for 'two pillar' cooperation between the United States and Western Europe failed in the political and military spheres. However, better results were achieved in the economic sphere. The Kennedy round, the sixth in the series of tariff negotiations within GATT, was the most important event. The participating countries together represented 75 percent of total world trade. In 1967, these negotiations resulted in major reductions in tariff rates. Two-thirds of the reductions on tariffs for industrial goods were of the order of 50 percent or more. Tariff duties on such products in the United States, Western Europe, and Japan were now approximately 10 percent. However, little was accomplished with regard to agricultural trade.

The EEC had negotiated as a single entity during the Kennedy round. This was a victory for European integration. The liberalization that resulted from the negotiations could be said to be a victory for the philosophy of Atlantic cooperation, although GATT comprised many more countries than the United States and the Western European nations.

The dollar was the most important international currency. It was for Western economic cooperation what nuclear weapons were for military cooperation. More than three-fourths of the trade among non-communist countries and of the central banks' reserves was in dollars. In the course of 1967–68, the most important currencies—the dollar, the pound, the franc and the mark—all experienced crises, demonstrating that the foreign exchange market was not effectively under control.

In 1969, a system of special drawing rights (SDR) was established to try to stabilize the market. In a longer perspective, SDR could possibly replace the dollar as the most important currency unit. The new value of currencies was not to be controlled by the United States alone, but by a group consisting of the ten most important industrialized countries within the International Monetary Fund.

In many ways the negotiations during the Kennedy round and the agreement on SDR represented a climax of the post-war period in terms of Western cooperation on trade and currency. US imports from what later became the nine EC countries rose sharply during the 1960s, in both absolute and relative figures. US exports to the same countries also increased. Both imports and exports represented about 25 percent of the total US figures in 1968. Most dramatic were the changes with regard to US investments in Western Europe. Their value rose from approx. 4 billion dollars in 1957 to approx. 24 billion in 1970, or from 15 to 30 percent of total US foreign investments. All in all, the United States became more dependent on the outside world economically than it had been previously, although foreign trade was still less significant for the United States than for nearly all the other industrialized countries.

Even so, the signals of a new and more difficult era were strong even at this stage. After 1968 the volume of US imports from Western Europe declined, while exports to Western Europe were better sustained. Western Europe's trade with the rest of the world, and not least the EC countries' trade with each other increased much more rapidly than trade with the United States. On the part of the United States, the Pacific region became increasingly more interesting in the course of the 1970s.

In 1966, the EEC had reached agreement on an agricultural policy that was clearly protectionistic, particularly in relation to the United States. US exports of the goods the Europeans protected fell dramatically. The EEC's various preference agreements with countries outside Europe created new problems. An enlargement of the EEC would have political advantages, but economically the discrimination against the United

States would be extended further. The tremendous growth in US invest-ments in Western Europe resulted in pressure for limitations and control in several areas. Finally, and not least in importance, Japan's flourishing economy and new status as an economic superpower caused major adjustment problems for the international trade system.

The United States had long struggled with a deficit balance of pay-ments, largely as a result of the military and economic commitments Washington had assumed. In 1971, the country experienced a trade defi-cit as well for the first time since 1883. This was mainly due to the large deficit in trade with Japan, but in the following year even the United States' traditional trade surplus in relation to Western Europe was changed to a deficit.

The complicated SDR system proved not to be a success. The foreign exchange market was still not under effective control. The dollar re-mained the currency all the others were measured against, and the Euro-peans became increasingly more irritated at being tied to a currency they did not have the slightest control over.

The many and complicated economic problems of the United States diminished Washington's willingness to sustain its internationally orien-ted economic policy. The measures of the Nixon administration in August 1971 represented a breakthrough in that respect. The convertibility of the dollar vis-à-vis gold was abolished, and a 10 percent import duty was levied on all dutiable goods. When this duty was removed shortly thereafter, the United States devalued the dollar. International exchange rates were allowed to float. Washington also demanded changes in the EC's agricultural policies and in the organization's general preference system. Here, however, little was achieved. All in all, the new policy could be said to signalize the collapse of parts of the Bretton Woods system as it had been established in 1945.

The United States and Western Europe after 1973: Tensions Increase

From the Year of Europe to Ronald Reagan

There had almost continually been some forms of disagreement within the Atlantic cooperation, but the differences had often been between the United States and perhaps only one of the European countries, especial-ly France, or they had been linked to specific problems, such as the Suez

crisis or the Vietnam war. At the close of the 1960s, differences of opinion began to appear between the United States, on the one hand, and
most of the countries of Western Europe, on the other. This tendency
would be reinforced during the 1970s and 1980s.

Every president since Kennedy had accused his predecessor of having
let relations with Western Europe decay. Kennedy's own plan for 'Atlantic interdependence' had been a success in one area at best: the economic
sphere. Nixon and Kissinger's Year of Europe in 1973 was the next major
initiative on the part of the Americans. The Year of Europe was an
attempt to give allied cooperation primary importance after US diplomacy had long been concentrated on the Soviet Union, China, and Vietnam. As under Kennedy, these efforts were supposed to lead to a statement that would partly outline the foundation for the existing cooperation and partly bring new life to it.

The Year of Europe was a fiasco. The Nixon administration was so
weakened by Vietnam and Watergate that its negotiating strength was
minimal. 1973 was dominated by conflict in the Middle East and the oil
crisis, resulting in new tensions across the Atlantic. Europe expressed a
clearly more pro-Arab attitude than the United States did. Moreover, the
French stood by their resolve and were still not interested in laying a new
foundation for Atlantic cooperation.

The Europeans were generally more concerned about the basis for political cooperation in the enlarged EC than about strengthening the Atlantic
ties. In many ways, European political cooperation experienced a breakthrough in 1975. At the Conference on Security and Cooperation in Helsinki, the EC position was presented by a joint spokesman. In that same year,
the Lomé agreement was signed between the EC and 46 developing countries, and the dialogue with the Arab countries was increased. In addition,
the EC members coordinated their policies with regard to a new economic
world order and to a somewhat lesser extent their policies within the UN.

The increased foreign policy cooperation could not conceal the fact
that the EC also had major problems. If there had been problems in a
system of six countries, they were even greater with nine members. There
was considerable opposition to the EC within Britain, especially with
regard to its agricultural policies and financing arrangements. Ireland
was not a member of NATO, a fact that made it difficult to introduce
the most direct security issues in the EC.

The coordination of foreign policy within Western Europe did not
contribute to reducing tension across the Atlantic. However, Carter felt

that a change of president would improve relations. Now the US allies would finally receive at least as much attention as the country's adversaries. Consultations were to replace dramatic initiatives in US policy.

The Carter administration could not prevent new difficulties from developing in US-European relations. The most important concrete controversy concerned the deployment of neutron weapons in Western Europe. Carter did not want to effect deployment unless the European countries in question expressed a desire for the new weapon. The Western Europeans would have preferred the United States to assume the responsibility for such a controversial decision. The entire matter was postponed. Neither the decision itself nor even less the process leading up to it strengthened Atlantic unity.

The economic problems between the United States and Western Europe merely continued to grow. The international recessions in the 1970s reinforced the difficulties, as protectionism and the subsidizing of industries in difficulties, such as the steel industry, showed. In 1979, the so-called Tokyo round within GATT was completed after more than six years of negotiations. A certain degree of further liberalization was achieved for trade in industrial products, but despite the lofty phrases in other areas the actual results were small. The discussion between the United States and Western Europe concerning the agricultural policies of the EC became ever sharper, especially after both sides tried to solve their surplus problems through exports. In 1981 Greece became the tenth member of the EC. In 1986 Spain and Portugal joined as numbers eleven and twelve. The new members created additional economic problems, particularly with regard to agriculture, between the United States and Western Europe.

The rate of economic growth in Western Europe was now even lower than in the United States. In contrast, the countries in the Pacific region still enjoyed substantial growth. US trade with the countries in the Pacific region increased rapidly, in 1978 for the first time becoming greater than trade across the Atlantic. Economic interdependence between the Western countries became stronger, but international control was greatly decreased. No single organization could assume the leadership role the United States had previously exercised.

After Carter's vacillation, Reagan wanted to recreate unity through firm leadership. 'The free world' was to be unified under American leadership against the communist threat. Defense was to be strengthened substantially and contacts with the Soviet Union reduced (see pages

138–140). However, the traditional system based on US leadership could not be re-established. The Reagan administration lacked the necessary insight. Even more important was the fact that the United States no longer held the same leading position and, partly for that reason, was not willing to make the generous contributions that had helped sustain the previous order.

When the United States at the end of the Carter administration and particularly under Reagan shifted to a harsher policy towards the Soviet Union, it was only partially followed by Western Europe. Even the conservative governments in Britain and West Germany favored maintaining a greater degree of contact with the Soviet Union and also placed greater emphasis on negotiations for arms control than the United States did (see pages 173–174). An example of the altered relations was the fact that whereas Washington had managed to persuade Bonn to halt the gas pipeline deal with Moscow in 1962, not only Bonn, but London and Paris as well refused to give in to similar requests in 1982–83.

The United States and Western Europe also differed on many Third World questions. Where Reagan often saw conflicts in an East-West perspective and favored military instruments, the Europeans put more emphasis on the local dimension and on political solutions. Such differences were evident in the disagreements over US actions in Nicaragua and Grenada, in the European reactions to Washington's policies towards Lebanon, Libya, Angola and even elsewhere (see pages 140–143).

Underlying Attitudes and Explanations for the Controversies

Beneath the concrete controversies, unmistakable strains of distrust could be observed between the United States and Western Europe in terms of their deeper politico-psychological assessments of each other. On the European side, there was increasing doubt as to the maturity of the United States in foreign policy affairs. US policy could swing dramatically and was considered unpredictable. There were long-term fluctuations, from isolationism during the period between the wars to sending over half a million men to a relatively unimportant area such as Vietnam. The pendulum had swung back and forth in terms of US evaluation of the Soviet Union. The same was true of the size of the defense budget. At certain times and in certain areas human rights were important, in others not. And regardless of what the United States stood for, the leaders in Washington at any given time were equally convinced of the rightness of the policies they pursued. Presidents such as Carter and Reagan were almost completely lacking in foreign policy experience. Relations were not improved by the fact that there was almost always an intense struggle going on between various views within the bureaucracy.

On the other hand, the Americans felt that the Western Europeans did not always know exactly what they wanted from the United States. No matter what the United States did, to many Europeans it was wrong. If Washington cooperated closely with Moscow, the suspicion came creeping in that the two superpowers were trying to dictate developments in the world. Only one thing seemed worse: when Washington did not cooperate with Moscow. If the United States did not consult Western Europe, that was wrong. If emphasis was placed on consultations, that was a sign of lacking US leadership. The Europeans protested when they were accused of being regional in their perspective. But if that was not the case, why then did they care so little about Soviet expansion in Africa and Asia?

In the military sphere many Europeans, but not necessarily their governments, were fond of criticizing NATO's emphasis on nuclear weapons, but repeated US attempts to strengthen conventional defense had met with little response. The Europeans could request new US weapons for the defense of Western Europe, but when this gave rise to domestic controversy they withdrew, leaving the responsibility to the United States. In the economic sphere complaints were heard when the dollar was low, for then European goods were not competitive. If the dollar was high, that reflected a high interest level, with the result that European capital was attracted to the United States. That was at least equally bad.

There were many reasons for the increased level of tension between the United States and Western Europe. The media often placed primary emphasis on the persons in positions of leadership both in the United States and in the major Western European countries. Individual leaders could be important enough. The personal ties between leaders in the 1970s and 1980s were never as close as those that had existed between the politicians who were shaped by the cooperation during and just after WW II and who dominated Atlantic politics until the mid-60s. For some of the youngest European leaders, Vietnam and Watergate took the place the Second World War and the Marshall Plan had had for the oldest ones.

The geographic distance across the Atlantic had increased to some extent, despite improved communications. In the United States the political center shifted to the west and south in line with the population trend. The influence of the Eastern states was reduced, and thus to some extent the level of interest in and knowledge about Europe. In Europe, on the other hand, the focal point of leadership moved eastwards. Britain's role was diminishing as the post-war period progressed. At first France claimed a leadership role, then from the beginning of the 1970s West Germany became the leading power economically, politically, and to some extent militarily as well. West Germany's relations with the United States were much weaker than Britain's both historically and in terms of language, culture and politics.

The dramatic shifts, particularly in the relative economic strengths of the United States and Western Europe (see pages 23–24), were bound to express themselves as tensions within the Western alliance. The Western Europeans were concerned about being heard to an entirely different extent than previously. The United States could no longer determine Western policy more or less on its own. However, the Americans made it clear that Western Europe's new strength would have to express itself in greater contributions to Western defense. Why should the United States use approximately twice as much of its national product for defense as the Europeans did, when several European countries had now become wealthier than the United States? It was easy enough for both Europe and the United States to claim the advantages of their new status, but it proved more difficult to relinquish the benefits of the past.

Despite the shifts in economic and political strength, the United States remains a global power, whereas the former European colonial powers have become more regional than they were previously. In 1967 the British Labour government under Harold Wilson decided to withdraw all British troops east of Suez, with the exception of the forces in Hong Kong. This policy was basically confirmed by Edward Heath when the Conservatives took power in 1970. The difference in geographic perspective reinforced differences that had also been evident earlier. Roughly speaking, it could be said that the Europeans often feared a strong US involvement outside of Europe. At the same time, they had seldom been afraid that the United States would engage itself too strongly in Europe.

In the final analysis, perhaps the controversies between the United States and Europe are a result of the fact that these two parts of the world have different histories and different geographic locations. The

United States and Western Europe do not have the same view of essential political phenomena such as socialism and capitalism. The two regions' experiences of war and peace have differed. Western Europe's geographic location makes this area more vulnerable than the United States in the event of an East-West conflict, but it also offers the greatest advantages during periods of detente. The country that was most easily influenced by fluctuations in the international climate was West Germany.

The United States and Japan, 1945–1986

Developments in US relations with Japan were at least as striking as developments in relation to Western Europe. In Japan the US role was considerably more dominant to begin with. Japan was the country outside the Western hemisphere in which US control was the strongest in the years just after 1945.

By the mid-80s, Japan was still not as independent in international politics as Western Europe was. But the difference was not as great as it had been in 1945. The Japanese gross national product was in the process of surpassing that of the Soviet Union. Economically, the country would thus become the world's second greatest power. Japan's political freedom of action was growing and was substantial compared with the occupation years, but it was still not proportionate to the country's economic strength. Japan was even weaker in military terms.

1945–1960: Occupation and US Dominance

Japan was occupied by the United States alone. The role of the other allied countries here was almost as modest as the role of the Western powers in the former Axis states of Eastern Europe, where the Soviet Union determined the course of developments virtually alone. The Soviet Union complained about its lack of influence in Japan, as did Britain, Australia and several other countries. Even the administration in Washington could feel disregarded at times. Although Washington determined the main course of action, the policies of the occupation authorities under General Douglas MacArthur were relatively independent.

During the US occupation, sweeping changes were instituted in Japanese society. Article 9 in the Japanese Constitution of 6 March 1946 established that Japan should not have military forces and that the country should not practice warfare. The political system came to resemble British parliamentarism on Japanese soil. The emperor was granted only a symbolic role. The national assembly, the Diet, became the seat of power, with the prime minister elected by the lower house. Women gained the right to vote, trade unions were established, comprehensive land reforms were instituted, the educational system was expanded, and decentralization encouraged.

As in Germany, the cold war soon influenced occupation policy in Japan. The purging of nationalistic elements was limited, while the dismantling of the large companies—the zaibatsus—ceased, and in some cases the process was even reversed. When it became evident that communists and left-wing socialists would have a strong position in the new trade unions, their rights were curbed.

From 1947 onwards, ever greater emphasis was placed on the reconstruction of Japan. A harsh policy of deflation was implemented in order to bring the country back on its feet. As with Germany, Japan could not be kept weak without the neighboring countries suffering serious economic consequences. But not until 1954–55 did the country again reach pre-war levels by most standards.

MacArthur wanted a prompt peace treaty that could make Japan what he called the Switzerland of the East — without military forces and without US bases. This dream of his was shared by many Japanese, but in this matter Washington did not concur with the General nor, for that matter, with the Japanese. The Department of Defense in particular insisted that a peace treaty had to be accompanied by a security agreement granting the United States comprehensive base rights. After the outbreak of the Korean war and the transfer of US troops from Japan to Korea, the pressure to get Japan to build up semi-military self-defense forces increased sharply as well.

Although the peace treaty of 1951–52 formally marked Japan's re-entry into the international arena, the country was still closely linked to the United States. The Soviet Union and its allies, including China, did not sign the treaty. US influence was further emphasized when the Senate, as a price for ratifying the treaty, insisted that Japan promise to recognize Taiwan. Again the Japanese had to give in, although many Japanese doubted that Japan's economy would be particularly viable without close relations with the Chinese mainland.

As early as in the 1950s, however, there were signs indicating that Japan would come to play a more independent role. In terms of domestic policy, a number of distinctively Japanese characteristics were preserved despite the tremendous US influence. As the decade progressed, Japan's economic growth began to accelerate in earnest. In terms of foreign policy, the Japanese criticized the US nuclear test detonations in the Pacific, re-established diplomatic relations with the Soviet Union, initiated a cautious trade with communist China, and joined the UN and international economic diplomacy through membership in the World Bank, the International Monetary Fund, and GATT. However, Japan's participation in the international economy in particular was encouraged by the United States.

1960–1986: Economic strength and greater political independence

The most obvious sign of a new climate was the rapidly growing criticism of the 1951 security agreement. The Eisenhower administration realized that comprehensive changes would have to be instituted if good relations were to be preserved and the governing liberal democratic party was to maintain its position vis-à-vis leftist groups. Thus Washington agreed in 1960 to make the agreement valid for 10 years, with an option for renewal, instead of the apparently permanent agreement of 1951; US troops were divested of their right to interfere in domestic Japanese affairs; and changes in US policy with regard to nuclear weapons in Japan could be effected only after consultations with the Japanese government. After Eisenhower had had to cancel a planned visit to Japan and Prime Minister Kishi had had to resign because of all the political unrest related to the security agreement, this issue again faded into the background for a few years.

Kennedy tried to instill new life into US-Japanese relations by promising Japan, like Western Europe, 'an equal partnership' with the United States. Relations between the two countries improved in many ways, but there was no equal partnership to speak of. Militarily and politically Japan was still highly dependent on the United States.

Economically, however, Japan was in the process of becoming a major power. In the course of a seven-year period from the mid-50s, the Japanese national product was doubled, representing what was perhaps the most rapid growth any major power had ever experienced. The United

States contributed to this growth by keeping the US market open for Japanese goods for the most part, while Washington accepted Japan's import restrictions on US goods—measures that to some extent went back to the occupation period. Most of the Western European countries, however, discriminated against Japanese goods even after Japan joined GATT. The primary interest of the United States in relations with Japan, as in Europe, was the establishment of an international political and economic system under US leadership. That required a willingness to pay the price certain aspects of this policy entailed.

In the course of the 1960s, new attitudes gradually began to emerge in Washington. Whereas the Americans enjoyed a large surplus in their trade with Japan until 1965, the United States now acquired a large deficit. Despite its participation in the international economic system, Japan not only had been but in many ways still was protectionistic. Free trade had never been a dominant philosophy in Japan. The country felt vulnerable since it had such limited natural resources. Moreover, the criticism from abroad was considered unfair since so many countries discriminated against Japanese exports.

In 1968, Japan surpassed West Germany and became the world's third greatest power, measured in terms of gross national product. Although a liberalization of Japanese import policies did take place, Japan's exports caused problems of an increasing magnitude. From the end of the 1960s, Washington began in earnest to pursue a policy encouraging 'voluntary' Japanese limitations on exports to the United States.

The feeling that Japan did not contribute its fair share to the defense of the Western world grew as Japanese prosperity increased. It was true that the US forces in Japan were reduced to a level of 30 000 men by 1972, and that Japan's defense appropriations were increased, but even so most Americans felt that Tokyo kept too low a profile. Defense expenditure remained at less than one percent of Japan's gross national product and even declined in some years. Nor did Japan offer more than superficial support to the United States in Vietnam.

Once more the security agreement with the United States became a focal point of interest. The US bases in Japan, and on Okinawa in particular, were highly significant for US warfare in South-east Asia. The crucial question was Okinawa, which only formally had been Japanese since 1945. For all practical purposes, the island was American. Again Washington had to make concessions to maintain good relations with Japan. In the so-called Sato—Nixon communiqué of 1969, the United States returned Okinawa to Japan, and the bases there acquired the same status as the other bases in Japan. In return, the Japanese gave Washington reason to believe that they would play a more active role in the defense of their region, including South Korea and Taiwan.

Relations between the United States and Japan seemed to return to relative tranquillity, but this was to be short-lived. In 1971 Japan suffered two blows, both inflicted by the Nixon administration. First the Americans initiated relations with China, then the United States levied a 10 percent import duty and devalued the dollar.

Japan had long been interested in better relations with China but had harmonized its policies with those of the United States. Now Washington terminated its quarantine of China without consulting Japan. The economic measures were aimed more at Japan than at Western Europe, but again no consultations preceded Washington's actions.

The tensions between Japan and the United States induced Moscow to attempt to improve its relations with Tokyo. Political contacts were expanded, trade increased and the Kremlin showed an interest in involving Japan in major industrial projects, particularly in Siberia.

However, there were clear limitations on how good Japanese–Soviet relations could become. The crucial issue was the Soviet-controlled islands north of Japan. In 1945, Japan had had to cede the Kurile Islands, but Tokyo was not willing to relinquish its claim on the southernmost four of them. The Soviet Union, which had evidenced a certain degree of flexibility in the 1950s in particular, finally refused to honor this claim. Moreover, in the course of the 1970s the Pacific fleet became the part of the Soviet fleet that grew the most rapidly. The increased Soviet military presence near Japan could not contribute to improving mutual relations. Nor did the ambitious Japanese-Soviet industrial projects in Siberia really get off the ground.

China's entry into the international arena also caused problems. Although Japan tried to improve relations with both communist countries at the same time, traditionally Japan had had closer ties with China. The military and political problems were now smaller, and the volume of trade became much greater with China than with the Soviet Union. Thus in 1978 Japan decided to sign a cooperation agreement with China, a decision that was not warmly received in Moscow.

During the first years following WW II, leading American politicians had been concerned as to whether Japan would manage to become economically self-sufficient. In the 1970s, their concerns were quite the opposite: that Japan would outstrip the United States, as it had outstripped most of the rest of the world. By 1986 Japan had become the world's greatest creditor. The traditional leader in that field, the United States, had in the course of a few years become one of the world's largest debtor countries.

Could economic competition be combined with political and military cooperation? Japanese foreign policy had long consisted primarily of creating favorable conditions for economic growth. In this perspective, the Japanese had for the most part willingly left military and political commitments to the United States. The United States, on its part, encouraged Japan to do more, for instance for its own defense.

As in its relations with Western Europe, Washington assumed that even a strong Japan would cooperate closely with the United States. Japan had gradually begun to play a greater political and military role. In the 1980s the defense budget was increased substantially, although less than Washington desired. At the May 1983 summit in Williamsburg, Virginia, the economic consultations among leading Western industrial nations were extended to include military cooperation vis-à-vis the Soviet Union. In 1986 Japan finally decided to abandon the self-imposed limit of defense expenditure not surpassing one percent of the country's gross national product. It seems reasonable to assume that economic strength will express itself as increasing political independence on the part of Japan as it has done in Western Europe, although the process has not gone as far in Japan as in Western Europe.

8. The Soviet Union and the Communist Countries, 1945–1986

During the first years after the Second World War, Communists gained control in vast new areas: Eastern Europe, North Korea, China and North Vietnam. Later, new Moscow-oriented regimes emerged—on Cuba, in Indo-China, and in Afghanistan. The Soviet Union obtained a footing in African countries such as Angola and Ethiopia.

Even so, in some ways the position of the Soviet Union became weaker as the post-war era progressed. There was no longer a world-wide communist movement with the Soviet Union as its indisputable leader. As early as in 1948, Tito's Yugoslavia had shown that a victory for communism was not necessarily a victory for the Soviet Union. In time, there would be more instances illustrating this fact.

Most important of all was the conflict with China, which in the late 1960s and during the 1970s surpassed the cold war with the United States in intensity. In Eastern Europe, the various countries chose different courses: a few relatively independent of the Soviet Union, most of them still more traditional. What was significant was that the national Communist parties, within certain limits, could decide for themselves exactly how closely they wanted to follow Moscow. This was true to an even greater extent outside Eastern Europe, in countries such as North Vietnam and Cuba and in the Communist parties of Western Europe.

Expansion and Conformism, 1945–1953

Whereas to a great extent the United States was invited to play an active role in Western Europe in the years immediately following WW II, this was seldom the case for the Soviet Union in Eastern Europe. The United States had a considerably wider range of instruments to choose among in its foreign policy than the Soviet Union had. The capitalist superpower could offer economic assistance and military guarantees. The Soviet Union had little to contribute economically. The Western powers were never considered the threat in Eastern Europe that the Soviet Union came to represent in Western Europe, which meant that the question of military guarantees was seen in an entirely different light in Eastern Europe.

The level of support for the Soviet Union and the Communist party varied in Eastern Europe. It was undoubtedly highest in Bulgaria and Czechoslovakia, lowest in Hungary, Poland, and Romania. Bulgaria had cooperated with the USSR/Russia on many occasions. Moreover, Bulgaria and Czechoslovakia had a past history that was characterized by scepticism of the Western powers. In Bulgaria, this went way back to the 1870s, in Czechoslovakia to the Munich settlement of 1938.

In Poland, Hungary, and Romania, hostility towards the Soviet Union had deep roots. Although the fear of a new strong Germany could increase understanding for the Soviet Union, especially in Poland, and although more or less opportunistic reasons dictated support for the governing party, there was a weak local basis for the dominant position the Soviet Union assumed.

Soviet expansion in Eastern Europe was primarily based on the Red Army (see pages 46–50). Hungary, Bulgaria, and Romania had fought on the side of the Axis powers. That made Soviet control especially extensive here in the first years after the war. Washington and London granted Moscow the chief role in the occupation of these countries. The Red Army also assumed a central role in developments in Poland, as it soon became evident that the Lublin group of pro-Soviet Poles enjoyed limited local support. (With regard to the situation in East Germany, see page 52.) Czechoslovakia was the only country from which the Soviets withdrew—which they did in December 1945—but where Moscow and the local Communists obtained full control nonetheless.

Soviet control was evident in most areas of society. Politically, the countries in the region were governed at first by coalition governments under varying degrees of Communist/Soviet influence. In 1947–48, these coalitions were dissolved. The non-communist parties disappeared as independent entities. They were soon followed by the communist leaders who could be suspected of wanting national independence. In Hungary, Rajk had to pay with his life, as did Kostov in Bulgaria; in Romania, Patrascanu was purged, as was Gomulka in Poland. In 1951-52 Slansky in Czechoslovakia and Pauker in Romania, both known for their subservience to Moscow and both of them Jews, were purged. Slansky, general secretary of the Communist party, was even executed.

The Eastern European economies were subjugated to the Soviet economy. Not only was trade skewed to the east, but the conditions of trade were to the advantage of the Soviet Union to an extreme degree. The joint Soviet—Eastern European companies were often a mere cover for Soviet exploitation. By demanding war reparations and by confiscating German-controlled property, Moscow could further consolidate its position. All in all, the Soviet Union's transfers from Eastern Europe probably amounted to more than the assistance the United States gave Western Europe under the Marshall Plan.

After a few years of relatively balanced reconstruction, from 1949-50 onwards Eastern Europe was built up according to the Soviet pattern, with five-year plans that clearly favored large-scale and heavy industry. In most countries the government even took over small handicraft firms. Much of agriculture was collectivized, although the pace varied somewhat from one country to another. An organization for economic cooperation, COMECON, was established in 1949, but acquired little significance at this time. As the various Eastern European countries placed priority on many of the same areas, there was little need for trade and cooperation. Moreover, the boundaries between countries were under close surveillance.

This enforced conformity can be explained on the basis of several considerations. The Soviet Union, like other powers in similar situations, transferred its own system of government to the countries it controlled. As the United States exported Western capitalism with considerable strains of pluralism, the Soviet Union exported communism, a communism in which divergence from prevailing norms was not allowed, especially during the Stalin era. Eastern Europe occupied a central position in ensuring Soviet security, and that strengthened Moscow's demands on the regimes that were established.

The demands for loyalty gradually increased. This was partly a result of the fact that Moscow got more time to shape the region in its own image and partly a reflection of international and local factors. The cooling temperature in the cold war meant that fewer and fewer deviations were tolerated. The lines between East and West were to be drawn even more sharply than previously. Several of the Eastern European countries, most particularly Czechoslovakia, were interested in participating in the Marshall Plan. The Kremlin's dissatisfaction on this account was part of the background for the Communist coup in Czechoslovakia in February 1948, a coup that quickly brought the country in line with the rest of Eastern Europe. Locally, the first important act of the Communist Information Bureau (COMINFORM), established in October 1947, was to expel Yugoslovia. The split between Stalin and Tito in June 1948 meant the initiation of a witch hunt for any elements that could be said to represent the slightest degree of independence in relation to Moscow.

The Yugoslavs were accused of having embraced ideological deviation. The fact that they had gone far in encouraging revolution in Western Europe was considered 'leftist deviation'. Tito had pursued a harsh course in relation to the United States and Britain, particularly in Trieste and by supporting the insurrection in Greece. Nationalization of industry and collectivization of agriculture had also begun earlier and progressed further than otherwise in Eastern Europe. Tito's 'national' deviations were examples of 'rightist deviation', such as his opposition to joint companies and Soviet exploitation, control and surveillance. Tito was now compared to Trotsky; it was not possible to sink much lower.

The most important basis for the split was the fact that Tito and the Yugoslavian communists had risen to power on their own, with little help from the Red Army. This was also the primary reason that Yugoslavia survived the total isolation the country was subjected to from the other Communist countries and parties. Tito had built up an army, a party, and an administration that for the most part remained loyal to him.

In only one other Eastern European country was the situation similar to that of Yugoslavia, and that was in Albania under Enver Hoxha. But here the bitter conflict between Yugoslavia and Albania contributed to Hoxha seeking close cooperation with the Soviet Union to prevent the country from being absorbed as a province of Yugoslavia. Thus the independent power base of the regime could for the time be combined with a pro-Moscow policy.

The Chinese Communists had at least an equally independent power base, but even they naturally looked to Moscow as the world's communist capital. The cooperation agreement of 1950 linked the two countries to each other. For the Chinese, the leadership of Stalin and the Soviet Union was a matter of course. When Stalin died on 5 March 1953, Mao Tse-tung spoke of his 'sublime wisdom' and 'burning love' for the Chinese people. (For the stance of the Soviet Union during the Chinese civil war, see pages 65–67.)

The Reins are Loosened (1953–1956) and Tightened (1956–1958)

A number of conditions diminished Soviet control over Eastern Europe and the world-wide communist movement during the course of the 1950s.

The most important single factor was Stalin's death. No one could take the place of 'the greatest genius of the present age', to use another of Mao's phrases at the time of Stalin's death. Although Khrushchev gradually emerged as the unmistakable top man, he never attained the authority Stalin had had, neither in the Soviet Union itself, in Eastern Europe, or in the other communist countries and parties.

The Soviet Union was still the model for the other countries, but with the thaw that was now taking place the content of this model was no longer so clear-cut. Power was shared among more persons and bodies, first in the Soviet Union and then in Eastern Europe. The position of the security police was reduced, and most of the political prisoners released. There were signs of discussion, and the various factions in the Eastern European parties could with varying degrees of justice invoke support from different centers of power in Moscow.

The position of the Soviet Union grew weaker. Trade agreements were revised, and the joint companies were changed in character or dismantled. Greatest were the concessions in relation to China (see page 218). These changes were partly a result of freer conditions, but it was also admitted that Stalin had made grave mistakes. Khrushchev's denunciation of the deceased leader at the Twentieth Party Congress in February 1956 tore the former deity down from his pedestal in earnest. This denunciation probably strengthened Khrushchev's position at the moment, but in a somewhat longer perspective it was bound to weaken his and the Soviet Union's possibilities of assuming the same leadership role as before. The Soviet Union had made serious mistakes in the past. The same could happen again.

One of Stalin's greatest mistakes, in Khrushchev's opinion, was the fact that he had thrust Tito out into the cold. The split in 1948 was considered unnecessary. Yugoslavia was again to be brought into the fold of communist countries. In 1955, Khrushchev journeyed to Belgrade for reconciliation. Tito was rehabilitated and declared a good communist. That could gain Moscow greater influence in Yugoslavia, but in the rest of Eastern Europe the consequences were the exact opposite. If there were now different roads to communism, that had to apply not only in Yugoslavia, but in other countries as well. Reconciliation with Tito was also bound to have consequences for the many Eastern European leaders who had been accused of 'Titoism' and 'national deviation'. They had not all lost their lives. In April 1956 COMINFORM was dissolved.

Destalinization was far from painless in the Soviet Union. Even so, the problems were small compared to those in Eastern Europe. In the Soviet Union, nationalism had been absorbed in the communist system to a great extent, in contrast to what was the case in Eastern Europe. There nationalism was an anti-Soviet and anti-communist force in most of the countries. The domestic political situation in these countries was less stable in other ways as well. The Communists had only been in power for a few years, and the attachment to traditions other than communism was far stronger than in the Soviet Union.

The new tensions were first expressed in the June 1953 demonstrations in Czechoslovakia and East Germany. In Czechoslovakia, the authorities managed to quell the unrest in Pilsen and other cities. In East Germany, a strong desire for liberalization coincided with a power struggle in the local party—a power struggle with ramifications in various factions in Moscow—and with the continuation of harsh economic policies. Only direct intervention by the Soviet occupation troops re-established socialist law and order in East Berlin and other East German cities.

The Revolts in Poland and Hungary in 1956

During the summer and autumn of 1956, revolts broke out, first in Poland and immediately thereafter in Hungary. In many ways, it was only to be expected that these countries presented the greatest problems.

Poland and Hungary had long historical traditions of struggling to resist foreign subjugation and sustain national independence. Moreover, the most deeply rooted anti-Russian sentiments were to be found in Hungary and especially Poland (and in Romania as well). The economic tensions were great. Whereas East Germany and Czechoslovakia were industrialized countries and Bulgaria and Romania were agricultural countries, Poland and Hungary were in an intermediate position. The rate of investment had been very high, with the sacrifices that necessarily entailed. Even more importantly, in 1956 the party leadership was in a period of transition which stimulated expectations and uncertainty. In Poland, Bierut died after having heard Khrushchev's disclosures of Stalin's outrages. In Hungary, the hated Rakosi had to resign after having tried various strategies to survive politically.

The workers' revolt in Poznan in June was aimed at economic conditions such as wages and prices. The authorities never managed to bring the situation fully under control. Ochab, the new party leader, could not unite the party, much less the nation. In Poland, the party's leading 'revisionist', Gomulka, had been sentenced to prison and thus escaped execution. In April he was released from prison; in October he was elected leader of the Communist party.

The Soviet leadership, which in many ways had initiated the thaw, was sceptical towards Gomulka. It tried to prevent his being elected general secretary. But considering the support he enjoyed in the party, in the population, in the police force, and in much of the army, Gomulka was the only person who could unite the country. If the Soviets chose to intervene with military force, it could be that they would be met with open opposition. Gomulka had to be given a chance. Then the revolt in Hungary broke out. Moscow soon became more preoccupied with Hungary than with the situation in Poland.

Rakosi's Hungary had pursued what was perhaps the harshest policy of repression in all of Eastern Europe. In July, this dictator had been forced to resign under Soviet pressure, a situation that could partially be seen as a result of the rapprochement with Tito.

The new party leader, Gerø, was so discredited that his take-over could not have any other purpose than to discourage Rakosi's supporters. As in Poland, Hungary moved into a transitional phase in which the new leaders did not manage to get the situation under control. The events in Poland stimulated developments in Hungary.

In Poland, the party had rallied around Gomulka. In Hungary, Imre Nagy was appointed prime minister on 24 October following large-scale demonstrations in Budapest. But the party was still divided. An appeal was sent to the Soviet troops to re-establish the socialist order. Clashes ensued in several places. Janos Kadar replaced Gerø as general secretary of the party.

The Soviet troops were withdrawn from Budapest, at the same time as preparations were made to send reinforcements into Hungary. Events unfolded rapidly. Pressured by the oppositional groups that sprang up everywhere, Nagy first allowed several parties and then established a coalition government. Thereafter he announced Hungary's withdrawal from the Warsaw Pact (see page 156) and established the country's neutrality. On 4 November, the Red Army intervened with its full force. In the course of a few days it had taken control. Kadar became the new strong man.

After the dramatic events of October-November 1956, Moscow tightened the reins once more. Khrushchev's policy of destalinization had suffered a defeat. Although he survived the 1957 challenge from his conservative rivals in the Soviet leadership, the course had to be altered. The attitude of the Soviet Union towards Tito became more sceptical. The cultural and political thaw was replaced by a colder climate once more. Collectivization accelerated anew in the Eastern European countries. COMECON and the Warsaw Pact were to be used more actively as instruments to control developments in Eastern Europe. In December 1957, a new communist world conference was held. Soviet leadership was emphasized. Attacks on 'revisionists' were far stronger than attacks on 'dogmatists'.

Despite its tighter grip, Moscow's dominance could never again be what it had been. Instead, the split in the communist camp would soon be greater than ever before.

The Split between the Soviet Union and China

There was no doubt that friction between the Soviet and the Chinese party leaders had existed for a long time. It was natural, at least in retrospect, for the Chinese to reproach Stalin for his cooperation with the Kuomintang that had resulted in the massacre of the communists in 1927. The popular front policy of the mid-30s suited the Chinese well in their struggle against Japan, whereas the 1941 Soviet non-aggression treaty with the same adversary can not have been in the interest of the Chinese. Likewise, it is unlikely that Stalin's recognition of Chiang Kai-shek as China's legitimate leader in August 1945 pleased Mao.

As we have seen, the Soviet support to the Chinese communists during the civil war was very limited (see pages 65–67). Both before and after the communist take-over, there were unmistakable signs that Moscow would try to maintain a special position in the parts of China that bordered on the Soviet Union. It is highly likely that Mao, for his part, wanted to limit the Soviet influence within the Chinese Communist party. Those who were considered most pro-Soviet were isolated. Kao Kang was frozen out of the leadership, and Wang Ming does not even seem to have been granted entrance into China.

Despite these occurrences and despite the harsh statements Mao himself issued after the split between the Soviet Union and China had become open and bitter, caution should be observed in describing Sino-Soviet relations as strained at too early a date. Throughout most of the 1950s, these two countries cooperated quite well.

In the first place, their systems of government were based on a shared Marxist-Leninist ideology. There were shades of difference in the two countries' interpretation and practice of this shared legacy. But there was no disagreement as to the fact that the Soviet Union was the undisputed leader within the communist movement.

For the most part Mao followed Soviet policies until 1958. Five-year plans were drawn up, the level of investment was very high, and giant projects within heavy industry were given priority over light industry and agriculture. Within agriculture, land redistribution was soon replaced by collectivization. Political fluctuations largely followed those in the Soviet Union. Mao's large-scale campaign, launched in May 1956 under the slogan 'Let a hundred flowers bloom, and a hundred schools of thought contend', could be seen as a local variant of destalinization. Both Moscow and Peking changed their policies towards the Third World. As late as at the world conference in December 1957, there were few participants who emphasized the leadership position of the Soviet Union as clearly as the Chinese, although they stressed their conviction that this leadership had to be accompanied by a special responsibility for cracking down on revisionists within the communist movement.

In the second place, the intensity of the cold war contributed to keeping the two countries together. The Soviet Union and China had one mutual enemy, the United States. The Chinese Communists needed Soviet support during the Korean war and in their conflict with Taiwan. As far as Korea was concerned, the Chinese may well have been disappointed at the business-like conditions on which the Soviet Union granted its military assistance. The same was true of Moscow's lukewarm stance during the Quemoy-Matsu conflicts of 1954–55 and 1958 (see page 154), but this was probably more evident in retrospect than at the time, Although the suspicious Stalin must have feared a new Tito in Mao, there could be no doubt in the Soviet Union that the Chinese Communists' victory had strengthened the USSR in relation to its main enemy, the United States. The 30-year alliance against Japan and countries

'China-Soviet friendship will safeguard peace'.
Woodcut by Li Hua, 1950.

allied with Japan that was established in February 1950 was an expression of this solidarity (see page 70).

In the third place, Soviet assistance to China was significant. It was true that the 300 million dollars Mao was granted in 1950 after his three-month visit in Moscow was quite certainly less than he had hoped for. However, the Soviet Union was the only country the Chinese could expect to receive economic and military assistance from. After Stalin's death this assistance was stepped up. New credits were granted, and entire factories were built by Soviet technicians, often in return for deliveries from those same factories. The Soviet Union relinquished its privileges in Port Arthur, in Dairen, in Manchuria and Sinkiang. Stalin had promised to terminate them in 1952, but they had been extended because of the Korean war. 6 500 Chinese students went to the Soviet Union to study, and, perhaps most significantly, the Soviet leaders promised in 1957 to help China develop nuclear weapons.

However, there were developments even in the 1950s that had a negative effect on Sino-Soviet unity. Khrushchev could never attain the position Stalin had enjoyed. Moreover, the Chinese were only partially in agreement with Khrushchev's criticism of his predecessor. Moscow's overtures towards Yugoslavia, emphasizing the several possible paths to communism, meant greater scope for China as well, although the Chinese would strongly distance themselves from Tito ideologically.

The events in Eastern Europe in 1956 illustrated the Chinese role in an interesting way. The Chinese defended Gomulka and the initial phase of the events in Hungary. However, when Moscow intervened it did so with Peking's support, as Nagy had abandoned fundamental communist principles. The fact that the Soviet Union wanted international approval of its intervention strengthened China's position. Finally, the incipient policy of detente with the West reduced both the willingness and the need to stand shoulder to shoulder against the United States. As we shall see, these two powers would also assess the advantages of detente differently.

In 1959, the Soviet Union reneged on its agreement to help China develop nuclear weapons. In the following year, economic assistance was stopped and the Soviet technicians suddenly withdrawn. The public polemics had already begun. From 1960 to 1962, these verbal attacks were indirect as the Chinese heaped abuse on the 'revisionists', particularly the Yugoslavs, while the Soviets thundered against 'dogmatists' and Albanians. However, few people were in doubt as to the true addressees.

The first minor border skirmishes took place as early as in July 1960. In 1962-63, the polemics changed to open, direct accusations. From 1965 relations between the two parties were nearly severed. In the course of the 1960s, the official relations also deteriorated rapidly, although there was never a formal diplomatic break. The border clashes increased in number and intensity, climaxing in March 1969 at the Ussuri River. On one occasion the Soviet Union suffered about 60 killed and wounded, while the figure for China was probably several hundred.

In 1967 the Soviet Union had 15 divisions along the Chinese border. In 1973 this figure had risen to 45, or 25 percent of the total Soviet forces. The Chinese had even more men on their side. Mao feared a Soviet attack and asked the Chinese people to 'store grain and dig deep tunnels' in anticipation of the war that might erupt. The situation became so strained that each of the two communist countries came to consider the United States a much lesser evil than the other side. (For the US-Soviet-Chinese triangle, see pages 110–112.)

Explanations for the Split

Many different factors must be included in order to explain the antagonism between the Soviet Union and China. They can be grouped into certain main categories. The ideological issues comprise one such group, the national issues another. The territorial disputes may be considered either a third group or an aspect of the national issues.

The ideological differences were in many ways the most conspicuous. They spanned a wide spectrum. In terms of foreign policy, Moscow emphasized its conviction that the socialist countries had now become so strong that war could be avoided and that peaceful co-existence between East and West should be possible. Peking agreed that socialism had grown stronger. It had actually become so strong that the imperialists ought to be forced to make concessions. Hand in hand with the Chinese scepticism towards peaceful co-existence went an emphasis on the socialist countries' duty to support 'wars of national liberation'.

As far as relations between the socialist countries were concerned, for a long time there was concurrence regarding the Soviet leadership role. However, after the split had widened, Peking placed primary emphasis on their conviction that relations ought to be based on the principles of equality and independence.

In terms of domestic policy, the possibilities for a peaceful transition to socialism were a primary concern. At least from the time of the Twentieth Soviet Party Congress in 1956, Moscow had maintained that such a transition was possible under certain conditions. The Chinese rejected this idea and stood firm on the premise that only a revolution could lead from capitalism to socialism. The Kremlin also claimed that when the proletariat had won its struggle, such as for instance in the Soviet Union, the dictatorship of the proletariat could be modified or even come to an end. The Chinese considered this too a dangerous heresy that would merely give bourgeois elements a new chance to gain influence. They felt that this had happened in the Soviet Union.

Domestic policy differences were most prominent during Peking's most ideological periods, the Great Leap Forward (1958–61) and especially the Cultural Revolution (1966–69). The Great Leap Forward represented China's liberation from the Soviet model. The level of ambitions was extremely high. Instead of relying on isolated giant projects within industry, built with Soviet assistance, more emphasis was now to be placed on small and medium-sized enterprises throughout the entire country. Agriculture was also to be incorporated in a more balanced manner than previously. Organizationally, the basic unit was to be the people's commune, which surpassed anything else within the communist world in its degree of collectivism. In many villages common eating and sleeping quarters were established.

The Great Leap was far from the success the authorities tried to give the impression of at first. The results were particularly poor within agriculture. Several million people probably lost their lives during the famines that were experienced in many areas.

The fiasco resulted in a weakening of Mao's strong position. He had to relinquish the office of president to Liu Shao-chi. However, attempts by more pro-Soviet circles, led by Defense Minister Peng Teh-huai, to exploit the situation to the advantage of rapprochement with the Soviet Union were unsuccessful. Peng was dismissed and replaced by Lin Piao.

A somewhat more moderate policy in China meant little in a larger context. The same was true of the transition from Khrushchev to Brezhnev and Kosygin. After a brief respite from the polemics following Khrushchev's demise, they were soon resumed, more bitterly than ever.

The Cultural Revolution resulted in a further escalation of the conflict. Now the enthusiasm of the masses was to save the Chinese revolution from bureaucracy and lead it on towards the highest form of communism in record-breaking time. The Soviet path was denounced in the sharpest possible terms as an attempt to reintroduce capitalism in the socialist world. At times, members of the Red Guard blockaded the Soviet embassy in Peking. Mao's standing reached new heights; he was the subject of a tremendous personality cult. He was considered the great renewer of world communism (and of the art of swimming: he ostensibly swam 15 kilometers in 65 minutes, not bad for a man of 72).

The many ideological disputes between Moscow and Peking were significant enough. But it is difficult to determine to what extent they were decisive in themselves, or whether they primarily reflected other factors that were subsequently cloaked in ideology.

On several issues, however, a substantial gap between theory and practice could be perceived. The Chinese issued exhortations on the need to combat capitalism and imperialism and proclaimed that several hundred million Chinese would survive even a nuclear war. In most practical contexts, however, they were reserved.

Thus Hong Kong and Macao were allowed to continue as 'imperialist enclaves' on Chinese soil. In contrast, although the Soviet Union emphasized the possibilities of peaceful co-existence, neither in theory nor in practice did that preclude support to 'wars of national liberation' in Africa and Asia.

Moreover, there was a clear tendency for the ideological accusations to play a lesser role in the 1970s than they had done in the 1960s. Certain accusations were almost the opposite of what they had been previously. Whereas the Chinese had long accused the Soviet Union of pursuing a weak, yielding course of policy, they later claimed that the Soviets' objective was world hegemony. 'Proletarian internationalism' grew increasingly weak, while anti-Soviet sentiments grew stronger. In several countries China supported anti-communist regimes on the basis of their resistance to Soviet influence (the Shah in Iran and Pinochet in Chile).

The different ideologies were not detached from reality; they had a source. To a great extent the ideological differences mirrored differing historical developments in the two countries. For instance, it was natural that the Soviet Union emphasized the role of industrial workers as a revolutionary vanguard, whereas the Chinese placed greater emphasis on the role of the peasants. From this basic difference arose divergent assessments of the relationship between city and countryside, between heavy industry, light industry, and agriculture.

The national issues were probably of the greatest significance. As in relations between the United States and Western Europe, an external threat and economic dependence could draw the two sides together. When the threat declined and dependence decreased, the antagonism became more open. This was even more evident in relations between the Soviet Union and China than between the United States and Western Europe.

Two countries seldom or never have identical interests. Two countries that were as different, as strong and as proud as the Soviet Union and China certainly did not. The Soviet Union was a world power and was used to other communist countries submitting to Soviet leadership. Perhaps China was not a major power at the moment, but the Chinese traditionally considered themselves the center of the world and believed they had a great future.

It was as natural for the Soviet Union to want to limit the number of nuclear powers as it was for China to want to develop such weapons. After the break in Sino-Soviet nuclear cooperation in 1959, Peking was bound to perceive the signing of the test ban agreement in 1963 as one more attempt to hinder China's production of nuclear weapons. China's and the Soviet Union's respective assessments of the horrors of nuclear war were influenced by the fact that for a long time both sides took it for granted that it was the Soviets and not the Chinese who would make the decision, if any, to start such a war.

In the Quemoy-Matsu issue, Peking's concern was the liberation of areas everyone agreed were Chinese. For the Soviets, relations with the United States were more important, a consideration which dictated the avoidance of a superpower conflict regarding these islands.

In the efforts of the Soviet leaders to improve relations with the countries of the Third World, India was of primary importance. The Chinese perspective on India was somewhat different. The boundaries were still in dispute, and this fact became more pressing after the Chinese had quelled the revolt (against China) in Tibet, and Dalai Lama had fled to India. In 1958-59, minor skirmishes took place between India and China. In 1962, open war ensued, in which the Chinese inflicted on the Indians a decisive defeat. The Soviet Union did not commit itself to either side during the war, but carried out a planned sale of Mig fighter planes to India.

The Cuban crisis in 1962 also resulted in polemics between the two communist countries. First, Peking criticized Moscow for having evidenced unwarranted boldness by stationing intermediate-range missiles on Cuba. When the missiles were withdrawn, Chinese criticism of the Soviet Union was harsh for having given in to US pressure.

On 23 August 1968, Prime Minister Chou En-lai described the Soviet invasion of Czechoslovakia as 'the most barefaced and typical specimen of Fascist power politics played by the Soviet revisionist clique against its so-called allies? Once again the perspectives were different. The Soviets were concerned about stopping tendencies towards dissolution within its Eastern European empire. The Chinese, who had supported the Soviet intervention in Hungary in 1956, now protested sharply. Peking was especially troubled by the so-called Brezhnev doctrine, which assigned Moscow the role of policing developments in the other socialist countries. The Chinese leaders feared that such a doctrine could justify even an invasion of China.

The territorial disputes concerned first and foremost the boundaries between the two countries. In 1858, 1860, 1864, and 1881, China had ceded large land areas in Central Asia and along the Pacific coast, amounting to a total of 1.5 million square kilometers, to Russia. It had long been Chinese policy, supported by both Chiang Kai-shek and Mao, to consider these agreements the result of coercion and thus unjust. Lenin had shown understanding for this point of view, although Moscow never proposed concrete changes in the boundaries.

A few years after the Soviet privileges in China had been relinquished in 1954–55, the Chinese cautiously began to re-open the boundary issue. From 1963 onwards they pursued it to the full. They did not demand the return of all the territory in question. Their point of departure was that the Chinese cession was to be considered invalid in principle. Thereafter the two countries were to negotiate on boundary changes, but it remained unclear which areas China would actually claim. Until agreement was reached, Peking was prepared to accept the status quo.

The Soviet Union dismissed all changes of any significance and was only willing to negotiate on minor details. To some extent, the disputed territories were important in themselves. Moreover, concessions could establish a dangerous precedent in relation to other countries, regardless of how unjust the old Czar agreements may have been at one time.

A number of other issues also involved the border areas. The Soviet position in Outer Mongolia was one of them. Although China had accepted Outer Mongolia as an independent nation in 1946, it was obvious that Peking wanted to bring the country within the Chinese sphere of influence and away from its close ties with the Soviet Union.

In the 1950s, the Soviet Union first wanted to import Chinese laborers to Siberia; then it began to fear that such an import could complicate the border issue. Moscow was also interested in acquiring submarine bases and radio stations on Chinese soil. The Chinese rejected this proposal, which they considered practically an attempt to undermine China's sovereignty.

China was far too vast to be dominated by outside powers, as the Soviet Union was not the first to experience. The fact that the communists in China had risen to power by their own efforts gave them an independence that most of the other communists lacked. This independent basis was undoubtedly one of the most important conditions for the split between the Soviet Union and China, as it had been between the Soviet Union and Yugoslavia.

The Soviet-Chinese-US Triangle after 1972

One of the chief controversies during the initial phase of the Sino-Soviet conflict was the question of relations with the capitalist countries, especially the United States. Peking had been highly negative to Khrushchev's policy of detente. However, this condemnation could not prevent rapprochement between the United States and China in 1971-72 (see pages 110-112).

Relations between the United States and China became steadily better throughout the 1970s, and a climax was reached in 1978-79 with full diplomatic recognition, a substantial increase in trade, and a number of cooperation agreements in various fields. Early in 1980 the United States declared its willingness to sell 'non-lethal' military equipment to China. Whereas Washington had had fairly good relations with both Moscow and Peking in the early 1970s, contact with China was much better than with the Soviet Union at the end of the decade. Both China and the West considered the Soviet Union an expansive power, in southern Africa, on the Horn of Africa, in Afghanistan, and in Indo-China.

Although the border clashes between the Soviet Union and China decreased in intensity after 1969, and although attempts were made to improve relations between the two communist nations, there was no real rapprochement between Moscow and Peking during the 1970s. The climax in US-Chinese cooperation coincided with a new, although temporary, deterioration in Sino-Soviet relations. In 1979 there were large-scale clashes between Vietnam and China, a situation that was mostly attributable to the Vietnamese invasion of Cambodia. Peking obviously wanted to teach Hanoi, now allied with Moscow, a lesson for having invaded a pro-Chinese nation. The Soviet invasion of Afghanistan in December 1979 represented a further strain on Sino-Soviet relations.

At the same time, cautious new signals could be perceived, signals that grew stronger in the course of the 1980s. The major controversies persisted, but the polemics were toned down. Trade and other contacts increased. Meetings took place between high-ranking representatives for the two countries. Initiatives were taken to improve the situation, both in terms of border disputes and party contacts.

This new mood had several causes. Important changes took place in China. Although the Cultural Revolution was on the wane after 1969, there were still radical elements among the party leaders. The fear of a 'Soviet-revisionist contagion' persisted. As long as Mao Tse-tung was alive, it seemed unlikely that the climate could be changed. After Mao's death in 1976 and after the moderates had consolidated their power under Teng Hsiao-p'ing's leadership in 1978-79, conditions were more favorable. The new leaders were prepared to have pragmatic relations with other countries, primarily to promote a large-scale modernization campaign based on a unique combination of communist and capitalist ideas. This dictated more tranquil relations not only with the United States, but with the Soviet Union as well.

The fear of a Soviet attack was also abating. At the close of the 1960s the atmosphere had been characterized by the Brezhnev doctrine, extensive border clashes, and Soviet hints of the use of nuclear weapons against China. Even during the Sino-Vietnamese conflict and the Soviet invasion of Afghanistan, the tension level did not reach the heights it had manifested ten years earlier. After Gorbachev took over in 1985, he made determined efforts to improve relations with China. The climate did improve further, but the basic issues remained unresolved.

The two countries' relations with the United States were also significant. The situation in the 1970s had given Washington a central role. The Americans could, if they chose to, alternately favor the one or the other of the two rivals. The Soviet Union and China did not have the same maneuvering possibilities. Both Peking and Moscow must have perceived the negative consequences this situation entailed for them.

At the end of Carter's presidency, new tension arose in relations between China and the United States. The question of Taiwan was a primary reason. Both sides agreed that Taiwan was a part of China. The United States had also promised, as early as in 1972, to re-evaluate its commitments to Taiwan in light of the overall situation in the region. But although US forces on the island had been reduced to 2 500 men, advanced weapons were still being sold to Taiwan.

Reagan's assumption of office resulted in increased tensions. During his election campaign he had promised to strengthen relations with Taiwan. The objective was a two-China policy. The president belonged to the Republican right wing, with its traditional partiality to Taiwan. Dissatisfaction with the new administration's stance was one factor behind China's somewhat improved relations with the Soviet Union.

Even so, Reagan did not go as far as he had first given the impression of. The need for a partner against the Soviet Union steadily increased and proved to be stronger than the conservative ties to Taiwan. The Chinese, on their part, needed US support, partly in relation to the Soviet Union, but just as much to accomplish their four-fold modernization program (industry, technology, defense, and agriculture). All in all, there were thus not such great changes in China's relations with the United States under Reagan. In 1984–85 Reagan even approved the sale of further types of weapons to China.

Soviet Relations with Eastern Europe after 1958

The split between the Soviet Union and China had dramatic effects on communist unity. The fact that the world's most populous country so openly challenged Moscow had consequences in virtually all the communist parties in the world. As long as the conflict was carried out within certain limits, Peking's criticism expanded the spectrum for what deviations in opinion the Soviet Union had to tolerate. After the breach was complete, the Kremlin's need for support in its struggle against the Chinese was exploited by the other Communist parties to their own advantage. Some of the parties even chose to follow the Chinese pattern. Moscow's authority could never be the same after the exchanges of verbal abuse between the Soviet Union and China. Finally, the strife demonstrated both that there were many paths to communism and that its victory had certainly not quashed nationalism as a driving force in relations between communist powers.

Even little Albania struck out an independent course. The country's relations with the Soviet Union were still largely a reflection of Yugoslavia's relations with the communist superpower. After the rapprochement between Khrushchev and Tito in 1955, the Albanians distanced themselves from the Soviet Union, subsequently to enter into cooperation with China against the Yugoslavian-Soviet revisionists. When revisionism began to appear even in China at the close of the 1970s, 'Europe's lighthouse' chose to remain quite isolated ideologically.

The process towards greater scope for the various countries of Eastern Europe could not be reversed. Under a surface of loyalty to the Soviet Union and the communist system, the various governments would pursue different policies in many areas, both in domestic policy and to some extent in foreign policy as well.

The factors that had previously contributed to weakening the position of the Soviet Union continued to have effect, including events within the Soviet Union itself. Stalin's death was the great watershed, but the fall of Khrushchev in October 1964 had a similar effect. Most of the leaders in Eastern Europe had had, or at least had developed, close relations with Khrushchev. Now the most powerful man in the Soviet Union was quite simply deposed. From the perspective of the Eastern European leaders, this could establish a dangerous precedent both in relation to their own parties and in relations with the Soviet Union. Thus they were more convinced than ever that in addition to goodwill in Moscow they needed a local power base that was preferably strong enough to make them more or less immune to shifts in the Kremlin.

Yugoslavia persisted on its independent course. After relations with the Soviet Union had been strained for a number of years because of the events in Hungary in 1956, they improved again, although they did not return to the level of 1955—early 1956. In 1964 Yugoslavia became an associate member of COMECON, but the country carried on extensive trade with the OECD and EEC countries at the same time. Yugoslavia was also one of the leading spokesmen for the non-aligned nations. This represented a substantial spectrum of contacts, which many Eastern Europeans regarded with envy.

A number of factors would further weaken the position of the Soviet Union in Eastern Europe, as in the rest of the communist world. The shared ideology deteriorated into ritual incantations, with little or no innovative thinking. In Eastern Europe, as in the Soviet Union, it became a modest superstructure over an enormous party apparatus. There was little left of the enthusiasm that had characterized at least certain parts of the population previously.

The policy of detente increased the freedom of action of Eastern Eu-

227

rope as well. The Kremlin established a network of contacts in the West and could not deny the Eastern Europeans the possibility of doing the same. Trade increased, as did imports of Western technology. If the Eastern Europeans were dissatisfied with the conditions Moscow had to offer, they could now turn to the West to some extent. The increased economic freedom of action was accompanied by political contacts. Both Moscow and the various capitals of Eastern Europe were, to varying degrees, interested in preventing Western ideas from creeping in with the political and economic contacts, but in several countries detente contributed to a certain degree of fragmentation of the communist power monopoly.

The policy of detente also made it difficult to use the danger from the West as an argument for solidarity within the Eastern bloc. The threat represented by 'German revanchism' had been of primary importance in this connection. Instead, for most of the Eastern European countries West Germany now became the most important trade partner and political contact in the Western world. The consequences of this new attitude would be particularly great in Poland, where anti-German feelings had been the strongest.

Eastern Europe acquired a position of increasing freedom in relation to the Soviet Union. Even so, there were clear limitations to these countries' freedom of action. The Soviet Union still had great influence, because of its geographic proximity and because of the instruments of power Moscow had at its disposal. With the exception of Yugoslavia and especially Albania, there were still close political, economic and military ties between the Soviet Union and the countries of Eastern Europe. In addition, most of the local communist leaders had a distinct need for support from the Kremlin. Their local power bases were not so strong that they could act too independently in relation to Moscow.

The countries that represented the least problem for the Soviet Union were Bulgaria and East Germany. Sofia stood by the close cooperation Bulgaria had always had with Moscow. East Germany was militarily, politically, and to some extent also economically highly dependent on the Soviet Union. Party leader Walter Ulbricht feared that the Soviet Union would enter into agreements with Bonn without his knowledge. He did not like the Soviet policy of rapprochement with West Germany, and in 1971 he was replaced by Erich Honecker.

During the 1980s, and especially in 1983-84, East Germany began to show signs of greater independence. The country had the highest standard of living in Eastern Europe. Its existence had finally been universally recognized. For both economic and political reasons, East Berlin was now more interested than Moscow in maintaining good relations with the West, particularly with West Germany. However, the Soviet Union placed clear limitations on how far Honecker could go in his efforts to sustain the policy of detente between the two German states in an era characterized by frostier relations between East and West.

In the 1960s, Hungary embarked on a more liberal course of domestic policy than any other country in Eastern Europe (with the exception of Yugoslavia). Cultural life enjoyed greater freedom. From 1968 onwards the economy was less centrally controlled, and market forces were granted more latitude. In terms of foreign policy, Budapest pursued a course that was more faithful to Moscow. All in all, Janos Kadar, the hated leader from 1956, managed to make himself perhaps the most popular leader in Eastern Europe.

The fact that there was no correlation between a liberal or dogmatic domestic policy and dependence on or independence of Moscow was illustrated by developments in Albania and Hungary, and by Romania as well. Under Gheorghiu Dej, and from 1964 under Nikolae Ceausescu, Romania pursued a dogmatic course in domestic policy. In terms of foreign policy, this country was the most independent of all the members of the Warsaw Pact.

The Soviet troops were withdrawn from Romania in 1958. As soon as they were gone, new attitudes cropped up. The occasion was the Soviet attempts at division of labor and integration within COMECON. Those who were to be 'industrial countries'—the Soviet Union, East Germany, and Czechoslovakia—were far more satisfied with the plan than those who were to be responsible for agricultural production. Among the latter category, Romania, which had traditionally been sceptical of Russia, reacted the most vehemently. Instead, the country embarked on an industrial build-up based on its own resources and increased trade with the West. During the 1970s, machines and entire manufacturing plants were imported from the West.

There was no question of Romania withdrawing from the Warsaw Pact, but the country became more and more passive in this organization. The Romanian leaders even questioned the Soviet takeover of Bessarabia—northern Bukovina. In the Sino-Soviet conflict, the Romanians tried to remain as neutral as possible and were eager to act as mediators.

A genealogical tree
(Jusp in *Wir Bruckenbauer*)
(Zürich)

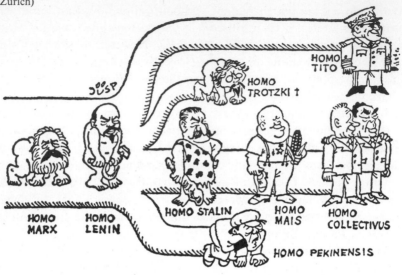

Relations with France were good, and Romania was often described as the France of the East bloc. As the first Eastern European country after the Soviet Union, Romania recognized West Germany in 1967. During the conflict in the Middle East in that same year, Bucharest sustained its relations with Israel. The Romanians did not take part in the invasion of Czechoslovakia, and they, together with the Yugoslavs, clearly warned the Soviet Union against taking similar actions in other countries. Romania's independent foreign policy continued during the 1970s and 1980s.

Czechoslovakia—1968

The events in Czechoslovakia in 1968 arose from internal conditions. The rate of economic growth had long been among the highest in Eastern Europe. However, it leveled off altogether in the early 1960s. In order to stimulate the economy once more, reforms were instituted. Whereas growth would stimulate cultural liberalization in Hungary, economic failure led to similar changes in Czechoslovakia.

As in Poland and Hungary in 1956, time would show that a partial dictatorship was a more difficult form of government for the authorities than a firm dictatorship. Those who favored reforms thought that the reforms fell short. The dogmatists felt they went too far and became disillusioned. In January 1968, the strong man ever since 1953, Antonin Novotny, was forced to withdraw as general secretary of the party. He was replaced by the party leader in Slovakia, Aleksander Dubcek.

Dubcek and his collaborators felt they had learned from the events of 1956. Liberalization had to be limited. Two limits were absolute: Czechoslovakia's participation in the Warsaw Pact could not be questioned, and a system with more than one party could not be allowed.

Even so, the course of developments soon gave rise to concern in the Soviet Union and even more so in East Germany and Poland. The repeal of press censorship meant that the authorities had sacrificed an important instrument of control. The dogmatists were pushed aside. New, independent persons took over. Parties that agreed to cooperate with the Communist party under its leadership were to be allowed. What would be next?

On 20 August, the Red Army invaded Czechoslovakia, with the support of smaller units from Poland, East Germany, Hungary, and Bulgaria. As usual, we know little of the decision-making process on the part of the Soviet Union. But the situation in Czechoslovakia seemed steadily more disquieting for the Kremlin. The Fourteenth Party Congress was expected to result in further replacement of elements that were loyal to the Soviet Union. Ulbricht and Gomulka applied pressure, as did the party leader in the Ukraine, Pjotr Shelest. He, too, feared that the 'Czechoslovakian disease' would spread. Domino theories were easy to resort to, in Moscow as in Washington. The risk an invasion entailed was small. The Western powers would not respond in military terms, and there were indications that even the political reaction would be more limited than could be feared.

The invasion was justified by the Brezhnev doctrine. A socialist nation was duty bound to intervene in another socialist nation if the socialist form of government as such was threatened. The invasion did not meet with any military opposition, and the deaths were few. In April 1969, Dubcek was replaced by Gustav Husak. Some people hoped that Husak, who himself had been imprisoned under Novotny, would become a new Kadar: a leader who would embark on a liberal course once he had got the situation under control. This would prove not to be the case. The resemblance to Gomulka was greater.

Developments in Poland

The invasion of Czechoslovakia showed that the Soviet Union had effective means of stopping the process of dissolution in Eastern Europe, if it went too far in the Kremlin's opinion. But such means could only be employed in extreme situations. Developments in Poland would demonstrate how difficult it had become to repeat operations such as those in East Germany in 1953, in Hungary in 1956, and in Czechoslovakia in 1968.

There had been high expectations focused on Gomulka when he assumed power in 1956. Important reforms were instituted. Collectivization of agriculture was largely done away with. The church was granted a freer position than in any other Eastern European country. Soviet influence was reduced. But Gomulka was no liberal. After a short time, the grip was tightened once more. Cultural and intellectual life was closely controlled. At the end of the 1960s, the repression was the harshest since the Stalin era.

In 1970 Gomulka was aging, ailing and exhausted. The economy was in serious difficulties. In order to increase government revenue, the prices of consumer goods were raised substantially just before Christmas. That resulted in a repetition of 1956, the only difference being even more extensive demonstrations and protests. The new man the party rallied round was Edward Gierek.

Gierek concentrated on large-scale imports of Western technology to increase investments and economic growth. This policy showed good results during the first years. After that the economy declined once more.

New wide-spread demonstrations erupted in 1976. Once again, the economic situation was the point of departure. Again the authorities had to go back on proposed price increases. The situation did not improve after 1976. The economic crisis grew steadily worse and the political base for the regime narrower. In contrast to the party's dwindling authority was the church's ever stronger position, clearly manifested in the 'Polish' Pope John Paul II's journey to Poland in the summer of 1979.

In August 1980, extensive strikes broke out in protest against new price increases. Effective cooperation was instituted between workers and intellectuals, who jointly demanded free trade unions.

The new trade union, Solidarity, under the leadership of Lech Walesa, soon established itself as a third center of power, alongside the party and the church. The trade union was to pursue union concerns and keep clear of political issues that could undermine the position of the Communist party. This delimitation was bound to be unclear. Calls for the repeal of censorship, a more democratic Communist party, and finally free elections demonstrated the fact that Solidarity's demands had acquired clearly political dimensions.

The Soviet Union watched developments in Poland with the greatest unease. Through military maneuvers and other forms of pressure, the Kremlin tried to limit the party's concessions, without success. Direct intervention was hardly an alluring alternative. It could meet with considerable opposition from the Polish population in general and perhaps from parts of the army as well. The Western powers warned that a Soviet invasion would produce greater consequences than had been the case in similar situations previously. Poland's economic distress was considerable and its dependence on the West was great, which indicated that Moscow was bound to be interested in limiting its direct responsibility for developments in the country.

The unexpected solution was that the Polish army under General Jaruzelski took control and declared a state of emergency in December 1981. Jaruzelski had become party leader as early as in October 1981. The Western powers, led by the United States, responded with a limited economic boycott. Although the party had practically collapsed, the new leadership managed to stabilize the situation after a fashion.

The Soviet Union and the Communist Movement Elsewhere

Certain countries outside of Eastern Europe were also highly dependent on the Soviet Union. Outer Mongolia was one such example. This country's ties to Moscow went back to the 1920s and largely reflected a desire for protection against China. Mongolia was admitted to COMECON in 1962, and large numbers of Soviet troops were stationed in the country. In Afghanistan, the Karmal regime, which was installed in December 1979, would probably have had a short life span if it had not been for the massive Soviet military effort (see page 131).

Cuba and North Vietnam also supported the Soviet Union. They accepted the leadership of the Soviet Union, but did so mainly for their own reasons. These regimes had not risen to power with the help of the Red Army, but on the contrary had independent power bases. It was another matter that they could gradually become more closely bound to Moscow than they may have intended at first.

After Castro's Cuba had shown clear signs of independence during the 1960s, such as in its attempts to export the Cuban revolution to other countries in Latin America, and in its attitude towards the Sino-Soviet conflict, the country gradually began to pursue a clearly pro-Moscow course. Castro approved of the invasion of Czechoslovakia, supported the Soviet Union against China, and cooperated with the Soviet Union in Africa. In 1972 Cuba became a member of COMECON.

North Vietnam, which acquired control over South Vietnam and then over Laos in 1975, and from 1978 in Cambodia, abandoned the balancing act between Moscow and Peking that had characterized the country prior to the mid-70s. Hanoi now supported the Soviet Union openly. In 1978, Vietnam joined COMECON and entered into a 25-year friendship and cooperation agreement with Moscow. The Soviet Union acquired base rights in Vietnam.

Cuban and Vietnamese support for the Soviet Union was to a considerable extent situational. Cuba sought protection against the United States in Moscow, and the Cuban economy had become dependent on the Soviet economy. Vietnam had also received support against the United States. After the end of the Vietnam war, Hanoi came into serious conflict with Peking over boundary issues and over developments in Cambodia. That tied Vietnam even more closely to Moscow.

The split in the communist movement expressed itself more clearly in Moscow's relations with other major Communist parties. In North Korea, the country's leader, Kim Il-sung, wanted to keep on good terms with both of its large neighbors. To a great extent he managed to secure his own and North Korea's interests during the bitter Sino-Soviet dispute.

The largest non-governing Communist parties were to be found in Indonesia and in Italy. The Indonesian party had embarked on a pro-Chinese course in the 1960s, but was completely crushed during the chaotic events of the coup and counter-coup in the autumn of 1965. The army's assumption of power ushered in a witch hunt for true and imagined Communists, and approximately 500 000 persons lost their lives.

The Italian Communist party had shown signs of independence even before the death of party leader Togliatti in 1964, but the breakthrough came with the denunciation of the Soviet invasion of Czechoslovakia. Later, the party would distance itself further from Moscow. The Italian Communist party (PCI) refused to take a stand in opposition to China and accepted Italy's membership in NATO and the EC. In terms of domestic policy, the party placed emphasis on appearing both as a defender of democratic rights and as a spokesman for broad cooperation in the trade union movement and in the national assembly. Even so, the Communists were not accepted as members of the government. They did not effect a complete break with the Soviet Union. They still considered themselves a part of the world-wide communist movement, but with the right to determine their own policies.

The Italian version of 'Euro-communism' enjoyed support to some extent in France as well. For a time the small Spanish Communist party pursued its independence even further than the Italian, whereas the French party returned to a more traditional stand in 1978-79. This was apparently due to the need for a sharper profile in relation to the growing socialist party. Thus the change of course arose primarily from domestic French considerations. Moscow no longer had the authority to dictate developments in the Western European parties. But the new course gradually helped bring the French communists down to the 10 percent mark, while the Italian party, still a major political force, attracted almost one voter in three in 1985–86. But even the Italian party was losing votes.

In few places were the changes in the position of the Soviet Union greater than in Africa. Moscow could achieve success from time to time, but setbacks had a tendency to follow close on its heels. During the 1960s the Kremlin pinned its hopes on Ghana and Guinea. Ghana in particular proved a disappointment seen from a Soviet perspective. Then Egypt became the primary partner for cooperation, until the Soviets were thrown out in 1972. The same thing happened in Somalia in 1977.

The Marxist-inspired parties in Africa were quite different from ordinary Communist parties. Their ideological content could be highly syncretic. Thus Moscow had to concentrate more on ideological schooling. At the close of the 1970s the Soviet position was the strongest in Angola, in Ethiopia, and to a lesser extent in Mozambique (see pages 128–130). In Angola and Ethiopia the Soviet-Cuban presence was extensive. The Kremlin gave substantial military and economic assistance to all three countries. Twenty-year friendship and cooperation agreements were signed with Angola (1976), Mozambique (1977), and Ethiopia (1978).

But in 1984 there were signs that Soviet influence was declining even in these countries. Mozambique entered into a non-aggression treaty and Angola a cease-fire agreement with the hated regime in South Africa.

The Africans were eager to strengthen economic relations with the West. In the economic sphere it was still the case that the Communist countries could hardly compete with the Western powers. On the other hand, the unsettled internal political situation and, in Angola and Mozambique, the continued problems with South Africa maintained their ties with the Soviet Union and Cuba.

9. Decolonization

When the United Nations was established in 1945, the organization had 51 member nations. By 1986, this figure had risen to 159. Most of this growth was attributable to new states in Asia and Africa. During the course of the 1940s most of the Asian colonies became independent. In Africa there were still only four formally independent countries: Ethiopia, South Africa, Liberia, and Egypt. By 1976, when decolonization had been completed for the most part, this figure had risen to 48.

A revolution had taken place in international politics. This revolution had many different causes. Following the model developed by the historians Ronald Robinson and Wm. Roger Louis, I shall relate these causes to three levels—the international level, the national level (the colonial powers), and the local level (the colonies).

Changes on the International Level

The Second World War meant a sharp reduction in the international influence of the traditional colonial powers. There was a relative shift of power away from Britain, France, and the smaller European colonial nations to the two new superpowers, the United States and the Soviet Union. They were both characterized by an anti-colonial heritage and would accelerate the process of decolonization, in their own separate ways.

The principles on which Washington's attitude was based were clear enough. The existence of colonies conflicted with the right of national self-determination. As the United States had once torn itself loose from Britain, it was inevitable that other colonies would attain their freedom. It was the Americans' duty to hasten this process.

This point of departure had not prevented the United States from acquiring colonies. The most important of them was the Philippines, which the United States took over from Spain after the Spanish-American War of 1898. The time perspective for independence could be extremely long-term. Even such an anti-colonialist as Franklin Roosevelt was convinced during WW II that it could take 50 or 100 years before many of the colonies would gain their independence. After the war, opposition to colonial rule was accommodated to other objectives, such as the need to cooperate with allies and to contain communist expansion.

All these modifications could not change the fact that the United States was an important factor behind decolonization. In the first place, as early as in 1935 the United States had promised the Philippines their independence. Washington actually proceeded more quickly than some of the colony's own leaders appreciated. In 1946, the Philippines became independent. Relations with the United States were still very close in both the economic and the military spheres, but even so the United States was the first country to divest itself of a non-white colony. The example was bound to have certain liberating effects.

In the second place, the US attitude contributed to establishing the basis for changes in the policies of the more traditional colonial powers. Especially during WW II, Washington encouraged the institution of reforms, and in their long-term planning the British in particular took this into consideration. When India was promised independence and the African colonies significant although far less comprehensive reforms, the US attitude was one of many factors behind these commitments. The willingness of the United States to apply direct pressure in order to influence the European colonial powers was greatest where the colonial power was weak and the liberation movement clearly anti-communist. US policy in relation to Indonesia was the best example of this fact, although Washington waited until as late as 1948–49 to take an unequivocal stand even against the Netherlands (see pages 67–68).

In the third place, the liberation movements played on the attitude and powerful position of the United States. One of many examples of this was the fact that the Vietnamese independence declaration of 2 September 1945 followed the US declaration of independence of 1776 in several respects. This was an attempt to engage the United States on the side of the Vietnamese. But as France was an important power in European politics and the liberation movement in Vietnam was under communist leadership, US pressure here was much weaker than on the Netherlands in Indonesia.

The influence of the Soviet Union on the struggles for independence was also many-faceted. Moscow's policy line was clearly anti-colonial. All colonies had to be granted independence (with the exception of the areas in Asia that Russia itself had assumed control of during the 1700s and 1800s, of course). Marx had proclaimed imperialism the highest stage of capitalism. Local communists were often among those who were most active in the struggle for liberation. It was another matter that Moscow showed limited interest in what took place in most of Asia and Africa. Moreover, shortly after WW II Moscow began to consider many of the nationalist leaders 'Western lackeys' (see pages 68–70). This attitude often caused strife between communists and others who were fighting for their country's independence.

During the post-war era, it became increasingly more important for the colonial powers to institute reforms at such an early stage that the independence movements in the various areas did not become more radical and fall under communist leadership. If armed struggle ensued, the Soviet Union could supply weapons. Thus the Soviet Union influenced the actions of the colonial powers both through its policies and by its mere existence. But once a movement had become 'communist', and the definition of communism could vary considerably from one capital to another, the colonial powers almost always became less willing to grant independence. France's policy in Indo-China was to some extent determined by such considerations.

On the international level, it was also significant that organizations were created that placed limitations on the freedom of action of the colonial powers. This had already been illustrated under the League of Nations during the period between the two world wars. The mandate system of the League hastened the process of independence. The British granted Iraq independence in 1932. In 1944–46, Syria and Lebanon, former French colonies, attained their independence, as did Jordan, a British colony. Even so, these mandates—formerly Turkish—were considered so unique that developments there had little influence both on British and French colonial policies and on independence movements in general.

After the Second World War, the remaining mandates were placed under the UN supervision system along with the colonies Italy and Japan had to relinquish. The trusteeship system that was established tended towards reform, although it only affected a small number of areas, and although the colonial powers had a tendency to treat them in the same way as the other colonies they controlled. For instance, this was true of Britain's policies in the previously German Tanganyika, which the

239

British took over just after WW I. Libya, which had been Italian, represented a different course. International influence, combined with major power rivalry as to who should have control, resulted in this colony acquiring its independence as early as in 1951.

The UN accelerated the process of independence in other ways as well. Chapter XI of the UN Charter contained vague promises of future independence even for 'non-self-governing territories'. The new nations that gradually joined the organization were naturally preoccupied with independence for the remaining colonies. They questioned the policies of the colonial powers almost incessantly. This pressure was strongly reinforced by the support the new nations' viewpoints enjoyed around the world, primarily in the colonies, but in the Soviet Union and the United States as well and even within the colonial powers themselves.

The National Level: Changes within the Colonial Powers

After 1945, major changes took place in the colonial powers' capacity and willingness to retain their colonies. Their capacity was influenced by their weakened international position, by economic problems, and by many other considerations. These factors were important enough, although they were more relative than absolute in the sense that none of the European colonial powers actually had fewer resources than they had had in the period between the wars, at least not after the reconstruction years were over. Their will was thus at least as important as their capacity. Many politicians and segments of public opinion changed their attitudes towards colonies altogether, and even larger groups no longer wanted to use the force that was necessary to retain forms of rule that violated the ideals they acclaimed in their own countries. The significance of this factor was emphasized by the fact that the poorest and least democratic of the colonial powers, Portugal, retained its colonies for the longest time.

British Policies

The United Kingdom was the leading colonial power, both by virtue of controlling the largest areas and by setting an example in many ways to which the others had to accommodate themselves. The British colonial empire rested on a thin veneer of control. The British had only 4 000 bureaucrats in India in the 1930s, along with 60 000 soldiers and 90 000 civilians, mostly businessmen and ecclesiatical personnel, in a country of about 300 million inhabitants. This huge empire could only be sustained if the British enjoyed a certain amount of active or at least passive support from their Indian subjects.

For a long time the British were able to enlist such support. A combination of reforms and the use of force ensured the necessary control. Force alone was not politically acceptable in the long run. The Amritsar massacre in 1919, where British soldiers opened fire on an Indian public meeting, killing several hundred persons, had demonstrated this fact. The incident had occasioned sharp protests, not only in India, but in Britain as well. Without the use of force it was merely a question of time until the entire empire would collapse. The only difference was the somewhat unequal pace of developments in the various regions.

One theory of decolonization has been that it was more or less a logical process that would inevitably result in the dismantling of the colonial empires. This process had actually begun with the achievement of US independence from Britain in the 1770s and 1780s. The United States was followed by the white dominions of Canada, Australia, New Zealand, and South Africa. The Spanish empire collapsed as far back as after the Napoleonic wars.

India was supposedly the next rung on the ladder of history. The British gradually relinquished local control over the country. The most important stages in this process were the two Government of India Acts of 1919 and 1935. The first of these instituted an Indian Parliament with very limited power, as well as local assemblies with more extensive authority. The second Act increased the freedom of action of both the national and the local governing bodies. Independence ensued in 1947. Thus the floodgates were opened for the non-white colonies. In the wake of India followed the other British colonies in Asia, and from Asia the wave of independence swept over Africa. What Britain had begun, others had to complete: the Netherlands, France, Belgium, and finally Portugal as well.

This theory does contain elements of truth, but it is far too condensed and makes decolonization a much simpler process than it actually was. Most of the colonies were acquired after the first ones had already gained their independence. One colonial power did influence another, but there were still substantial differences among them. For a long time the purpose of the British reforms was not to prepare the colonies for future independence, but instead to lay a better foundation for retaining control more easily. Finally, it was quite clear, at least at the time, that the differences were tremendous between the policies that could be pursued in Asia and the policies that could be implemented in the far less developed Africa. For that matter, the differences were also great within such vast areas as Asia and Africa.

Before and during the Second World War few, if any, leading politicians foresaw the pace and extent of decolonization that would take place in Asia and particularly in Africa during the post-war era. In November 1942, Churchill said that he had not become the King's Prime Minister in order to preside over the dissolution of the British empire. However, developments in Asia were in the process of outdistancing the British prime minister. Equally memorable, and perhaps more representative of the sentiments of the common people, was the comment of Labour's deputy leader Herbert Morrison, that independence for the African colonies would be 'like giving a child of ten a latch-key, a bank account, and a shot-gun'. In France and Portugal, there was talk long after the war of an unending union between mother country and colonies.

During the war, both the Conservatives and Labour opposed the demands of the Indian Congress Party for immediate independence. London long refused to discuss this question until the war was over, although there was little doubt that India would then have to be granted at least a high degree of self-government. The Indian 'Quit India' movement of 1942, combined with the need for support in the war against Japan and Germany, made the British prepare themselves for further concessions. It became the official policy that India would be granted full dominion status after the war, with the right even to leave the Commonwealth. Exactly how quickly this process would proceed was somewhat unclear as yet. Although Labour, assuming power in the summer of 1945, did not have a set schedule, they were more willing than the Conservatives to make concessions to the Congress Party.

In February 1947, Prime Minister Attlee declared that Britain would withdraw from India by June 1948. In reality, events would unfold even more rapidly. Because of pressure from the Congress Party leaders and Britain's strained economy, India was declared independent already in August 1947. The Attlee government also had to abandon attempts to keep India unified. Pakistan was partitioned off as a separate country. Hindus opposed Moslems, a division the British had previously tried to exploit through the tactic of 'divide and rule'. Burma and Ceylon, too, became independent in 1947–48.

Few if any members of the British colonial administration believed that the events in India would have much relevance for the African colonies. The Labour government envisioned a period of several decades of social and economic reforms that perhaps in the long run would lay the foundation for political independence there. In 1945 there was not yet a single party in any of the British colonies in Africa that had complete independence on its political platform.

Although the actors of the day did not see them, in retrospect we can see forerunners of the events that were to ensue in the 1950s. The first of a series of sporadic Pan-African Congresses was held as early as in 1900. The first elected representatives of the local legislative councils had assumed their seats at the beginning of the 1920s, and the constitutions of 1946 increased their power considerably in the Gold Coast and Nigeria. Minor reforms led to demands for more reforms, and it was not possible to halt this process without using physical force to an extent that was unacceptable.

The Sixth Pan-African Congress had been held in Manchester in October 1945. For the first time, the Africans were in a majority in relation to the American Negroes they had learned so much from. The conference approved a highly radical program: complete independence for a unified Africa based on a socialistic economy. One of the participants at the conference was Kwame Nkrumah. A unified independent Africa was an unrealistic demand; the same was true of a unified West Africa. Nkrumah returned to the Gold Coast to lead the struggle for independence there.

The revolt in Accra in 1948 stimulated forces that had long undermined British control. In 1949 Nkrumah founded a new political party, the Convention People's Party, which pressed for dominion status. This party employed methods that had been developed by the nationalist leaders in India. Like them, Nkrumah landed in jail, but as had been the case for the Indian leaders, that did not diminish his popularity. In 1951 his party won an overwhelming election victory. The British had either to make concessions or resort to harsher measures. In many ways, the outcome was obvious. In 1957, the Gold Coast, under the name of Ghana, became the first of the new independent nations of West Africa. Nigeria followed suit in 1960. Major regional problems slowed the process there compared to in Ghana.

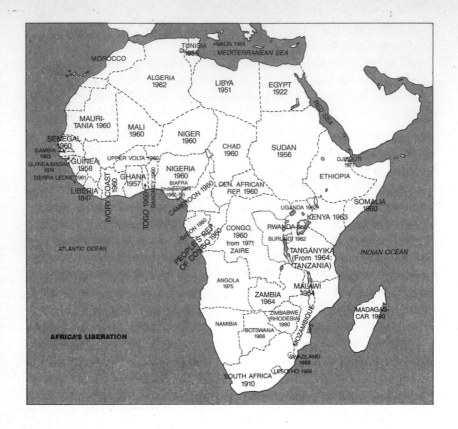

The British, and conservative circles in particular, perceived great differences between West and East Africa. In East Africa the white minority was larger and the level of cultural and economic development among the Africans not as advanced as in West Africa. In areas such as Kenya and Southern Rhodesia, the settlers had a particularly strong position, and there had been a substantial amount of immigration after 1945. Thus the white population of Kenya rose from 12 000 in 1945 to more than 50 000 ten years later. In Southern Rhodesia, the corresponding figures were 80 000 and more than 200 000. As late as in April 1959, Colonial Secretary Alan Lennox Boyd stated that he was 'unable to envisage a time when it will be possible for any British Government to surrender the ultimate responsibilities for the destinies and well-being of Kenya.'

244

However, the process leading to independence continued to accelerate. Sudan had acquired its independence as early as in 1955, but was considered an exception as the country had formally been governed as a British-Egyptian condominium. The concessions London had to make in West Africa could not be denied in East Africa. In Ghana, it took 32 years from the time of the election of the first members to the local assembly until the country became independent. In Tanganyika, which represented the great breakthrough in East Africa, the same course of developments took 39 months. Nigeria had 9 years of local autonomy before gaining complete independence, Ghana 6 years, and Tanganyika 19 months.

Conservative British governments wanted to build up federations partially controlled by whites in East and Central Africa. Even so, Tanganyika's independence in 1961 was succeeded by Uganda's in 1962, and then by Kenya's in 1963. The federation that was actually established further south was short-lived. Malawi and Zambia became independent nations in 1964. Thus Southern Rhodesia was the only remaining colony. In 1965, the white minority under Ian Smith declared themselves 'independent' in an attempt to halt developments towards a majority government. Even in Southern Rhodesia, however, retaining white control proved hopeless. The major Western powers applied political and economic pressure to the country, and the nationalist movement grew steadily stronger. In 1979-80, Southern Rhodesia attained complete independence under the name Zimbabwe.

South Africa had acquired dominion status as early as in 1909. Particularly after 1948, Pretoria built up a strict apartheid system between the white minority and the black majority. The country also had control over the previously German colony of Namibia. South Africa became subject to strong international condemnation and withdrew from the Commonwealth in 1961. The struggle against the racist regime increased within the country as well, and from the autumn of 1985 the regime's apartheid policy came under stronger pressure both internationally and locally than ever before.

French Policies

French colonial policies were quite different from those of Britain. Instead of decentralization, with local assemblies which gradually received more power, the French model was based on Paris as its center, with a strong governor general as the capital's local representative. Whereas the British policy gradually led to a considerable degree of local autonomy, finally—although somewhat reluctantly at first—to culminate in full independence, France's attitude was that the local population was gradually to be assimilated within French culture, thus in theory attaining rights as French subjects within a French union. This union was still to be controlled from Paris, but the local populations would be increasingly better represented in the National Assembly there.

In the defense of French great power status, of French culture and long-range assimilation, the French were willing to use considerably harsher means than the British were. In 1946, several thousand Vietnamese died when the French bombarded Haiphong in order to drive the Vietminh forces out of the city. In the following year more than 80 000 persons were killed on Madagascar in an attempt to quell the nationalist movement there. On the whole, Paris considered British decolonization a process that both would and should have little influence on French areas. France could sustain its rule even if the British gave up.

The French, too, realized that the Second World War was bound to produce major changes in relations between mother country and colonies. This was expressed at the Brazzaville conference of 1944, where the free French forces, together with officials in the French colonies that supported them, were represented. The educational system was to be expanded, there was to be an end to compulsory public service, and the Africans were to be granted greater electoral influence. These reforms would create a new foundation for permanent French rule, or as the Brazzaville declaration stated: 'Any idea of autonomy, any possibility of evolution outside the French bloc, as well as the eventual, even far-off, constitution of self-government in the colonies, must be set aside.'

There were differences among the attitudes of the French parties towards the colonies. However, with the exception of the Communists, particularly after they had been thrown out of the government in May 1947, these differences were small. Even many African leaders, such as Houphouet-Boigny in the Ivory Coast, long pursued a policy placing greater emphasis on having a voice in Paris than on local independence.

But French policies, too, would come up against a local reality that could not be forced into a pattern worked out in a distant capital. Indo-China was France's most important colony in Asia. Here, it was more the capacity than the willingness to retain control that was lacking. In 1954,

246

France suffered a political and military defeat, a defeat that was confirmed at the Geneva conference that same year (see pages 80–81). Developments in Indo-China merely made the French all the more determined to maintain their colonial empire in Africa.

In North Africa, British-dominated Egypt had formally gained its independence in 1922, in reality in 1952. The example of Egypt and a strong, but moderate nationalist movement resulted in independence for Tunisia and Morocco in 1956. Although there were great differences between Africa north and south of the Sahara, this illustrated that the process of independence could not be kept out of French Africa. Concessions had to be made in Togo as well, as the country, a former German colony, was under the UN trusteeship system.

The reforms that were introduced through framework legislation *(loi cadre)* in 1956 still had as their objective the retention of control over the African colonies. However, the colonies were granted better representation in Paris, at the same time as local assemblies acquired significant influence for the first time. This new policy modified the course of integration that had been dominant. Assimilation was abandoned for the most part.

France's most uncompromising stand was made in relation to Algeria. This area was still considered an integrated part of France itself, and French policy had fluctuated between harsh repression of the Arab majority and attempts at assimilation. The French minority, about ten percent of the population, owned the best land and controlled the most important sectors of the economy. They were firmly determined to prevent any development that might reduce their dominance.

The nationalist movement, the FLN, had initiated an uprising in 1954 that soon assumed vast dimensions. French involvement was escalated sharply in 1956 under a government led by social democrat Guy Mollett. This, together with the earlier stand in Indo-China, showed that the social democrats, too, were part of what political scientist Tony Smith has called 'the French colonial consensus'. French participation in the Suez invasion that same year was largely dictated by the war in Algeria. Paris wanted to bring to an end the foreign support believed to sustain the FLN. The Suez expedition was a failure (see page 190), as French policy in Algeria would also prove to be.

After de Gaulle rose to power in 1958, changes began to take place in French colonial policy in earnest. In close cooperation with Houphouet-Boigny, the government drew up the sections of the French Constitution that were to transform the French Union into the French community (communauté). The colonies were given the choice between independence or continued close cooperation with France, with local autonomy. With the exception of Guinea, which thus became the first independent black country in French Africa, all the colonies chose the latter alternative.

The new *communauté* was to have a joint foreign policy and a joint defense policy, as well as a common economic policy for the most part. In theory, these common policies were to be determined by an executive body consisting of the presidents from all the member states. In reality, the French viewpoint was usually decisive. On the more symbolic level, French remained the official language, the 'Marseillaise' the national anthem, and the French tricolor the common flag.

In 1960, this system was replaced by formal independence. The individual countries could now decide freely in the spheres that had previously been subject to joint policy. The ties between the French colonies and Paris long remained close, much closer than between London and the British colonies. There were many reasons for the rapid course of developments from 1958 to 1960. The example of Guinea was one reason, British decolonization another, internal rivalry among several of the colonies in French West Africa yet another.

Finally, the French war in Algeria played a part. The French colonies wanted to distance themselves further from the France that was waging a bloody war in Algeria. But the French had to yield even in Algeria. Four hundred thousand French soldiers finally managed to bring the military situation under control, but the price proved to be extremely high. Political opposition to the war was growing, not only in Africa but in much of the rest of the world as well, and, most significantly, in France itself.

De Gaulle first tried to satisfy the interests of France, the local French population and the FLN through a policy based on local autonomy. This course failed. The President then advocated full independence for Algeria, a course that meant a complete break with many of those who had placed their confidence in the General. In 1962, Algeria finally became independent.

Belgium and Portugal

The other colonial powers, too, had to yield, although both Belgium and Portugal long believed that they could retain their colonies despite developments elsewhere.

Belgian policy in the Congo has often been described as paternalistic. Through a general improvement in the standard of living, the Belgians expected to be able to postpone political demands, if such ever arose. They considered themselves far more conscientious than other colonialists, as in fact they were in certain ways. Great emphasis was placed on education, but only on basic education. In 1955, the Belgian authorities proclaimed with pride that 10 percent of the population of the Congo attended school, while the corresponding figures were 7 percent in Ghana, 6 percent in India, and 3 percent in French Equatorial Africa. However, there were only 16 Africans with university educations in all of the Congo in 1960.

As late as in 1958, no preparations had been made for independence. A revolt broke out in early 1959. Political factions were formed, and with them a race to declare independence as soon as possible. Belgium was not willing to use extensive force to stop this process. The objective was to retain the best possible relations with the Congo. The moderate forces had to be supported. This could be done by realizing the demands for independence. The Belgians dismantled their administration in great haste. The new state contained many tribes and languages, and the governing bodies soon collapsed. Five years of unrest ensued until the country achieved a sort of stability under the leadership of General Mobutu (see pages 91–92).

The Portuguese were even less affected by the general decolonization than the Belgians were. Lisbon tried to pursue the French policy of assimilation even further than Paris did. The Portuguese colonies were still integrated parts of the mother country. Politically, the Africans would be allowed to participate when they had attained a specified standard of 'civilization.'

Portugal's colonial policy was closely linked to the domestic situation at home. In a dictatorship, spreading ideas of freedom and a gradual build-up of self-government was inconceivable. Decolonization could mean the collapse of the Salazar regime. But the costs of retaining control were tremendous as the independence movements grew stronger. Thus Portugal's colonial policy was much of the reason for the fall of the regime in 1974.

Even after the revolution in Lisbon, some of the new leaders spoke of decolonization taking a generation. But the radical forces in Portugal applied pressure, and the liberation movements were strengthened substantially. Guinea-Bissau became independent already in 1974. Angola and Mozambique followed suit the following year (see pages 129–130).

249

There were many reasons for the differences in the colonial powers' attitudes. The reason that was perhaps most significant has already been mentioned: the relation between colonial policy and the dominant ideologies in the mother country.

As an extension of this factor, it was significant that Britain had a feasible pattern for its colonial policies. The white dominions had after all developed a model that could be followed when the political will to grant the colonies their independence arose. Moreover, developments in India could create a pattern for possible events in Africa. The ultimate transfer of power was a process that was fairly undramatic for the British.

In contrast, France was caught up in a vicious circle in several areas. Partly due to its unwillingness to grant independence, Paris had to face radical liberation movements. This was most evident in Indo-China and, to a lesser extent, in Algeria. Radical movements meant that France in turn became even more intransigent in its policies. Thus developments in certain colonies reinforced themselves.

The British governments were also far more viable than the French. Dismantling colonial rule required strong governments, particularly in areas where substantial interests were linked to the maintenance of the status quo, such as in Algeria and in some of the British colonies in Central and East Africa. It was easier for British governments, even Conservative ones, to resist the pressure from settlers and their supporters, than it was for the rapidly changing French governments. However, de Gaulle's rise to power paved the way for the final decisions regarding decolonization.

Considerations of prestige and great power politics were other factors influencing the attitudes of the colonial powers. Rivalry among the European powers had been a central factor in the establishment of the colonial empires. This rivalry had ceased. Both Britain and France were nations on the wane in an international perspective. The colonies were now partly seen as necessary in order to defend their roles as the third and fourth-ranking major powers in the world.

Britain's international influence was clearly stronger than that of France. Thus it was easier for Britain to make concessions. France had a tremendous need to re-establish its pre-war status to some extent. Paris was largely unwilling to make concessions to its colonies. If a war had broken out, it had to be won. Because France had lost in Indo-China, it had to fight all the harder in Algeria.

250

The countries' relations with the United States were also significant. Washington's stand had greater impact in London than in Paris because Britain's relations with the United States were so much closer than France's. This factor was also important for the smaller colonial powers. The Netherlands, like Britain, pursued a relatively Atlantic policy. When the United States, in 1948-49, decided to support Indonesia's independence, that was bound to have great effect. Portugal dreamed of still maintaining a certain international position, and through the US need for bases on the Azores Salazar could long secure at least neutrality from Washington.

The colonies had varying significance for the different mother countries. The British economy was only dependent on the colonies to a slight degree. In 1938, only 8.5 percent of British imports originated in the colonies, and 12.5 percent of their exports went to the colonies. For France, trade with the colonies accounted for almost one-third of both exports and imports. Where settlers were numerous and the economic interests especially great, such as in Southern Rhodesia for Britain and in Algeria for France, this was a factor that delayed independence. The white minority consistently opposed plans to transfer power to the local majority.

However, it gradually became clear to the colonial powers that independence did not necessarily entail such great changes in relations between mother country and colony. Economic, military and cultural ties could still persist. The greater the chances of this happening, the easier it was to grant political independence. There could be advantages to not having to spend large sums of money to retain administrative control. Independence would also mean that the colonial power would be spared from having sole responsibility for local development programs.

The relation of the Philippines to the United States was a good example of this. The US bases remained, economically the country was still closely linked to the United States, and the same social groups governed in Manila now as previously. For Britain, relations with former colonies such as Canada, Australia, South Africa, and the United States illustrated that economic relations could even be strengthened after the colonies had gained political independence. Even so, the British placed little emphasis on this experience during the first years after 1945. But later experience confirmed that the consequences of decolonization were often far less sweeping than they had imagined immediately after the war.

The maintenance of close ties with the mother country was also a condition for the changes that took place in French colonial policy in the years 1958-60. In Africa south of the Sahara, in Morocco and Tunisia (in contrast to in Indo-China and to some extent in Algeria), the French largely succeeded in retaining the new nations' orientation towards France. The smaller colonial powers (the Netherlands, Belgium, and Portugal) had difficulties in maintaining the former ties. They were simply not strong enough, neither economically nor militarily.

The Local Level: Independence Movements Grow Stronger

Independence may have been something the colonial powers granted, but it was also something the colonies seized. Although there were differences in the colonial powers' attitudes, independence was almost always something the national leaders had to struggle for, at least until developments began to unfold almost under their own momentum during the 1960s.

Local conditions in the various colonies differed tremendously. Distinctive local features were one important factor determining when the individual colonies gained independence. Generalizations about the course of developments are necessarily more accurate for some colonies than for others, but certain basic features can be outlined.

The establishment and expansion of control by the colonial powers had often led to revolts, but these tended to be more or less spontaneous, without any national ideology as a unifying factor. They could be protests against taxes, against the loss of land, against enforced labor, modernization, religious repression, racial discrimination, etc. The most important shared feature was that they tried to return to the order that had existed before the colonial power had arrived. The Senussi rising in Tunisia in 1881 may serve as an instance of a protest at the establishment phase, while the Indian mutiny of 1857 largely broke out in areas that had long been under British control.

Such revolts could represent sources of inspiration for the nationalist movements that later emerged, but ideologically they were quite distinct. The revolts pointed back to a bygone era; the nationalist movements tried to establish a new order. However, the transition between these two phases could be a state of flux. The revolts in some of the African colonies just before and after the turn of the century seem to some extent

to have been precursors for those that were to follow. The Saya San revolt
in Burma in 1930 was another example of such an intermediate incident.

The Three Stages

The historian Geoffrey Barraclough has divided the struggle for independence into three schematized stages that can be identified in the
course of development of many of the colonies. The first stage was
dominated by what he calls 'proto-nationalism.' During this period colonial rule was accepted, but new social groups and political movements
emerged that strove for reforms within this system. The Congress Party
was established in India in 1885, but until 1905 it was largely a debate
forum for a narrow upper class. British civilization was considered superior. The most important demands for reform included limited local
autonomy and more job opportunities for educated Indians. In Indonesia, this first stage began with the creation of the religious-nationalist
movement Sarekat Islam in 1911. Similar movements were established in
important African colonies such as the Gold Coast, Nigeria and Tunisia
around 1920.

Barraclough identifies the second stage as 'the rise of a new leadership.' Nationalism began to gain ground in a growing middle class. The
demands the new leaders made on the colonial power were expanded
substantially, and independence was considered at least a future goal. In
India, this second phase can be said to have lasted from 1905 to 1919.
Although the social base for the Congress Party was expanded, it was
still far from a mass movement. Demands for independence were raised,
but this was not a unifying common goal. In Indonesia, Sarekat Islam
commited itself to independence as early as in 1917. Even so, the Partai
Nasional Indonesia was not established until 1927. Similar turning
points can be said to have been reached in Tunisia and Nigeria in 1934
and 1944, respectively.

The third stage was a nationalist movement with 'a mass following'
working actively to achieve independence. Nationalist movements grew
so strong that the use of force had to be stepped up in order to maintain
the colonial system. Whereas the colonial power had formerly been able
to play the masses off against the narrow social groups that led these
movements, this was now more difficult, although there were still many
who were not directly engaged in the political struggle. Again, India

serves as the model. Under Gandhi's leadership, from 1920 onwards the Congress Party established clear lines from the political center to India's tens of thousands of rural villages. The objective was now clearly independence. In Indonesia, the PNI under Sukarno's leadership did not manage to launch a comparable mass mobilization until during WW II. This stage was initiated in Tunisia as well during the war. In Nigeria, the initiation of the third phase occurred in 1951. In the Gold Coast, the second phase and the beginning of the third phase almost converged during the years 1947–49.

Thus these stages were not equally distinct everywhere. The process tended to extend over the longest period of time in the British colonies. In the French colonies in Africa south of the Sahara, the entire course of development could take a mere 10–20 years. In some instances it went even more quickly. In the Belgian Congo, for instance, there were hardly any demands for independence until 1955. Even then, local leaders thought that it might take 60 to 100 years before the colony became independent.

Economic and Cultural Development

The three stages were closely linked to economic and cultural developments in the colonies. The establishment of mass parties which at least to some extent felt that they had ties to the nation, and not primarily to regional, tribal or upper class interests, tended to presuppose economic modernization and a certain minimum level of cultural strength based on an educational system.

To a considerable degree, the colonial powers contributed to shaping the reactions against themselves. The leaders of the independence struggles were very often educated in Western countries, most likely in the mother country itself. The central names of the Indian-Pakistani freedom struggle exemplify this fact, although they were highly influenced by non-Western cultures as well. Jinnah, Ali Khan, Nehru and to some extent Gandhi had all been influenced by British political and judicial ideas during prolonged stays in Britain. Western influence was even stronger in Africa, as illustrated by Nkrumah, Nyerere (Tanganyika) and Kaunda (Northern Rhodesia). If nationalist leaders in the British colonies were influenced by British ideas, the leaders in the French areas were even more characterized by French ideas. Houphouet-Boigny in the

Ivory Coast and Senghor in Senegal were two clear, though differing examples of this French influence.

The national idea as such was frequently a product of Western impulses. This was most evident in Africa. The recently established colonial territories of Africa did not have a common past and a shared cultural tradition to fall back on to the same extent as in Asia. As Nkrumah wrote in 1958, it was Europeans who 'set the pattern of our hopes, and by entering Africa in strength ... forced the pattern upon us. Likewise, it was the colonial powers, through the borders they established, who decided what territory each individual 'country' was to comprise.

This Western influence could have beneficial aspects. But the point is rather that the colonial system had disruptive effects, effects that strengthened the independence movements. Communications were expanded, a factor that contributed to reducing the traditional boundaries within the individual colonial areas. Cities grew rapidly and with them educational institutions and new elites. Lagos, for example, had 75 000 inhabitants in 1914, 230 000 in 1950 and 675 000 in 1962. The corresponding figures for Accra were 20 000, 135 000 and 325 000. In the years just after WW II, more than 600 000 children attended school in Nigeria, more than 250 000 in Kenya and 120 000 in the Gold Coast. Universities were established in the Gold Coast, Nigeria, Uganda and Sudan. Previously there had been only one university in the British-controlled colonies in Africa south of the Sahara, and that was in Sierra Leone.

In Africa, modernization was largely responsible for the creation of new groups such as clergy, teachers, shopowners, politicians, etc. In Asia, the numbers of people in these groups grew. Racial discrimination, which in many ways was strongest in the British colonies, became intolerable. Those who had gained a little under the colonial system wanted more. Those who had got nothing, protested, and the protests became steadily better organized.

The native soldiers who had participated in the Second World War did not want to return to the old colonial system after having fought for the triumph of democracy. The large-scale production of persons with primary education created a group that became important supporters for the new elites in the struggle against the colonial powers. Trade regulations of various types often limited the opportunities for the native population. Conflicts arose continuously regarding wages and working conditions. These were circumstances that primarily affected the cities.

But the independence movements themselves were largely urban pheno-mena, especially in Africa south of the Sahara.

Reactions against the colonial powers arose first and most strongly in the areas where there were both highly developed native cultures and a strong, early Western influence. Once again India was the clearest example. The country had thousands of highly educated persons as well as strong religious and cultural traditions. Comprehensive social changes had taken place during the years of British rule. The areas which most resembled India in these respects were Indonesia, Vietnam and Islamic North Africa.

The independence movements of East and Central Africa were the weakest. Western influence could be too strong. In these areas the oppo-sing forces, most easily measured by the number of local whites, were substantial. Of all the British colonies, those in this area had the least experience in local self-government. Few Africans had higher education. As late as in 1963, there were only 8 Africans among the 116 top admin-istrators in Nyasaland (Malawi). In the following year the country be-came independent.

The Influence of International Events

A number of events in various parts of the world contributed to strength-ening the independence movements (or to weakening the mother countries—the two aspects are difficult to keep entirely separate). Among the earliest of these may be mentioned the black Ethiopians' vic-tory over the white Italians at Adua in 1896; the Boer war, which resulted in independence for South Africa while at the same time strengthening anti-colonial sentiments in Britain; Japan's victory over Russia in 1904-05, which showed that the white man could also be defeated by the yellow man; the First World War, which brought hundreds of thousands of natives from Asia and Africa to Europe as soldiers and workers at a time when radical ideas and slogans flourished; the Russian Revolution, which created highly conscious Communist groups that would act as a vanguard in many of the independence movements.

However, the Second World War was the most important single factor. This war led to changes on the international level, and it contributed to the creation of new attitudes towards the colonies in their mother coun-tries. At least equally important were the changes the war caused in the colonies, especially in Asia. The Second World War had many of the same effects there as the Napoleonic wars had had on the Spanish and Portuguese colonies in South and Central America.

Japan occupied all Asian colonial areas up to the Indian border. The European colonial powers were decisively defeated by Asians. The Japanese occupation would strengthen the independence movements in a number of other ways as well. New governing structures were created and psychological barriers broken down. Partly to gather support against the allies and partly as a step on the way towards Japanization, the Japanese promoted nationalism in several areas. National leaders were given offices and to some extent power that they were certainly not prepared to relinquish when the war was over. National languages were encouraged in Indonesia and Burma, national armies established. Independence was even proclaimed for the Philippines and Burma in 1943 and for Vietnam, Laos and Cambodia in 1945, although this was primarily a formality. Those who cooperated with the Japanese, such as Sukarno in Indonesia, Aung San in Burma and Roxas in the Philippines, were seldom seen in the same light as the Quislings of Europe.

Of course there were conflicts between Japan and the national movements as well. The Japanese concessions were always too limited. Brutal economic exploitation stimulated revolt and opposition.

In the areas Japan did not occupy, the war meant that the colonial powers had to exert themselves to the extreme in order to secure material and political support. As we have seen, such considerations were an important factor behind the India declaration of 1942, which laid the foundation for the country's independence after the war.

Perhaps most important of all was the vacuum that arose when Japan suddenly capitulated in August-September 1945. The Japanese were defeated without the Europeans having advanced into their former areas. Vietnam and Indonesia received, or rather seized, their independence and were not at all willing to relinquish it when the colonial powers were eventually in a position to send in troops. France and the Netherlands never managed to re-establish the control they had had before the war.

The liberation of Asia necessarily had substantial consequences for Africa as well. As the historian D.A. Low has stressed: 'It is not fanciful to assert that many of the critical battles for British colonial Africa were fought, not on the banks of the Volta, the Niger, or the Zambezi, but on the Ganges.' After all, four-fifths of the population of Britain's colonial territories lived in India. The floodgates were opened and the pattern established, not only for the British colonies, but for all colonies.

The Non-Aligned Nations in World Politics

The vast majority of the new nations that emerged first in Asia and then in Africa were firmly determined to keep at a distance from the two major power blocs. Some form of non-alliance was nearly self-evident. Geographically, many of these new nations were located far from the two blocs. The ideology of independence was strong; independence meant revolt against a Western power, which in itself made alliance with the Western bloc difficult, or even impossible; yet very few of the new nations carried the anti-Western sentiment so far as to tie themselves to the East bloc.

The question of cooperation with other liberated nations became highly relevant. There could hardly be a question of a third 'bloc', because in the opinion of the non-aligned nations the bloc policy was responsible for much of the tension that existed in the world. Even so, the movement needed a foundation on which to stand. Defining this foundation would prove difficult.

The first meeting among African and Asian countries was held in Bandung, Indonesia, in 1955. All the independent countries from these two parts of the world were represented, with the exception of North and South Korea and Israel. Western-oriented states such as Turkey, the Philippines, and South Vietnam, and Communist nations such as China and North Vietnam all took part. The twenty-nine participants concentrated their efforts on condemning colonialism, emphasizing the need for economic growth in the Third World, and calling for a decrease in international tension based on the principles of cooperation and peaceful co-existence.

Shortly thereafter, two of the conference's leaders, Nasser from Egypt and Nehru from India, travelled to Yugoslavia to have talks with Tito, the most prominent neutral leader who had not participated in Bandung. In a joint statement they expressed their support for the resolutions from the meeting that had been held and moreover sharply attacked the two major power blocs. Thus non-alignment was focused in a much clearer way than at the Afro-Asian meeting, where representatives for the two blocs had participated.

The first summit meeting of the non-aligned nations was held in Belgrade in 1961 with 25 nations participating. The clearly bloc-oriented countries that had been in Bandung were excluded, as were the so-called Brazzaville nations, the most pro-French of the former French colonies. On the other hand, Yugoslavia and Cyprus had been added from the European countries and Cuba from the Latin American countries. The participants in Belgrade placed primary emphasis on the struggle for peace in the world. The meeting was dominated by the belief that non-alignment would be different from traditional neutrality. Non-alignment was to be active and positive, whereas neutrality had been passive and negative.

New conferences were held in Cairo in 1964, Lusaka in 1970, Algiers in 1973, Colombo in 1976, Havana in 1979, New Delhi in 1983, and Harare in 1986. The number of participants increased each time, from 25 in 1961 to 100 in 1983. The African and Asian nations consistently composed the core, but Latin American countries also joined the movement in increasing numbers. Such European countries as Sweden, Finland, and Austria took part in some of the conferences as observers or guests.

Defining non-alignment precisely proved impossible. The criterion that was the most important for a long time was that the participants could not grant the major powers military bases, but even this was far from strictly practiced. Cuba and Vietnam have been among the most Soviet-oriented participants, the Philippines, Saudi Arabia, and Pakistan among the most pro-USA. In addition to them there were the many African countries that retained their close ties with France. The level of development was also widely divergent, from the wealthy oil nations of the Middle East to the poorest of the poor in Africa. Nor have conflicts and wars been unusual among the participants, such as between India and Pakistan, Vietnam and Cambodia, Iran and Iraq.

The conferences of the non-aligned nations all concentrated their efforts on decolonization, economic development, and anti-bloc policies. The balance among these themes varied. Decolonization became less relevant as the vast majority of the colonies gained their independence. Even so, the non-aligned nations were highly concerned about the remaining areas, such as Namibia and South Africa. The Palestinian problem was also considered in this light. The same was true of the Falkland islands (the Malvinas), where Argentina's claim enjoyed support. (In 1982 the islands were seized by Argentina but then re-taken by British troops.)

Demands for a new economic world order became increasingly prominent. As early as in 1964, the non-aligned countries had been instrumental in bringing about the first United Nations Conference on Trade and Development (UNCTAD). The economic problems of the 1970s reinforced the concentration on these issues. Most of the oil nations and certain others enjoyed strong growth, but the majority suffered from economic stagnation. In the 1980s growth became even slower (see chapter 10).

The non-aligned nations long tried to distribute the responsibility for the bloc policy fairly equally between East and West, between the Soviet Union and the United States. The emergence of the new nations probably contributed to strengthening the forces within the two blocs that favored an easing of tensions, as an uncompromising policy could repel the non-aligned nations. However, this was far from a decisive factor, as the later worsening of the international climate has shown.

Even so, the verbal attacks on the colonial empires and the demands for a new economic world order almost inevitably meant a focusing of attention on the Western powers. They were the ones that still had colonies, and they were the ones who dominated the international economic system the developing countries protested against. Criticism of the West varied somewhat from one summit to another with the meeting in Lusaka in 1970 as the most moderate.

Condemnation of the bloc policy faded somewhat into the background during detente in the late 1960s and early 1970s. When relations between East and West became more strained once more, this condemnation increased again. At the fifth summit in Colombo and the sixth in Havana, there was a clear tendency to place the primary responsibility for this increased tension on the Western powers in general, and on the United States in particular. To a great extent the non-aligned nations rallied round the Cuban charges against the Western powers and at least indirectly supported Soviet stands on several important issues. During the 1960s Fidel Castro had represented the most radical wing. Now his stand was shared by increasing numbers of non-aligned nations, despite Cuba's close ties with the Soviet Union.

The meeting in New Delhi contributed to returning the non-aligned movement to a more balanced course once more. Vietnam's policy in Cambodia and that of the Soviet Union in Afghanistan resulted in a sharper tone towards Moscow, but criticism of Washington was still the harshest. The same general tone was noticeable also in Harare in 1986.

In 1986, the non-aligned movement represented about two billion people and is thus the most extensive organization in the world after the United Nations and its subordinate organizations. Cohesion has proved greater than could be expected in consideration of the large number of members and the many conflicts between various participants. When voting in the UN these countries have on the whole shown a higher degree of agreement among themselves than was to be found both among the Western-oriented nations and among the neutral nations that do not participate at the non-aligned meetings.

The non-aligned nations have to a great extent managed to determine what issues the UN system is to concentrate its efforts on. The struggle for a new economic world order and against colonialism, racism, the arms race, and related issues have thus been recurrent themes on the international agenda.

However, the results have not been proportional to the time expended on these discussions. With the partial exception of decolonization, the resolutions passed by the UN and other bodies have resulted in very few concrete changes. The possibilities of applying pressure on the major powers have been very limited. Even small countries such as South Africa and Israel have largely been able to ignore continual condemnation from the non-aligned nations without much consequence. Endeavors to further develop cooperation among the member countries have had somewhat greater, although still limited, success. An office of coordination has been established to promote mutual interests, but the attempts at large-scale economic cooperation between developing countries have generally produced small results.

10. Economic relations between North and South, 1945–86

Political independence led to great changes. In terms of foreign policy, most of the new nations chose to avoid the struggle between East and West. Domestically, local leaders now controlled the government. Only a few of the countries followed the conventions of Western democratic government, but socially many of them underwent substantial improvements in such fields as health services and education.

Both the nationalist leaders and the population in general expected political independence to produce great results in the economic sphere as well. Kwame Nkrumah's advice to the other African countries was typical in that respect: 'Seek ye first the political kingdom and all else shall be added unto you.' It was not expected that everyone would become exactly wealthy, but the possibilities of material progress were considered extremely good.

In relation to these soaring expectations, the disappointments were tremendous. A few countries achieved substantial results. For many, however, independence seemed to mean little or nothing in the form of concrete economic results. In several countries foreign influence increased, at least in certain areas. Thus there were approximately 300 000 French citizens residing in Africa in 1983, or more than twice as many as during the colonial era. Radical politicians and social scientists began to question whether independence had actually altered the fundamental ties between the former mother countries and colonies, or between industrial countries and developing countries in general.

Two Theories concerning Development and Underdevelopment

A number of theories have been launched to explain the development, or lack of development, that has taken place in the 'developing countries.' There are nearly as many theories as there are authors. However, we can roughly identify two main schools, which in turn can be subdivided into numerous sub-groups. While such diverse views would not normally be grouped together, the primary issue at hand here is economic relations between North and South, and on this subject the degree of concurrence is great enough to defend such a schematic division.

The dominant school has long been the liberalist or traditional school. Despite the great diversity of views particularly within this school, its adherents all believe that there are mutual gains from economic contact to be realized by rich and poor countries alike. In contrast to this mainstream, there is the structuralist, underdevelopment or dependency school. Marxist theory may be considered an important sub-group within this school. Instead of a basic harmony of interests, this minority sees a conflict of interests between rich and poor countries.

Traditional neoclassical economists and even most Western development economists argue, although with varying degrees of intensity, that international trade has contributed to economic growth in both industrialized and developing countries and that the market ought to be an important control mechanism in the economy.

Within the liberalist school, we find relatively early development economists (Nurkse and Haberler), neo-classicists with great faith in the growth capacity of market economies (Bauer), stage theorists who are preoccupied with the developing countries' economic 'take-off' (Rostow), researchers who are primarily interested in the multinational corporations and who perceive positive effects from their presence in developing countries (Vernon), and even the many who place emphasis on how domestic conditions in the developing countries have impeded their growth, whether these conditions are problems within and among various economic sectors (Lewis) or general politico-economic weaknesses (Galbraith).

The liberalists believe in openness. There is not necessarily anything wrong with a country specializing its production to a considerable degree. To a great extent, such specialization is a necessary condition for international trade. Trade may even be more important for the developing countries than for the industrialized countries, as their domestic markets are smaller. Many liberalists consider export-based growth the most effective in promoting development.

Moreover, contact with industrialized nations can supply capital, technology, and so on. The multinational corporations are often important instruments for transferring resources of this type. The liberalists generally consider these corporations advantageous for the developing countries from an economic perspective.

As one such liberalist study of developments in seven countries (Argentina, Brazil, Mexico, India, Pakistan, the Philippines, and Taiwan) concludes:

> Emphasis should be placed on the development of exports so as to earn the foreign currency required to pay for essential imports, whether of machines, materials, or food, which cannot be economically produced at home. Administrative control should be replaced by better use of the price mechanism; and high cost internal production be replaced by a reorganized agriculture and industry, capable of gradually becoming competitive and assuming their place on the world market.

The liberalists deny that there are nearly absolute divisions between developed and developing countries. Industrialization began in Britain and spread from there. New countries will continue to join the ranks of the industrialized nations. Agriculture too may play an important role in the development process. If a nation has a fairly good resource base and pursues a reasonable economic policy, it will have the possibility of participating in economic prosperity.

Extreme liberalists may be sceptical to government intervention in the economy, but most of them would concur with moderate intervention both internationally and nationally. Some of them would even emphasize the need for reforms on both of these levels. Most liberalists will, contrary to the structuralists, emphasize the domestic determinants of underdevelopment (overpopulation, shortage of capital, insufficient national resources, unfortunate economic policies, social structures, corruption, climate, etc.).

In the 1950s leading leftist scholars such as Myrdal, Prebisch and Singer argued that, in Gunnar Myrdal's words, 'Market forces will tend cumulatively to accentuate international inequalities, [and] a quite normal result of unhampered trade between two countries, of which one is industrial and the other underdeveloped, is the initiation of a cumulative process toward the impoverishment and stagnation of the latter.'

During the 1960s and 1970s a number of writers went beyond the analysis of 'disequalizing forces' in the international economy. Prominent representatives of the new school of structuralists are André Gunder Frank, Samir Amin, Walter Rodney and Johan Galtung. Greatly simplified, this school maintains that the South became underdeveloped and has remained underdeveloped as a result of the development of the North. Structuralist theories are dominant in the developing countries themselves; they also have adherents among leftist intellectuals in the North.

According to this perspective, many international factors have produced the South's underdevelopment. The local economies in the colonies were adapted to and made dependent on the needs of the mother country rather than those of the colonies themselves. Thus agriculture was oriented towards export rather than towards self-sufficiency. Exports were often concentrated on a single product. In return, the colonies imported processed goods from the mother country or from other industrialized countries. The terms of trade between raw materials and industrial goods were biased to the advantage of the latter category. Attempts to initiate industrialization were stopped because of the colonial powers' own interests in this area.

The structuralists maintain further that although with independence the colonies attained greater freedom of action, they were so bound to the international capitalist structure that development was still difficult, if not impossible. They were still producers of raw materials. The terms of trade were just as biased as before. Feeble attempts at industrialization did not improve conditions noticeably. Investments by multinational corporations tended to make things worse, as their net effect was to withdraw more capital from the developing countries than they invested in them.

Thus the industrial countries continued to occupy the 'center', while the developing countries remained on the 'periphery'. The power of the center also depended on the ties it established with local elites in the periphery. These elites profited by the international economic system, although the system as a whole worked to the advantage of the North.

How were the masses in the developing countries to be included in economic development? It would not be easy in any case. The industrial countries and the local elites were prepared to use economic, political and military sanctions to defend their interests. The solution was to be found, according to the structuralists, in severing the links to the prevailing economic world order in some way or other. The individual country or groups of countries must direct their efforts towards increased self-sufficiency. The repressed majority in the developing countries must organize themselves and break the ties to the world market.

Most Marxists would be willing to accept the main features of the theory of underdevelopment, although there are clear differences between them and other structuralists. For one thing, Marxists place greater

265

importance on rivalry among the industrial countries, which in their opinion certainly do not always have coinciding interests. Marxists also emphasize their conviction that belonging to different classes produces different attitudes within both industrialized and developing nations. Moreover, as a point of departure Marx considered imperialism a progressive factor. At least in the short run it contributed to economic development in the colonies and was a necessary step on the path to socialism and communism.

Aid and Trade, 1945–1986

Before undertaking a more detailed evaluation of certain aspects of these theories, it may be useful to outline the most important features of the North's economic policies towards the South. These policies can be divided into three main phases, although the changes have been greater and the phases more evident in aid than in trade policy: from 1945 until the mid-50s, a phase in which economic assistance was initiated in earnest, but was kept at a relatively modest level and in which the international system of trade showed little concern for the South's interests; from the mid-50s until the late 1960s, characterized by an increase in development assistance, a considerable development optimism and gradually by international plans to regulate trade for the purpose of improving conditions for the developing countries; finally, a third period from the late 1960s that probably still pertains, with stagnation in development assistance from the large industrialized countries, strong tendencies towards development pessimism and an increasing gap between the developing countries' hopes for a trade policy the industrial countries ought to pursue and the policy they actually pursued.

1945–1956

The colonial powers undertook a number of investments in their colonies that could have the effect of promoting development, and after 1945 they launched substantial development programs financed primarily by the colonies' own budgets, but based on transfers as well. However, promoting economic growth in the independent nations was primarily the responsibility of the new nations themselves, supplemented by pri-

266

vate capital.

The first meager plans for assistance to the developing countries were laid through the UN Technical Assistance Program (1949), the US Point 4 program (1949), and the British Colombo plan (1950). Point 4 was an attempt to transfer the experience gained from the Marshall Plan to the less developed countries. The tasks were much more extensive than in Europe. The means were much smaller. The Colombo plan concerned modest assistance from the wealthier Commonwealth countries (Britain, Canada, Australia, and New Zealand) to the new nations in Asia. After the United States joined the Colombo plan, Asian countries outside the Commonwealth were also included.

The World Bank was not truly a world bank, as its efforts were long concentrated on conditions in the industrial nations. All in all, the Bank granted loans to the developing countries amounting to only 583 million dollars up to 30 July 1952.

The developing countries played a most modest role in terms of international trade policy as well. The charter for the International Trade Organization (ITO) left some room for their interests, but this organization did not materialize. Instead, GATT was established, placing virtually sole emphasis on the needs of the industrialized countries. For that reason, many of the new nations chose not to join GATT.

The industrial countries were eager to trade with the developing countries but did not make any serious attempts to adapt the international system of free trade to their special situation. The developing countries, on their part, were few and weak, and their policies were poorly coordinated. The depression of the 1930s and developments during the Second World War had stimulated a course of self-sufficiency in Latin America and in many of the colonial areas. This course was now maintained, emphasizing import substitution. The developing countries themselves were to produce many of the industrial goods they had imported previously. To some extent, this policy succeeded. Industrial growth was substantial in several areas.

1956–1968

During the course of the 1950s, changes could be observed in the attitudes of the industrialized nations. The amounts spent on development assistance were stepped up. World Bank loans to the new nations increased. New loan institutions were created: in 1956 the International Finance Corporation, four years later the even more important International Development Association, which granted cheap, long-term loans to countries in the Third World. Bilateral programs were increased considerably. In the United States, total development assistance increased from 2.0 billion dollars in 1956 to 3.7 billion in 1963. In Britain and France the corresponding figures showed an increase from 205 to 414 million dollars and from 608 to 863 million dollars, respectively.

The change of attitude in the industrial nations arose from at least three considerations. One factor was the many new nations that acted as a pressure group for increased assistance. International organizations were gradually dominated by these countries, and the established powers considered remaining on good terms with them essential. By 1959, the United Nations consisted of 122 member nations, among them 87 Third World nations.

A second important factor was the optimism that reigned — not only in the developing countries—regarding the possibilities of initiating economic growth. Many professional economists felt that if only a specified investment level was reached, the developing countries could 'take off' and create a self-generating growth. The clearest expression of this growth optimism was W.W. Rostow's book *The Stages of Economic Growth,* published in 1960. Growth in the developing countries would increase their purchasing power, which in turn would have favorable effects on world trade and the industrial nations' own economies. This optimism was largely based on the course of development that had taken place in North America and in Western Europe, but it fell on fertile soil in the newly independent countries as well.

However, the most important factor, particularly for the US stand, was the increased Soviet interest in the new nations. After Stalin's death, the Kremlin began to pursue much more active policies than previously (see pages 85–92). Assistance was granted, industrial projects initiated, political declarations of support made. In the West, the impression spread that Asia and Africa would be the primary arena in the cold war. If the Western powers did not take care, the new nations could drift in the direction of the Soviet Union. Especially the United States had to recognize its responsibility, as the country was the leader of the 'free world' and was not compromised in the same way as the former colonial powers.

With regard to trade, the industrial nations concentrated nearly all their attention on trade among themselves. Growth in this trade was very rapid, particularly within Europe. Most of the new nations still pursued the policy of import substitution. The growth in trade among the industrial nations in particular contributed to a fall in the South's share of total world exports from 31.6 percent in 1950 to 21.4 percent in 1960.

Even so, new signals could be observed. Import substitution seemed to produce poorer results as time passed. Countries that concentrated on exports, such as Taiwan, South Korea, and Singapore, began to enjoy a considerably more rapid growth in the 1960s than those that concentrated on protecting domestic industry.

The established trade organizations had shown little willingness to adapt to the developing countries' increasing demands for reforms. With the interest the Soviet Union now showed for the Third World, from 1956 onwards Moscow would support the creation of an organization separate from GATT, of which the Soviet Union was not a member either. The Western powers now tried in earnest to accommodate the wishes of the developing countries within GATT, but finally gave in to pressure for a new organization.

The result was a decision to establish the United Nations Conference on Trade and Development (UNCTAD). The first meeting was held in Geneva in 1964. The organization's first general secretary, the moderate Argentine structuralist Raul Prebisch, stressed the limitations of import substitution:

> The relative smallness of national markets, in addition to other adverse factors, has often made the cost of industries excessive and necessitated recourse to very high protective tariffs; the latter in turn has had unfavourable effects on the industrial structure because it has encouraged the establishment of small uneconomical plants, weakened the incentive to introduce modern techniques, and slowed down the rise in productivity ...

Through UNCTAD, the new nations' demands were to be placed on the international agenda in earnest: the industrial countries would have to remove restrictions on imports from developing countries, without their having to make similar concessions in return. The prices of commodities were to be stabilized, loan opportunities improved dramatically, and all forms of economic assistance stepped up.

269

There was no increase in development assistance from the late 1960s and throughout the 1970s. Instead, the contributions of the large industrial nations tended to decline. In absolute figures the amounts spent did increase, but because of the high rate of inflation there was an actual decline. This was most pronounced in the United States, where development assistance had amounted to 0.58 percent of the gross national product in 1965 and 0.32 percent in 1970. By 1982 this figure had dropped to 0.27 percent. Britain's reduced presence in the Third World contributed to a stagnation in development assistance there as well. In 1982 it amounted to 0.37 percent of the British national product. The strong increase that took place in assistance from some of the smaller OECD countries was not always sufficient to compensate for the drop in the larger countries' contributions. Moreover, an increasing share of the assistance was linked to purchases from the donor country, which further reduced its effect. Old loans finally fell due for repayment. The flow of capital out of the developing countries was thus often greater than the influx of capital.

The newly wealthy OPEC members gave far more than the OECD countries if assistance is measured as a percentage of the gross national product. But even OPEC's contributions declined from the end of the 1970s. Moreover, their contributions went primarily from one Islamic nation to another. Thus the geographical distribution of this assistance was limited.

This stagnation in development assistance was due to several considerations. The North's declining growth rate in the 1970s was undoubtedly one of them. In many industrialized countries development assistance became less popular. Much of the motivation disappeared when it became evident that economic assistance did not necessarily secure political support. Many began to doubt the economic efficacy of development assistance. There were numerous examples of support that appeared to have been futile. Assistance was only one of a great number of factors that influenced development in the various countries, and rarely the most important one.

With regard to international trade, negotiations between North and South proceeded slowly. After UNCTAD II in 1968, progress was limited, and the high expectations from the early 1960s disappeared, although OPEC's success in 1973-74 would temporarily give them new life again (see pages 283–284). The developing nations' trade did increase, but measured as a share of world trade there was no increase during the 1960s and 1970s. Their share remained largely stable. At least the decline from the 1950s had stopped. Despite the pessimism, several countries, particularly in South-east Asia and among the OPEC members, actually enjoyed rapid economic growth.

The proposals that had been put forward in 1964, and that had been considerably elaborated in 1974 through the call for a New International Economic Order (NIEO), led to few changes of any significance. New programs of assistance were initiated for the very poorest developing countries. The World Bank and the International Monetary Fund were granted more funds to administer. A commodity fund was established in 1980. The gap between demands and results was illustrated by the fact that whereas the developing countries had proposed a 6 billion dollar fund, the two programs that eventually materialized amounted to 750 million dollars. Several of the most important industrialized nations, led by the United States, refused to contribute to one of the programs. A system of trade preferences was established during the 1970s in principle, but with so many and such complicated exceptions for numerous goods that were of particular interest to the developing countries that it had little practical significance. Moreover, the importance of these preferences was undermined to a certain extent by the liberalization of trade among the industrialized nations.

Most of the developing countries concluded that the UNCTAD and NIEO process had been a failure. It was true that somewhat better results were achieved through regional agreements, of which the most important were the two Lomé agreements of 1975 and 1979. In these, the members of the EC extended themselves further than most other industrial nations, but only in relation to the 46—later 58—developing countries in the Caribbean, in Africa, and in the Pacific that were associated with the EC. Even here the practical results were quite small. A third agreement was signed in the autumn of 1984. It did not represent much of an improvement for the developing countries.

The United States proved even less willing to make concessions. The feeling of solidarity was weaker than in Western Europe. On the other hand, the degree of self-sufficiency was higher than in Western Europe and Japan, a fact that probably contributed to Washington feeling less of a need to make concessions. The Reagan administration believed that in this sector, as in other sectors, market forces and private interests, such as the multinational corporations, ought to play the dominant role. This conservative attitude was somewhat modified during Reagan's second term, in part in response to the Third World's rising debt problem (see pages 284–285).

The Soviet Union and North–South Issues

The Soviet Union and the Eastern bloc had an interesting position in the negotiations related to UNCTAD and a New International Economic Order. As mentioned, Moscow was one of the driving forces behind the UNCTAD process and supported the demands of the developing countries in principle almost without exception. As they were primarily aimed at the Western powers, all proposals for increased development assistance, remission of debt, integrated commodity funds and reduced tariff restrictions could be supported. Particularly until the mid-70s, most of the so-called 77 country group considered the Soviet Union an ally on these issues.

However, the negotiations would also represent a number of problems for Moscow. In the first place, the fact that the demands of the developing countries were a matter of reforms within a system dominated by the Western industrial nations had always given grounds for concern. In 1979, trade with the Soviet Union and Eastern Europe accounted for only 3.2 percent of the exports from and 5.3 percent of the imports to the countries of the Third World. The proposed reforms would not loosen these ties. On the contrary, they could tend to make them even closer. In the opinion of the Kremlin, a truly new world order could only be established by the developing countries breaking away from the capitalist nations. The New International Economic Order could thus at best be merely a first step on the long road to independence.

In the second place, the developing countries gradually became less willing to accept that the Soviet Union took the stand it did as to the demands they raised. Moscow could deny having any responsibility for the former colonies' poverty, but why shouldn't the Soviet Union, too, increase its development assistance, renegotiate debts, and import more? Soviet development assistance was modest. In 1982 it amounted to only about 20 percent of US development assistance. Debts were renegotiated only on an individual basis with nations that had proved themselves deserving of it. Even though the volume of trade increased substantially as time passed, it remained small compared with Western trade with the developing countries.

The Soviet Union became increasingly sceptical about the intrinsic authority UNCTAD developed. The political and economic expectations that the Soviet Union now became subject to had an unfortunate tendency to rise incessantly. The country's unwillingness to fulfill these expectations meant that the Soviet Union was considered an increasingly less interesting actor within UNCTAD and in the discussions concerning the New International Economic Order.

Some Comments on the Two Main Theories

The theories of the structuralists and the liberalists are far too comprehensive to be discussed in their full scope. Moreover, too little research has been carried out for anyone to give decisive answers to many of the most controversial questions. Furthermore, much of the research has had, and to some extent still has, more the form of political pamphleteering than of empirical inquiry. This was particularly true of the structuralists' early phase.

Much of this chapter is relatively speculative compared with the rest of the book. Four central issues in the discussion of economic relations between North and South will be considered: to what extent contact with the industrialized nations has contributed or not contributed to economic growth in the developing countries; the role of multinational corporations; the relative prices of raw materials and processed goods, including the significance export agriculture has had in the developing countries; the question of how dependent North and South are on one another.

The North's Development — The South's Underdevelopment?

The structuralists have emphasized that only by breaking the ties to the capitalist world order can the developing countries achieve development. As an extension of this thesis, they tend to maintain that there were highly developed cultures in many of the areas that were subjugated by the Western colonial powers. They often argue more or less explicitly that if developments had been allowed to continue unimpeded, many countries in the Third World would probably have been industrialized today. They frequently maintain that the growth that has taken place has been in relatively isolated states and preferably in periods when the developing countries had little contact with the international economy, such as allegedly during the world wars.

Our knowledge of conditions in Asia and Africa before colonialism is inadequate, opening for both idealization and the painting of gloomy pictures. An important counterfactual element is the uncertainty that will always remain as to what would have happened if the colonial empires had not arisen.

It is not difficult to find instances in which the colonial powers exploited their colonies economically. They are manifold, and the further we move into the past, the more numerous they were. But the examples of development effects are also numerous. The colonial powers' policies do not seem to be a sufficient or even a primary factor in explaining the developing countries' lack of development. This is particularly true for countries that were not colonies at all. Non-colonies such as Ethiopia, Afghanistan and, to a lesser extent, Thailand did not have a higher standard of living than their colonial neighbors. Traditional colonialism also seems to have limited validity as an explanation for conditions in Latin America, which became independent after the United States but before Canada, as an example from the Western hemisphere.

Nor do the industrialized nations that have had colonies seem to be or even to have been wealthier than others. The United States, Canada, and Australia are all among the world's wealthiest nations. They were colonies themselves at one time, and they were relatively highly developed at that time as well. Likewise, for such countries as Switzerland and the Scandinavian countries it must be unreasonable to maintain that their especially high standard of living is based on exploitation of the developing countries.

The industrialization of India is among the most controversial themes in this historical perspective. It is dubious to claim, as some structuralists do, that the country could have been an industrialized state today if developments had been allowed to continue along their original course. India was technically and economically far behind Europe in the 1800s. At the close of the century, however, a sizeable textile industry developed. Britain was undoubtedly interested in limiting this industry to promote its own. But in the first place it did not carry its policy particularly far. The Indians wanted to grant their industry special favors—that was the source of the controversy—and were allowed to do so from the 1920s onwards. London never tried to stop the process of industrialization, although it could probably have proceeded somewhat more rapidly with tariff barriers, at least in the short run. In the second place, the textile industry grew even when it was subject to free competition.

The problem is more what the British did not do than what they did. Of course they could have done much more to promote economic growth. The reponsibilities of government were quite limited during this period of history, especially under British liberalism. The government actually tended to be more active in India than in Britain itself. An era has to be understood in the light of the ideas of the time, not of the post-war period, when it became much more common for the government to enter actively into industrial projects.

If we move from traditional colonialism to the more general economic ties between North and South, a comparison of Argentina and Australia is interesting. They both began to grow quickly around 1850; they sold basically the same products; in 1913 they both had a per capita income that was among the ten highest in the world. Thereafter, their paths parted. What may be the explanation? Structuralists have pointed to the strong British and later North American influence to explain why no extensive industrialization took place in Argentina. Comparatively, however, this explanation is problematic because the extent of foreign influence was probably even greater in Australia. Many different local factors were undoubtedly more important than the international factors. The rigid social structure in Argentina, which limited both incentive and the possibilities for industrialization and further economic development, was probably of primary importance.

On the other hand, China and India are often compared to prove that sheltering the economy gives better results than openness. Economic growth has probably been somewhat higher in the more closed China, and China has generally done the most of these two countries to provide for the very poorest segments of its population. However, the points of departure were different in the two countries, and it is significant that the setbacks were great during China's most sheltered periods, the Great Leap Forward and the Cultural Revolution (see pages 220–221). Nor has the Indian economy, with its emphasis on import substitution, been particularly open in an international perspective.

The international economic system has not proved to be as rigid as it may appear in the structuralists' theories. Total production in the

Basic indicators

	Population (millions) mid-1983	Area (thousands of square kilometers)	GNP per capita Dollars 1983	GNP per capita Average annual growth rate (percent) 1965-83	Life expectancy at birth (years) 1983
Low-income economies	**2,335.4**	**31,603**	**260**	**2.7**	**59**
China and India	**1,752.3**	**12,849**	**280**	**3.2**	**62**
Other low-income	**583.0**	**18,754**	**200**	**0.7**	**51**
Sub-Saharan Africa	**245.2**	**15,451**	**220**	**—0.2**	**48**
1 Ethiopia	40.9	1,222	120	0.5	43
2 Bangladesh	95.5	144	130	0.5	50
3 Mali	7.2	1,240	160	1.2	45
4 Nepal	15.7	141	160	0.1	46
5 Zaire	29.7	2,345	170	—1.3	51
6 Burkina	6.5	274	180	1.4	44
7 Burma	35.5	677	180	2.2	55
8 Malawi	6.6	118	210	2.2	44
9 Uganda	13.9	236	220	—4.4	49
10 Burundi	4.5	28	240	2.1	47
11 Niger	6.1	1,267	240	—1.2	45
12 Tanzania	20.8	945	240	0.9	51
13 Somalia	5.1	638	250	—0.8	45
14 India	733.2	3,288	260	1.5	55
15 Rwanda	5.7	26	270	2.3	47
16 Central African Rep.	2.5	623	280	0.1	48
17 Togo	2.8	57	280	1.1	49
18 Benin	3.8	113	290	1.0	48
19 China	1,019.1	9,561	300	4.4	67
20 Guinea	5.8	246	300	1.1	37
21 Haiti	5.3	28	300	1.1	54
22 Ghana	12.8	239	310	—2.1	59
23 Madagascar	9.5	587	310	—1.2	49
24 Sierra Leone	3.6	72	330	1.1	38
25 Sri Lanka	15.4	66	330	2.9	69
26 Kenya	18.9	583	340	2.3	57
27 Pakistan	89.7	804	390	2.5	50
28 Sudan	20.8	2,506	400	1.3	48
29 Afghanistan	17.2	648		0.5	36
30 Bhutan	1.2	47			43
31 Chad	4.8	1,284			43
32 Kampuchea, Dem.		181			
33 Lao PDR	3.7	237			44
34 Mozambique	13.1	802			46
35 Viet Nam	58.5	330			64
Middle-income economies	**1,165.2**	**40,525**	**1,310**	**3.4**	**61**
Oil exporters	**542.6**	**15,511**	**1,060**	**3.3**	**57**
Oil importers	**622.6**	**25,014**	**1,530**	**3.5**	**64**
Sub-Saharan Africa	**148.2**	**5,822**	**700**	**1.9**	**50**
Lower middle-income	**665.1**	**18,446**	**750**	**2.9**	**57**
36 Senegal	6.2	196	440	—0.5	46
37 Lesotho	1.5	30	460	6.3	53
38 Liberia	2.1	111	480	0.8	49
39 Mauritania	1.6	1,031	480	0.3	46
40 Bolivia	6.0	1,099	510	0.6	51
41 Yemen, PDR	2.0	333	520		46
42 Yemen Arab Rep.	7.6	195	550	5.7	44
43 Indonesia	155.7	1,919	560	5.0	54
44 Zambia	6.3	753	580	—1.3	51
45 Honduras	4.1	112	670	0.6	60
46 Egypt. Arab Rep.	45.2	1,001	700	4.2	58
47 El Salvador	5.2	21	710	—0.2	64
48 Ivory Coast	9.5	322	710	1.0	52
49 Zimbabwe	7.9	391	740	1.5	56
50 Morocco	20.8	447	760	2.9	52
51 Papua New Guinea	3.2	462	760	0.9	54
52 Philippines	52.1	300	760	2.9	64
53 Nigeria	93.6	924	770	3.2	49
54 Cameroon	9.6	475	820	2.7	54
55 Thailand	49.2	514	820	4.3	63
56 Nicaragua	3.0	130	880	—1.8	58
57 Costa Rica	2.4	51	1,020	2.1	74
58 Peru	17.9	1,285	1,040	0.1	58
59 Guatemala	7.9	109	1,120	2.1	60
60 Congo, People's Rep.	1.8	342	1,230	3.5	63
61 Turkey	47.3	781	1,240	3.0	63
62 Tunisia	6.9	164	1,290	5.0	62
63 Jamaica	2.3	11	1,300	—0.5	70
64 Dominican Rep.	6.0	49	1,370	3.9	63

276

	Population (millions) mid-1983	Area (thousands of square kilometers)	GNP per capita Dollars 1983	Average annual growth rate (percent) 1965–83	Life expectancy at birth (years) 1983
65 Paraguay	3.2	407	1,410	4.5	65
66 Ecuador	8.2	284	1,420	4.6	63
67 Colombia	27.5	1,139	1,430	3.2	64
68 Angola	8.2	1,247			43
69 Cuba	9.8	115			75
70 Korea Dem. Rep.	19.2	121			65
71 Lebanon	2.6	10			65
72 Mongolia	1.8	1,565			65
Upper middle-income	500.1	22,079	2,050	3.8	65
73 Jordan	3.2	98	1,640	6.9	64
74 Syrian Arab. Rep.	9.6	185	1,760	4.9	67
75 Malaysia	14.9	330	1,860	4.5	67
76 Chile	11.7	757	1,870	−0.1	70
77 Brazil	129.7	8,512	1,880	5.0	64
78 Korea, Rep. of	40.0	98	2,010	6.7	67
79 Argentina	29.6	2,767	2,070	0.5	70
80 Panama	2.0	77	2,120	2.9	71
81 Portugal	10.1	92	2,230	3.7	71
82 Mexico	75.0	1,973	2,240	3.2	66
83 Algeria	20.6	2,382	2,320	3.6	57
84 South Africa	31.5	1,221	2,490	1.6	64
85 Uruguay	3.0	176	2,490	2.0	73
86 Yugoslavia	22.8	256	2,570	4.7	69
87 Venezuela	17.3	912	3,840	1.5	68
88 Greece	9.8	132	3,920	4.0	75
89 Israel	4.1	21	5,370	2.9	74
90 Hong Kong	5.3	1	6,000	6.2	76
91 Singapore	2.5	1	6,620	7.8	73
92 Trinidad and Tobago	1.1	5	6,850	3.4	68
93 Iran, Islamic Rep.	42.5	1,648			60
94 Iraq	14.7	435			59
High-income oil exporters	17.9	4.312	12,370	3.8	59
95 Oman	1.1	300	6,250	6.5	53
96 Libya	3.4	1,760	8,480	−0.9	58
97 Saudi Arabia	10.4	2,150	12,230	6.7	56
98 Kuwait	1.7	18	17,880	0.2	71
99 United Arab. Emirates	1.2	84	22,870		71
Industrial market economies	728.9	30,935	11,060	2.5	76
100 Spain	38.2	505	4,780	3.0	75
101 Ireland	3.5	70	5,000	2.3	73
102 Italy	56.8	301	6,400	2.8	76
103 New Zealand	3.2	269	7,730	1.2	74
104 Belgium	9.9	31	9,140	3.1	73
105 United Kingdom	56.3	245	9,200	1.7	74
106 Austria	7.5	84	9,250	3.7	73
107 Netherlands	14.4	41	9,890	2.3	76
108 Japan	119.3	372	10,120	4.9	77
109 France	54.7	547	10,500	3.1	75
110 Finland	4.9	337	10,740	3.3	73
111 Germany Fed. Rep.	61.4	249	11,430	2.8	75
112 Australia	15.4	7,687	11,490	1.7	76
113 Denmark	5.1	43	11,570	1.9	74
114 Canada	24.9	9,976	12,310	2.5	76
115 Sweden	8.3	450	12,470	1.9	78
116 Norway	4.1	324	14,020	3.3	77
117 United States	234.5	9,363	14,110	1.7	75
118 Switzerland	6.5	41	16,290	1.4	79
East European nonmarket economies	386.1	23,422			70
119 Hungary	10.7	93	2,150	6.4	70
120 Albania	2.8	29			71
121 Bulgaria	8.9	111			70
122 Czechoslovakia	15.4	128			70
123 German Dem. Rep.	16.7	108			71
124 Poland	36.6	313			71
125 Romania	22.6	238			71
126 USSR	272.5	22,402			69

Source: **World Development Report 1985**

developing countries increased by 4.9 percent annually from 1950 to 1960, by 6.1 percent from 1960 to 1973, by 5.5 percent from 1973 to 1980, and by 3.0 percent from 1980 to 1985. For all of these periods, the figures were actually higher than the corresponding aggregate figures for the Western industrial countries, although the differing points of departure must be taken into consideration.

Production has increased more rapidly in some developing countries than in others. Almost all the countries enjoying the strongest growth have also had close contact with the rest of the world. Several of the oil nations are among them, but they are such special cases that it may not be reasonable to place too much emphasis on developments there. Other countries experiencing strong growth have been South Korea (8.6 percent annually from 1960 to 1970, 9.1 percent annually from 1970 to 1981), Taiwan (9.0 and 7.7 percent for the two periods, respectively), and Brazil (8.4 percent from 1970 to 1981). A number of countries—about 20—have graduated into the category of newly industrializing countries—the NICs.

There are also examples of countries that have been relatively isolated from the international economy but that have experienced strong growth. The Soviet Union, especially during the period between the two world wars, is one such example. Several countries in Latin America had at least short-term benefits from the fact that their infant industries were spared from European competition during the First World War. Certain colonies that were fully or partially isolated from their mother country during the Second World War experienced an upswing. In French West Africa, for instance, this resulted in the establishment of a certain amount of industry based on import substitution, although the area remained one of the more underdeveloped segments of Africa. Finally, the highly developed Western industrial nations have not always favored free trade. The United States and Germany pursued protectionist policies vis-à-vis British competition during build-up phases. Japan has long combined free trade with clearly protectionist elements.

However, a great number of colonies experienced economic growth during the Second World War. Their very inclusion in the international economy, in the form of the enormous wartime demand, contributed strongly to this growth. W. Arthur Lewis has argued that the growth cycles in developing countries and in industrial countries have coincided closely. When the industrial countries experience growth, the developing countries grow. When there is a recession in the North, there is a recession in the South as well. Moreover, the examples of the United States, Germany and Japan merely illustrate that in the short term protectionism can be advantageous. The benefits of a long-term protectionist policy are considerably more questionable. Most economists today agree that import substitution has not produced the desired results in the developing countries that have maintained such a course for the longest time. Japan's remarkable growth also shows how a country can be transformed from being primarily an underdeveloped country to becoming an advanced industrial nation in the course of a few generations.

All the comparisons that have been carried out here are far from decisive evidence. The cause-effect relationship is often highly complex. For instance, in some cases it may be that it is the natural resources that have attracted the interest of the outside world, whereas countries with few or no natural resources have become isolated for that very reason. But it must be possible to conclude that the evidence seems weak for the claim that the North's development has led to the South's underdevelopment.

The Multinational Corporations

A corresponding line of reasoning can be applied to the role of the multinational corporations. Once more, there are many examples of them entering into unreasonable agreements, so unreasonable that they must be termed exploitation. When corporations pay little or no tax on huge profits over long periods of time, such as was long the case with the US copper industry in Chile, then that is exploitation. But sweeping generalizations concerning the role of multinational corporations cannot be made on the basis of a few such examples — nor a few to the contrary.

It is often impossible to determine what the alternatives to multinational investments may be. The structuralists often take as their point of departure the assumption that the alternative is government-owned businesses with the same efficiency as the foreign firms. Many liberalists go to the opposite extreme and assume that the alternative is no investment at all.

Empirical investigations seem to indicate that the multinational corporations normally have a positive effect on a country's national income and even on government revenue. However, it appears that their effect is more questionable with regard to the balance of payments. The corporations export much of their profits, whereas the original investments often originate in the local market. Moreover, they often obtain their production equipment and capital goods from abroad, so that the spill-over effect of such new industry is less than in developed economies.

It is misleading to consider the capital flows in and out of a country in a certain year in isolation as many structuralists do. For instance, when a company manages to take out more than it has contributed, an important reason may be the increase in value which has taken place in the meantime and which may also have expressed itself in terms of employment, taxes, etc.

Many multinational corporations have contributed to an uneven distribution of income because their employees have been relatively well paid in relation to the vast majority. Such investments can also result in a reduction in the number of jobs because new technology tends to re-quire fewer workers than the old processes did. Here as elsewhere, the differences can be great from one country to another and from one sector to another.

The structuralists claim that the ties between multinational corpora-tions and local elites are often so close that they make colonial control obsolete. Why send in troops when the local elite can do the job? Once more there are many examples of such coinciding interests. Many elites lack both the will and the capacity to control foreign firms. The number of corrupt and/or incompetent regimes in the Third World is substantial.

But governments of varying political persuasions have shown great ingenuity in terms of regulating the activities of such firms. A much dis-cussed phenomenon in this connection is the so-called 'host country's learning curve'. Governments are willing to provide favorable conditions in order to attract a firm. When it has established itself and committed its activity, the time is ripe to impose stiffer conditions. When one coun-try has struck out this course, others will follow.

The oil companies (often considered the strongest of the strong among the multinationals) and their course of development may be instructive. From having controlled the entire process, from exploration and exploi-tation to distribution and sales, and from having paid nearly symbolic taxes, in many countries they have now been reduced primarily to the role of distributors who pay large, increasing percentages of their profits in taxes. Particularly in the 1960s and 1970s many raw materials indus-tries were nationalized in Third World countries.

Even in Chile, the Christian Democrat Eduardo Frei was in the process of nationalizing the North American copper companies before Allende took over in 1970. After an interval conservative leaders have often continued where the radical leaders left off. In Iran, Mossadeq was deposed in 1953; the new Western-oriented government under the leadership of the Shah increased the country's share of the oil companies' profits from 68 percent in 1954 to 80 percent in 1970. In Venezuela, the dictator Jimenez and reform-minded elements such as Betancourt saw to it that the same share increased from 51 percent in 1950 to 70 percent in the 1960s.

The historian David Fieldhouse has shown in his analysis of the British-Dutch Unilever group's activities in Africa that strong governments have been able to influence a company's local policies to a great extent. Where this will or capacity was not to be found, the results naturally failed to appear. There has also been a clear tendency for governments to impose the condition that foreign capital cooperate with local capital. Before 1951, only 17 percent of the US companies in the Third World were subject to such limitations. During the years 1971–1975, 38 percent of new US ventures abroad fell into this category. The corresponding figures for European firms were 15 and 49 percent, respectively, and for Japanese firms 29 and 82 percent. The attractiveness of multinational corporations even in leftist countries under certain conditions is best illustrated by the fact that in the course of the 1970s even most of the communist countries, including the Soviet Union, began to show their interest in such investments. During the 1980s, China surpassed them all on this course.

Raw Materials and Processed Goods

The relative prices of raw materials and processed goods have been another central issue in the debate between structuralists and liberalists. Is it true that the price trend has been unilaterally in disfavor of raw materials and thus the developing countries? Prebisch was among those who first and most strongly claimed that this was the case. In 1950 he published a study based on Britain's terms of trade during the period 1870-1936. Later, several similar investigations have been carried out. The conclusions of these later studies are not as unambiguous as Prebisch's.

A number of methodological objections have been raised against Prebisch's study. He has largely ignored quality improvements and thus given a distorted impression of the increase in prices for processed goods.

Transport costs have not been 'correctly' calculated. Even so, the most important result of these studies is that a lot seems to depend on what goods and what time periods are considered. The relationship between commodity prices and the prices of processed goods has often, but certainly not always, been to the advantage of the latter. Another element is the fact that fluctuations have normally been greatest for raw materials, with the unfortunate consequences that entails. And in 1982 non-oil commodity prices, in relative terms, reached their lowest level in 50 years.

The developing countries do not export solely raw materials and the industrial countries solely processed goods. In 1975, 33 percent of exports from developing countries consisted of processed goods. This figure does not include the oil nations. Many developed countries, such as Australia, New Zealand, and Denmark, have joined the ranks of the richest nations of the world precisely by exporting agricultural products. The United States has long been the world's largest exporter of raw materials.

The structuralists have claimed that the colonial powers placed sole priority on exports of agricultural products, and that this took place at the expense of production for the local market, to some extent at the expense of the local population's ability to survive. There is little doubt that exports of agricultural products were an important aspect of the colonial powers' policies. The controversy concerns primarily the effect of this policy on the colonies.

Again it is difficult to make a decisive assessment. Local variation was considerable. India seems to illustrate the advantages of such a policy. Export agriculture was clearly the most dynamic. Exports paid for the import of other goods. Moreover, in many countries local sales were insufficient to satisfy basic needs. With rapid population growth, this would probably have become even more pronounced. Finally, for the most part agriculture for domestic use remained more important than agriculture for export. But it is a valid criticism of the colonial powers that they promoted export interests virtually everywhere, even in areas where there was little to be gained and perhaps more to be lost by such a policy, such as in Mali and Niger.

The Question of Dependence

It is one thing to claim that the industrialized nations' development has caused the developing countries' underdevelopment and that the latter group are trapped in the existing structure. However, the structuralists have enjoyed greater support when they emphasize the fact that the developing countries are highly dependent on the industrialized countries and that this dependence can have a series of unfortunate consequences for them, both politically and economically.

Whereas the vast majority of the poor countries are dependent on income from a single or a few export goods, the import of these goods represents only a small fraction of the industrialized countries' imports. Several developing countries often compete with one another, with the consequences this entails for both price and general bargaining position. An economic recession in the center has great effects in the periphery, whereas a crisis in the periphery need not have particular effect in the center. This imbalance in trade is accompanied by an even greater asymmetry with regard to investments.

In 1982, trade with the Third World accounted for 25.2 percent of the Western industrialized nations' exports and 27.2 percent of their imports, while those same numbers constituted 66.5 percent of the exports from the South and 61.2 percent of their imports. Whereas 51.8 percent of all trade by EC members was with other EC countries, the poor countries' trade with one another accounted for only 27.5 percent of their total trade. The tendency in recent years has been for the South to become somewhat less dependent on the North, but the lack of balance is still striking.

In certain areas, however, the dependency is primarily in the other direction, thereby demonstrating also to the North the problems of dependence. Yet there is a vast difference between this rather limited dependence and that of many poor countries which rely almost entirely on the export of one or two products. The North is most vulnerable in relation to the South in terms of certain strategic goods, such as oil, chromium, copper, manganese, nickel, tin, phosphates, etc. In general terms, Japan is more dependent on importing such goods than Western Europe is, although Western Europe is in turn more vulnerable than the United States.

Particularly with regard to oil, altered power relationships have had dramatic manifestations. The producers among the developing countries organized themselves in 1960 in the Organization of Petroleum-Exporting Countries (OPEC). Oil consumption continued to rise incessantly in the Western industrialized nations. The dependence on imports rose correspondingly as the industrialized nations' own production far from managed to keep up with consumption. The reversal was particularly great in the United States, which had long been self-sufficient, but which in 1977 imported almost half of the oil the country needed.

These long-term trends, combined with the solidarity the Middle East crisis of 1973 created among the Arab nations, were the background for the major price rises OPEC was able to implement in 1973–74, when prices were approximately quadrupled. In 1978-79, they were doubled once more. This time the trigger was the fall of the Shah and a strong decline in Iran's oil exports.

The oil shocks had sweeping effects in the industrialized countries. Among other things, they contributed to increasing further the rate of inflation that had been accelerating for some years already. US oil imports, and the exports to the oil nations that these nations' large incomes now enabled them to afford, were an important explanation as to why US dependence on foreign countries also increased sharply. As late as in 1970, exports and imports together accounted for only 11 percent of the US gross national product. By 1982 this figure had risen to 20 percent.

The oil nations' success in determining prices in 1973-74 created high expectations among other commodity producers as well. Producers' cartels were established or renewed for such products as copper, bauxite, iron ore, bananas and coffee. The developing countries applied pressure for a new economic world order.

However, it soon became evident that no one could copy OPEC. The other cartels did not manage to maintain high prices, especially when the effects of the economic recession of 1974–75 appeared in the West in earnest. Disagreement among producers could be substantial. With regard to bauxite, for instance, Jamaica, Surinam and Guyana reduced production in order to stimulate price rises, whereas Australia and Guinea increased their production. The demand for copper proved smaller than anticipated. Other cartels had additional difficulties because of their products' perishability and the possibilities of using substitutes in the industrialized countries.

In the course of the 1980s, the developing countries' dependence increased dramatically in two fields: foreign debt and food stuffs, particularly grain. The debt burden of the developing countries, with the exception of the OPEC countries, reached nearly 600 billion dollars in 1984. The situation was most critical in Latin America—in Argentina, Brazil, Chile and Mexico. The world recession of 1980-83, a combination of general inflation, rising oil prices and falling commodity prices, a stronger dollar and a high interest level in the United States created enormous problems. Several countries had pursued highly expansive policies, as had many banks in industrialized countries, and had to accept strict conditions in order to obtain new economic support from abroad.

If the debt burden was greatest in Latin America, the food situation was most grave in Africa. While grain production soared in India and China in the late 1970s, Africa's imports of grain increased from an average of 1.2 million metric tons in 1960–63 to 8 millon in 1980. But this could not prevent as many as 200 million persons—60 percent of the population of Africa—from having a daily calorie intake that was less than what the UN considered the subsistence level. The situation was most acute in Ethiopia and in the Sudan in 1983–85. The agricultural crisis had many causes, as did the debt crisis. As mentioned, the colonial countries had placed priority on exports; Africa was hit by serious droughts; the various governments pursued policies that in many different ways favored urban and consumer interests over rural and producer interests, despite the fact that approximately 60 percent of all Africans were still engaged in agriculture.

Then in late 1985-86 the oil market changed dramatically. The high prices had cut demand. Production from non-OPEC countries had increased. Feuding within OPEC also increased as several countries tried to combine high prices with higher production levels. In late 1985 Saudi Arabia refused to suffer the effects of stabilizing this complicated game any longer. The price of oil was cut in half. While the falling oil price represented a set-back for the producers, it was generally welcomed by the world's consumers, also in the Third World. Worse for most of the poor countries was the fact that other commodity prices remained at a very low level.

Why Poverty?

The debate on development has naturally not only concerned relations between North and South. A number of other factors also influence the situation in the South. In the first place it may be valid to ask what it is that actually requires explanation, and what is normal. Is it development or poverty? In a long-term historical perspective, rapid growth is the exception. Poverty and a lack of development have been the norm. This fact in itself is significant in order to understand the poverty of the developing countries.

In the second place, although breaking loose from centuries of accommodation to poverty has always been a difficult task, not least attitudinally, the difficulties related to initiating economic development are in many ways greater now than previously. Population pressure is substantial; death rates have sunk dramatically while birth rates have remained high. The number of industrialized countries is already high; the world is more closely-knit than before; the entrance ticket to industrialization in the form of advanced technology and investments is often more expensive. Moreover, the results of industrialization are sometimes less significant than previously. In the 1970s it was estimated that Brazil needed only 8 000 workers to produce a million tons of steel. When Britain, as the first country in the world, reached that level of production, 370 000 workers were required.

On the other hand, developing countries today do have certain advantages. Most forms of technology are more readily available now than formerly. Insight into how economic growth is created and controlled is greater than previously. The same is true of assistance from abroad, in the form of grants, loans and other resources. The balance between advantages and disadvantages can vary considerably from one sector to another and from one country to another.

In the third place, it is important to emphasize the diversity of the Third World, the local variation. The economist John Kenneth Galbraith distinguishes between three main models to explain why economic development has not taken place. They are extremely schematic, but these models may establish a point of departure for a discussion of this local dimension.

First is the model from Africa south of the Sahara. Most of the barriers to economic growth are to be found here, including those that will be mentioned in connection with the other two models. However, Galbraith places particular emphasis on the insufficient 'cultural base'. As late as in 1958, only about 10 000 Africans were studying at universities, more than half of them in Ghana and Nigeria. The situation in Zaire was the most extreme, where only 16 Africans had completed a university education before independence in 1960. Although the new states on the whole placed greater emphasis on education than the colonial powers had done, the countries south of the Sahara are still in a weak position in this regard. It is difficult to imagine development without education, including everything from university studies to many different types of practical training.

A number of other problems are more or less unique to much of Africa. The soil is poorly suited for agriculture, deserts and jungles complicate transportation, illiteracy has deep roots, regional disputes and tribal conflicts are still highly significant. It is true that there were highly adapted cultures in parts of Africa before the colonial powers arrived. On the other hand, sleeping sickness ruled out the use of draft animals and meant that important conditions for economic growth, such as the wheel and the plow, were not be found south of the Sahara. A feature many African countries share with several others is the fact that their regimes are so weak, corrupt and incompetent that they represent a significant obstacle to development in themselves.

The second model is the South-Asian model (which can also be applied to certain other countries, such as Egypt and Indonesia). Here the primary obstacles seem to be population growth and capital shortage. Population growth is so rapid that it often swallows up any progress that is made. Capital shortage makes investment difficult both within agriculture and more 'modern' sectors. The differences between the countries in this model and the African countries can be striking. A country such as India has an educational system that is good in many ways, both in terms of basic education and university education. There is a surplus of several categories of highly educated manpower, a surplus that is part of the background for the export of such personnel to industrialized countries such as the United States and Britain.

However, capital shortage and overpopulation are features that characterize other developing countries as well. Several countries in Latin America, the Middle East and particularly in Africa have had considerably higher population growth than e.g. India, Pakistan and Egypt. When such great attention is focused on precisely these two factors, the explanation is in part that it is difficult to identify other basic obstacles to development. However, a number of major and minor obstacles are to be found here as well: a hierarchic social structure, the pattern of ownership, particularly in agriculture, a paralyzing bureaucracy, wide-spread corruption, etc.

The third main model is the Latin American model (which is appropriate for several nations in the Middle East as well). These countries, too, enjoy a high level of education. To some extent they even have relatively substantial capital resources. On the other hand, the population pressure is great. Nevertheless, even this has not prevented some of the countries from achieving an impressive economic growth, measured in terms of gross national product. Thus Brazil and Mexico were among the growth successes of the 1960s and 1970s.

Their growth was of a type that has figured prominently in structuralist arguments. Several structuralists practically define development in such a way that it cannot take place in a capitalist society. 'Development' is largely reserved for countries that emphasize self-sufficiency. Such a definition does not seem particularly fruitful. However, a different point they make is of greater interest in this context—the significance of the internal distribution of growth. Growth that does not benefit the vast majority of the population has obvious drawbacks, both morally and politically. Even from an economic point of view, growth is retarded by the majority being largely excluded from taking part in it. What is more, many of the countries in this group have not experienced much growth at all, in part because the purchasing power is limited to a small minority.

In few places is the social structure more inequitable than in many Latin American countries. Land distribution is one example. Most of the small peasants find few opportunities for increasing production. If they manage to do so, others often make off with the profit for their extra effort. In the rapidly growing cities, a rather extensive industrialization may be taking place, but the profit here is often shared among three main groups, in a complicated mixture of cooperation and competition: the multinational corporations, the government, and the local economic elite. Society must also provide for other elites: the military, the clergy and the politicians. As there is seldom enough for everyone while making certain minimum concessions to the rest of the population, more and more money is printed. The result is that many of the highest inflation rates in the world are to be found here. They in themselves constitute an obstacle to further growth.

Latin America provides many examples of economic growth that has primarily benefited a minority. In Africa, Kenya and the Ivory Coast are countries that have experienced growth but inequitable distribution. But other capitalist growth successes, such as South Korea and Taiwan, have an income distribution that is fairly even according to most estimates. It is probably more even than in China, although the validity of comparing two such small countries with the world's most populous nation may be questioned.

Industrialization and growth have taken place under various conditions. No single model has brought the industrialized nations where they are today. Some scholars employ five main models—the English, the German, the French, the Japanese and the Soviet model. A corresponding view applies to the developing countries. Various paths lead to growth, just as various paths uphold poverty.

However, it appears as though the later industrialization has got under way, the more important the role of the state has been in the process. In most of the developing countries, too, strong government will probably be necessary to provide the required infrastructure (education, communications, etc.), to stimulate capital formation and moderate population growth, control foreign investments, implement reforms, etc.

Why have the countries of South-east Asia enjoyed more rapid growth than most other developing countries? Why did Brazil do better than Argentina and Chile in the 1960s and 1970s? What is the 'proper' balance between agriculture and industry in order to create economic growth? And, when we reach the individual level where the various decisions are made that together constitute 'development', what makes one person change whereas another remains in the traditional pattern?

With regard to development and poverty, as in most North— South and East—West issues, comprehensive explanations must be supplemented with a knowledge of local conditions. Such conditions tend to modify nearly any generalization. Local diversity is difficult to grasp and is easily forgotten in the stream of top-level international events. But in many ways the local determinants have become ever more important, in step with the weakening we have seen in the position of the superpowers, both politically and economically.

Bibliography

This bibliography has a limited objective. In the first place it shows what works have been most important for this book. An exhaustive list of all the literature that has been used would have been much longer than the present one. In the second place, the bibliography aims to give the interested reader ideas for further reading. Experience seems to indicate that if the number of titles is too great, it merely tends to discourage the reader. Those who may desire further suggestions will find many more in the books mentioned below.

General Surveys

A good survey of US-Soviet relations is to be found in Walter LaFeber: *America, Russia, and the Cold War 1945-1980* (New York, 1980). Among the abundance of surveys on US foreign policy after 1945, I recommend Seyom Brown: *The Faces of Power. Constancy and Change in United States Foreign Policy from Truman to Reagen* (New York, 1983). The standard work on Soviet foreign policy is still Adam B. Ulam: *Expansion and Coexistence. Soviet Foreign Policy, 1917-73* (New York, 1974). A useful version of history as seen from Moscow is *Soviet Foreign Policy. Volume II: 1945-1980* (Moscow, 1981).

Joan Edelman Spero: *The Politics of International Economic Relations* (New York, 1981) has been most useful, as it deals with economic relations between East and West, within the West and between North and South.

Much of the statistical material has been derived from The World Bank: *World Development Report 1985* (New York, 1985); the US Department of Commerce: *Historical Statistics of the United States. Colonial Times to 1970* (Washington, D.C., 1975); and from Herbert Block: *The Planetary Product in 1980: A Creative Pause?* (Washington, D.C., 1981).

The Cold War, 1945–1949

Herbert Feis: *From Trust to Terror. The Onset of the Cold War, 1945–1950* (New York, 1970) is a key traditionalist presentation, whereas Gabriel and Joyce Kolko: *The Limits of Power. The World and United States Foreign Policy, 1945–1954* (New York, 1972) presents an unequivocal revisionist version. The best post-revisionist book is John Lewis Gaddis: *The United States and the Origins of the Cold War, 1941–1947* (New York, 1972). My own analyses of this period are to be found in *The American Non-Policy Towards Eastern Europe 1943–1947* (Oslo–New York, 1975) and *America, Scandinavia and the Cold War 1945–1949* (New York–Oslo, 1980). Vojtech Mastny: *Russia's Road to the Cold War. Diplomacy, Warfare and the Politics of Communism, 1941–1945* (New York, 1979) is by far the best analysis of Soviet policy during the period in question.

The Cold War Becomes Global, 1945–1962

Russel D. Buhite: *Soviet–American Relations in Asia, 1945–1954* (Norman, 1981), is a useful survey of the two superpowers' Asian policies. William Whitney Stueck, Jr.: *The Road to Confrontation: American Policy Toward China and Korea, 1947–1950* (Chapel Hill, 1981) also contains interesting observations.

The central works on the Eisenhower period are Robert A. Divine: *Eisenhower and the Cold War* (Oxford, 1981) and Townsend Hoopes: *The Devil and John Foster Dulles* (Boston, 1973). The key book on the Cuban crisis is still Graham Allison: *Essence of Decision: Explaining the Cuban Missile Crisis* (Boston, 1971).

Valuable surveys of Soviet policy in the Third World are to be found in Roger E. Kanet, ed.: *The Soviet Union and Developing Nations* (Baltimore, 1974); Christopher Stevens: *The Soviet Union and Black Africa* (New York, 1976); and Robert H. Donaldson, ed.: *The Soviet Union in the Third World: Successes and Failures* (Boulder, 1981).

The Policy of Detente

Two key works on Soviet policy during this period are Michel Tatu: *Power in the Kremlin. From Khrushchev to Kosygin* (New York, 1972) and Robin Edmonds: *Soviet Foreign Policy: The Brezhnev Years* (Oxford, 1983).

For US policy, Henry Kissinger's monumental *White House Years* (Boston, 1979) and *Years of Upheaval* (Boston, 1982) are indispensable. They may well be supplemented with Seymour M. Hersh: *The Price of Power. Kissinger in the Nixon White House* (New York, 1983).

The most satisfactory presentation of the SALT I talks is John Newhouse: *Cold Dawn. The Story of SALT* (New York, 1973). With regard to the Middle East, Nadav Safran: *Israel. The Embattled Ally* (Cambridge, 1982) may be recommended, although it places greatest emphasis on the role of Israel, as the title indicates. More evenly balanced in this respect is Ritchie Ovendale: *The Origins of the Arab-Israeli Wars* (London, 1984). As far as Vietnam is concerned, much of the literature is still focused on the United States. Most useful among these books are George C. Herring, Jr.: *America's Longest War: The United States and Vietnam, 1950-1975* (New York, 1979) and Leslie H. Gelb and Richard K. Betts: *The Irony of Vietnam: The System Worked* (Washington, D.C., 1979).

Relations between East and West in Recent Years

The most exhaustive survey is to be found in Raymond L. Garthoff: *Detente and Confrontation. American-Soviet Relations from Nixon to Reagan* (Washington, D.C., 1985). Adam Ulam has written the sequel to *Expansion and Coexistence* in *Dangerous Relations. The Soviet Union in World Politics, 1970-1982* (Oxford, 1983). Among the many memoirs from the Carter period, Zbigniew Brzezinski: *Power and Principle. Memoirs of the National Security Adviser 1977-1981* (New York, 1983) is the most candid. Fred I. Greenstein, ed.: *The Reagan Presidency. An Early Assessment* (Baltimore, 1983) is interesting reading on the Reagan administration. Highly useful surveys may be found in the annual *America and the World* volumes of *Foreign Affairs*.

David E. Albright, ed.: *Communism in Africa* (Bloomington, 1980) provides useful insights on Africa. Strobe Talbott: *Endgame. The Inside Story of SALT II* (New York, 1979) is the best presentation in its field. He has analyzed Reagan's nuclear arms policy in *Deadly Gambits* (New York, 1984). A fascinating analysis of the Jackson-Vanik amendment may be found in Paula Stern: *Water's Edge. Domestic Politics and the Making of American Foreign Policy* (Westport, 1979).

Three key presentations of the arms race are Lawrence Freedman: *The Evolution of Nuclear Strategy* (New York, 1981); Michael Mandelbaum: *The Nuclear Question. The United States and Nuclear Weapons, 1945–1976* (Cambridge, 1979), and David Holloway: *The Soviet Union and the Arms Race* (New Haven, 1983). Thomas Wolfe: *Soviet Power and Europe, 1945–1970* (Baltimore, 1970) and The Harvard Nuclear Study Group: *Living with Nuclear Weapons* (Toronto, 1983) are also useful.

In the abundant literature on why the atom bomb was dropped on Hiroshima and Nagasaki, one book stands out from the rest. It is Martin J. Sherwin: *A World Destroyed. The Atomic Bomb and the Grand Alliance* (New York, 1973). Good on the role of the new weapon in early US nuclear strategy is Gregg Herken: *The Winning Weapon. The Atomic Bomb in the Cold War, 1945–1950* (New York, 1980).

An excellent general presentation of US security policy is John Lewis Gaddis: *Strategies of Containment. A Critical Appraisal of Postwar American National Security Policy* (Oxford, 1982). The most recent years are analyzed in Strobe Talbott's two books listed under the preceding heading.

Developments within the Western Camp

Robert Hathaway: *Ambiguous Partnership: Britain and America, 1944–1947* (New York, 1981) is an excellent book on relations between Britain and the United States early in the postwar period. Robert Osgood: *NATO. The Entangling Alliance* (Chicago, 1962) is still an important work. Alfred Grosser: *The Western Alliance. European–American Relations Since 1945* (London, 1980) contains a wealth of useful information, but is quite poorly organized.

A general survey of the course of development in Western Europe may be found in D. W. Urwin: *Western Europe Since 1945. A Short Political History* (London, 1981). Martin Sæter: *Det politiske Europa* (The Political Europe) (Oslo, 1971) gives a good presentation of European integration. Herbert Tint: *French Foreign Policy Since the Second World War* (London, 1972) contains a useful survey of French foreign policy. A similar survey for the United Kingdom may be found in Joseph Frankel: *British Foreign Policy 1945–1973* (London, 1975).

Relations between the United States and Japan are analyzed in Edwin O. Reischauer: *The Japanese* (Cambridge, 1978) and Charles E. Neu: *The Troubled Encounter: The United States and Japan* (New York, 1975).

The Soviet Union and the Communist Countries

Adam B. Ulam's two books listed earlier are indispensable. The key work on developments in Eastern Europe is Francois Fejtø: *A History of the People's Democracies* (Penguin Books, 1974). Zbigniew Brzezinski: *The Soviet Bloc. Unity and Conflict* (Cambridge, 1967) is also useful.

An excellent source publication on relations between China and the Soviet Union is Keesing's Publications Limited: *The Sino-Soviet Dispute* (London, 1970). Also useful in their own separate ways are O. Edmund Clubb: *China and Russia. The 'Great Game'* (New York, 1971) and John Gittings: *The World and China, 1922–1972* (London, 1974).

Jahn Otto Johansen: *Hva vil Sovjet? Sovjetisk utenrikspolitikk i perspektiv* (What does the Soviet Union Want? Soviet Foreign Policy in Perspective) (Oslo, 1969) provides a useful survey in Norwegian. The chapter on the conflict between the Soviet Union and China is especially good. Strobe Talbott, ed.: *Khrushchev Remembers. The Last Testament* (Boston, 1974) is a fascinating source from the Soviet side.

Decolonization

My presentation has been influenced by the chapter on decolonization in Geoffrey Barraclough: *An Introduction to Contemporary History* (London, 1964).

A wealth of information is to be found in Rudolf von Albertini: *Decolonization. The Administration and the Future of the Colonies, 1919–1960* (New York, 1971) and Henri Grimal: *Decolonization. The British, French, Dutch and Belgian Empires 1919–1963* (Boulder, 1978). A good anthology is Tony Smith: *The End of the European Empire. Decolonization after World War II* (Lexington, 1975).

With regard to Africa, this presentation is particularly indebted to Prosser Gifford and Wm. Roger Louis, ed.: *The Transfer of Power in Africa. Decolonization 1940–1960* (New Haven, 1982) and Jarle Simensen: *Afrikas historie. Nye perspektiver* (Africa's History. New Perspectives) (Oslo, 1983).

The best survey of the non-aligned movement is to be found in William M. LeoGrande: 'Evolution of the Nonaligned Movement', *Problems of Communism,* January–February 1980, pages 35–52. Useful information may also be found in Peter Willetts: *The Non-Aligned Movement. The Origins of a Third World Alliance* (London, 1978).

Economic Relations between North and South

An anthology containing several important contributions is Andrew Mack, David Plant and Ursula Doyle: *Imperialism, Intervention and Development* (London, 1979). A very exciting collection of essays is to be found in W. Arthur Lewis: *The Evolution of the International Economic Order* (Princeton, 1978). The present work is also considerably indebted to David K. Fieldhouse: *Colonialism 1870–1945. An Introduction* (London, 1981); C. Fred Bergsten, Thomas Horst and Theodore H. Moran: *American Multinationals and American Interests* (Washington, D.C., 1978); Malcolm Gillis, Dwight H. Perkins, Michael Roemer and Donald R. Snodgrass: *Economics of Development* (New York, 1983); and Gerald M. Meier: *Emerging from Poverty. The Economics that Really Matters* (Oxford, 1984).

John Kenneth Galbraith: *The Nature of Mass Poverty* (Cambridge, Mass., 1979) is important for understanding how difficult it is to create economic growth. A successful attempt at a survey of relations between North and South over a long period of time is Tony Smith: *The Pattern of Imperialism. The United States, Great Britain and the Late-Industrializing World since 1815* (Cambridge, 1981).

Index